MURDER PLUS

MURDER PLUS

True Crime Stories from the Masters of Detective Fiction

Marc Gerald, Editor

PHAROS BOOKS

A SCRIPPS HOWARD COMPANY

NEW YORK

First published in book form in 1992.
Compilation copyright © 1992 by Pharos Books
Introduction copyright © 1992 by Marc Gerald

Library of Congress Cataloging-in-Publication Data
Murder plus : true crime stories by the masters of
detective fiction / Marc Gerald, editor.
p.   cm.
ISBN 0-88687-662-1
1. Crime—United States—Case studies.
2. Homicide investigation—United States—Case
Studies. I. Gerald, Marc.
HV7914.M89   1992   92-12412   CIP

Printed in the United States of America

Cover design: Darlene Barbaria

Pharos Books
A Scripps Howard Company
200 Park Avenue
New York, NY 10166

10 9 8 7 6 5 4 3 2 1

Pharos Books are available at special discounts
on bulk purchases for sales promotions, premiums,
fund-raising or educational use.
For details, contact the
Special Sales Department,
Pharos Books, 200 Park Avenue,
New York, NY 10166

For Marla

CONTENTS

ACKNOWLEDGMENTS

So many people have been instrumental in helping me complete this book. To them, I am deeply indebted and sincerely grateful:

To my friends at *America's Most Wanted*, especially Peter Koper and Rebecca Campany, for their editorial and emotional support.

To all my pals, far and wide. You know who you are. Especially to Robert Polito, who has not only taught me much about Jim Thompson, but who has also taught the virtues of modesty and devotion to craft. I, like many others, eagerly await his forthcoming biography on Thompson, entitled *Savage Art*.

To Priscilla Ridgway of the Mystery Writers of America, Mark Goodman of Green Lion Books, Linda Martin from the Reference and Bibliography section at the Library of Congress, and Martin Greenberg, the unsurpassed "King of the Anthologists."

To my editor Eileen Schlesinger at Pharos and my agent Clyde Taylor at Curtis Brown Ltd. A writer couldn't hope for more helpful encouragement, counsel, and insight.

To my family, Dr. Michael and Gloria Gerald, my sister Melissa, and my two grandmothers, Esther Gruber and Ruby Gerald. You've always been there for me, and none of this could have been accomplished without your loving support and guidance.

But most of all, to my girlfriend, Marla Weinhoff. For all those long days and nights when the last thing you wanted to talk about was blood and guts, the least I can do is dedicate this little volume to you.

Marc Gerald
Washington, D.C., 1992

MEMORY AND THE ANGELS: AN INTRODUCTION

Maybe you've seen the magazine before? You know, the one with buxom babes in skimpy get-ups holding only the most lethal weapons—AK-47s, Uzis, Glocks, Colt 45s—a different girl, a different gun. And maybe you've glanced at the headlines that surround the girls. Lurid, titillating rapid-fire headlines like "She was hot enough to lure her victim and COLD ENOUGH TO KILL!" or "Pittsburgh sleuths winced at the bodies and agreed it was NO WAY FOR THE SWEET OLD FOLKS TO DIE!"

Perhaps you've even dared to open a copy? If so, you've no doubt read about a handyman, a dishwasher, a baby-sitter, a schoolteacher—an everyday ordinary "Joe," who for some reason—you fill in the blank—snapped and turned into a fiendish, raving, cold-blooded killer. And you've read about the hard-nosed detective who battled against high odds to bring the homicidal maniac to justice.

In case you haven't figured it out yet, I'm talking about *True Detective*, a magazine not on the margins of respectable popular culture but clear off the page. Once it was a cornerstone of a popular *pulp* culture and featured writing by some of the boldest authors of its day. But that culture has long since vanished. And while *True Detective* survives, it has been relegated to the back of the lowliest newsstands, the low-rent section, just behind *Tattoo Times*, just in front of *Superstars of Wrestling*.

It wasn't on the newsstand that I first discovered *True Detective*, but at the Old Worthington Barbershop on High Street back in Columbus, Ohio. I couldn't have been more than six or seven, but I still recall the nightmares—especially one about a shoelace strangler who did in a handful of coeds out in the heartland. I was terrorized but I kept reading, and as I reached my teenage years, my parents and teachers considered sitting me down on the couch as my appreciation for the magazine's cheap and gaudy pages grew into an obsession. Finally, twenty-two, idealistic, and fresh out of college, I ditched plans to go to graduate

1

school so I could pursue higher learning, pulp-style. I became the managing editor of *True Detective* and its sister titles, *Master Detective, Official Detective, Inside Detective,* and *Front Page Detective.*

It was 1988. For most in the business of crime, that was a good year. People were desperate. Times were violent. Uncertain. The stock market had crashed. Crack had hit the streets. Dozens of serial killers stalked the country hunting for prey. Mass murderers spontaneously erupted with alarming frequency: reports had it that about once a week someone killed more than four people at a time. And there were several new and improved ways to die: at the hands of carjackers, in drive-bys, as a mushroom victim, in kiss-eye killings. Things were so bad this nation even managed to elect a president based in part on trumped-up, racist commercials featuring Willie Horton, the Massachusetts man who, as a prisoner during the term of Michael Dukakis, was given a weekend furlough while serving a sentence for first-degree murder, only to resurface in Maryland where he raped a woman and tortured her fiancé.

Struggling to keep pace with this whirling frenzy of violence the true crime genre began to flourish. Books like Ann Rule's *Small Sacrifices,* Joe McGinnis's *Blind Faith,* and Jack Olson's *Cold Kill* soared to the top of best-seller lists. New tabloid shows dealing in murder and mayhem and scandal and sleaze, like "A Current Affair" hit television airwaves with a vengeance. So did reality-based crime shows like "Unsolved Mysteries" and "America's Most Wanted," which urged viewers to "Watch TV— Catch Criminals." Miniseries "inspired by actual events" emerged as a tool for networks during sweeps periods when ratings are essential in the pricing of commercials. And two notable movies based on real life cases were theatrically released: *The Thin Blue Line,* Erroll Morris's weighty documentary about a Texas man falsely imprisoned for killing a cop, and *Henry: Portrait of a Serial Killer,* John McNaughton's stark, unflinching account of Henry Lee Lucas, possibly the most prolific serial killer in the history of the United States, and his fun-loving accomplice Ottis Toole.

One might think the same impulse that brought these latter-day true crime forms to prominence would've also benefited *True Detective.* After all, they were our descendants, modern equivalents of what we had been doing for a long time. It wasn't to be.

True Detective's Manhattan headquarters were on the twentieth floor of a dilapidated, prewar Hell's Kitchen office building. They were a grim, unhappy place, for the future of the magazine was very much in doubt.

The detective titles were owned by RGH Publications, a father and son corporation. Even without the luxury of promotion and publicity, and with covers so shoddily produced they could only scare readers off, about 500,000 diehards still purchased the magazines every month. But our readership of blue hairs, shut-ins, Greyhound bus riders, cops and axe-murderers was growing old and dying fast.

The magazines turned a profit, but it was becoming an increasingly small one, especially since our kindly, withered, little ad man now found it impossible to place ads from the tobacco and liquor companies. Instead, he searched lower. Much lower. The back page was reserved for our biggest advertiser who sold fake speed which could make you "Explode with Energy." Other ads were 900 numbers and sex manuals for those who craved the pleasures of the flesh after reading about bone-chilling violence; mail-order courses teaching promising careers like how to be a private eye, a locksmith, a wig salesman; and for the lonely hearts, "Jewels of the Orient" and "Untouched Island Girls."

To keep the magazine afloat, the staff was pared down to the absolute minimum. Just six editors put out five magazines a month.

My boss was Art Crockett. Pushing seventy, he wore a fedora over his horseshoe of hair and a cardigan vest over white starched shirts. He walked with a cane, had a lame eye, a wisecrack for every occasion, and a two-pack-a-day cough though he'd recently cut down to a half a pack a day. Doctor's orders.

If Art looked and acted the part of the wizened, old, tough-guy editor, he had a right to. He had lived the life.

Raised a few blocks up from our office, Art received a Bronze Star and a Purple Heart as a radioman with the 100th Infantry Division in World War II. After his discharge, he worked a series of unsatisfying jobs—in a salt factory, a refrigeration plant, and as an elevator repairman. Then, with a wife and two kids to support, Art quit his day job, rolled the dice, and began hammering out plots fast and for money—a penny a word.

His first stories appeared in second-generation detective fiction pulps like *Manhunt, Pursuit, Menace,* and *Conflict.* In the early 1960s, he edited a bizarre string of sex-cum-violence magazines, unreasonable facsimiles of legitimate men's adventure titles like *Argosy* and *True* that featured lavishly illustrated covers of dolled-up girl-Nazis equipped with leather, whips, and chains. When they folded, Art left for the greener pastures of the True West publications. It was a short stay, for they, too, closed up shop, and when they did he turned to *True Detective.*

Art was a man of considerable literary talent although thirty-five years of high-speed writing had taken its toll. When necessary, he could still knock out a masterful yarn. Mostly, he just churned out tawdry blurbs and titles on his Royal manual, circa 1936, something he could do like nobody's business. ("The poor joker on the floor was literally beaten to death. That was bad enough. But what his blood-dimmed eyes beheld before the end came may have been even worse." Or "It was the ultimate humiliation for the man who was obsessed with sex, and no power on earth could stop her as she approached him with her menacing knife.")

Most of the stories in the magazine were composed by moonlighting reporters around the country, cops or former cops, and freelancers. Despite preposterous conditions, a handful managed to be quite good: Joseph Koenig (author of *Little Odessa*), Ann Rule (one a prolific contributor who had since hit it big and now wrote only sparingly), and Charles Sasser and John Dunning (both authors of many crime paperbacks, both fact and fiction). All turned out consistently action-packed, adventurously told yarns.

But most had been trucking along far too long to care. All-time pulp great Jack Heise had been two-fingering ten stories a month from his mobile home in Spokane, Washington, since 1936. And Bud Ampolsk, Bill Kelly, Bill Cox, and Walt Hecox each had spent thirty-five years in the trenches. As a writer, inspiration was hard to find, especially after all those years. It was even harder when one had to write on the fly just to survive: 5,000 words fetched $250 in 1988, or $50 less than writers made during the darkest days of the depression.

I loved *True Detective* dearly and with all my heart. I wished more people read it, and was bitter that they didn't. But there wasn't a hell of a lot I could do about it. Facts were facts, and the fact was, our Golden Age had ended forty years earlier, and the magazine was a far cry from its former glory.

True Detective was founded in 1924 by physical fitness fanatic Bernarr Macfadden, a man of singular creative genius and imagination, one of the major publishers of the first half of this century. For Macfadden, truth was always stranger than fiction. It was also more lucrative. Having already made a mint on reality-based true confession–style publications like *True Story*, *True Romance*, and *True Experiences*, he fashioned *True Detective* as a magazine that would realistically portray a world marked by chaos and uncertainty.

With prohibition in full swing, the 1920s were violent times much like our own, and the magazine derived its plot material from these horrors of everyday life. Hyperreal, *True Detective* was democratic in spirit in much the same way Dashiell Hammett, Carrol John Daly, and Erle Stanley Gardner were. In 1924, these authors were revolutionizing the detective fiction story in the pages of *Black Mask*—and in the words of Raymond Chandler were giving "murder back to the kind of people that commit it for reasons, not just to provide a corpse; and with the means at hand."

From the get-go, the magazine ran stories about real kidnappings, bank scams, forgeries, art thefts, cons, and swindles; but its specialty was always murder, and no matter where you lived, it was always too close to home. You could be one of humanity's rejects or beneficiaries—a ritzy socialite, a bored housewife, a bell boy, a bartender, a truck driver, a farmer, a gambler, or a bum—and still be a killer and still be killed. Murder happened by day or by night, and it happened anyplace—on the waterfront or a lonesome desert highway, at an amusement park or a rail yard, in an Appalachian shack or a Park Avenue flat. But most shocking, murder in *True Detective*, just as in real life, could happen for chillingly commonplace reasons—for chump change, for looking at someone wrong, just for the thrill of it, or for no apparent reason at all.

The 25-cent journey Macfadden offered into this dark, shadowy, frequently harrowing, always brutal world was fascinating. Its bodies and blood grotesquely real, it was also pretty damn scary. Macfadden realized this. He also knew that most of his readers, the same people for whom crime was the biggest threat, wanted their fears alleviated by the end of the story, no matter how horrible the crime or how formidable the criminal. That's why he dictated that justice would always prevail, that the criminal must always get his comeuppance at the hands of a heroic officer of the law.

And some heroes they were, these "clever, brainy, and brave men," who in the words of Macfadden, "investigate bizarre crimes committed by cunning men who leave no clues behind them . . . and "take the tangled knot of circumstances in their hands and slowly, patiently, unravel all its twistings and windings, until finally the great secret is disclosed and the criminal is brought to justice."

Stories were based on fact, but there was always a fantastic element to this police work, especially when you consider the magazine's heroes were deputies, detectives, fingerprint experts, and prosecutors from two-bit towns across the country. In real life, some of these law officers may have been tough, hard, and determined—in *True Detective* they all were . . . always.

Critics dismissed the magazine as low brow and low down: some were troubled by its savage, unrelenting violence; others by its hybrid form (not journalism and not fiction) and penchant for purple prose; others still by its formula, which unrealistically, in their opinion, transformed cops into superheroes. But readers flocked to it—and it is estimated that *True Detective* sold close to two million copies a month during its heyday.

The magazine was also a big hit with publishers, who found its formula easy to knock off and imitated it by the score. In all, some seventy-five magazines were developed, magazines that covered the same cases, used the same artists and designers, and posed the same models in elaborate reenactments of the crimes. Indeed, they were so similar from one to the next that even their titles blur together: *Daring Detective, Shocking Detective, Startling Detective, Big Book Detective, Detective World, Underworld Detective, Headline Detective, Headquarters Detective, Dragnet Detective, Complete Detective, Homicide Detective, Confidential Detective, 10 True Crime Cases, True Police Cases,* to name but a few.

Hundreds of writers were kept busy during this boom time trying to satisfy readers' bloodlust. They had to type fast. Crime junkies were out stalking newsstands waiting for every issue. As many as ten million copies a month were snatched off shelves before spiraling inflation, mismanagement, television, and paperback books all but killed off the genre in the early 1950s.

From a literary point of view, the majority of the stories from these pulps of old don't command our attention. Most were pounded out by talentless, no-name hacks who brought little creativity to the genre. Others were written by well-known, much respected true crime reporters like Edward Radin, Alan Hynd, and John Bartlow Martin. While their stories often fascinate, one must look past a style more closely resembling journalism, one that seems dated, its prose ponderous and clunky.

Side by side with these stories appeared others by a different group of authors, who brought to the genre the best of the novelistic imagination and the kind of reportage only a journalist can provide. This bold crew is best known for their detective fiction—and if some of the names surprise you, that is because only one, Jim Thompson, has any true crime in print today.

Long lost are stories by American crime noir writers Robert Bloch, Charles Burgess, Harlan Ellison, Robert Faherty, Bruno Fischer, Day Keene, Lionel White, and Harry Whittington, and mainstream mystery authors such as Leslie Ford, Brett Halliday, Dashiell Hammett, Erle Stanley Gardner, Nunnally Johnson, Eleazar Lipsky, Stuart Palmer, Patrick Quentin, Craig Rice, Lawrence Treat, and S. S. Van Dyne.

History was never kind to the true crime pulps, and it hasn't been kind to these stories. Considered instantly disposable entertainment even by pulp standards, little effort was made to preserve them, even by the Library of Congress which deemed only *True Detective* and *Master Detective* worthy of preservation. As a result, these writings have previously been hard to find. A few appear in little-known, now much sought-after paperbacks. Most have never before been reissued. They've been available only in the true crime pulps in which they originally appeared—their paper brown and brittle with age and found only at junk stores, garage sales, and flea markets and in the hands of private collectors.

Casting light on their most notorious fiction while reporting on some of the biggest cases of their day, these true crime gems by the masters of detective fiction are unearthed and collected for the first time in *Murder Plus*.

While some were already writing on all eight cylinders most were just off the starting line when these stories appeared. An excellent training ground, the willing pupil could learn many of the skills needed to write engaging fiction, such as how to plot events into a fast-paced narrative, develop and personify a character who might only exist in bones and scant remembrances, provide the right detail to capture time and place, and shift points of view while advancing a story every step of the way.

Like the game of chess, mastery was complex, but the rules were simple and unchangeable. Stories had to keep to the facts and be easy to follow, unpretentious, and definitely not experimental. Editors strove for stylistic conformity and kept blue pencils on their desk, sharp and ready. Those looking to recast the formula did so by degrees. A writer who stepped too far out of line learned quickly which conventions could be toyed with and which could not. And those who didn't learn went hungry.

Reporting on these crimes not only provided writers with skills they could use, but it also gave them scores of actual material they could use in their fiction: fascinating characters with odd quirks and traits, plot devices, settings, and scenarios. And many of them did.

Robert Bloch acknowledges this debt in a remarkable story entitled "The Shambles of Ed Gein," in which he tells how he based his 1959 classic novel *Psycho* on Gein, a necrophiliac with a sharp wit and an even sharper knife. In Dashiell Hammett's "Who Killed Bob Teal?" one discovers an odd plot turn he would later use to great effect in the *Maltese Falcon*. While one needn't be familiar with Jim Thompson's unforgettable novels to appreciate "The Case of The Catalogue Clue," one might recognize the chatty sheriff, the scheming bellboy, the unloved wildcatter and the once pastoral, now booming West Texas town. Each reappears some twenty years later in books like *The Killer Inside Me* and *Wild Town*. And then there's Harry Whittington, "The King of the Paperback Originals," whose practically immoral "Invaders from the Sky" may just be the perfect true crime story. He would go on to base his 1960 novel *The Devil Wears Wings* on this case about two hard-luck pilots who swoop down from the skies to rob banks and reclaim their pride.

It is inevitable that the law and order message is the one that sounds the loudest in these stories. Had it not they never would have been published in the first place. But in some of the most audacious works, other voices can be heard under its din.

Some are the agonizing, barely distilled cries of victims like Pauline Sokolowska, who is killed for the shabbiest of reasons in Leslie Ford's "Scar-Faced Fugitive and the Murdered Maid." While her life and death might never be the stuff of fiction, the cruel poignancy of her murder shows through in these blood-dripped pages.

And then there are those in which we hear the tormented, tortured voices of raging psychopaths for whom killing is out of their control. Lionel White, who is best remembered for meticulously plotted caper novels like *The Killing* and *Death Takes the Bus*, here gives us the truly horrifying "Case of the Poison Pen." This lean, terse, and unrelenting story features a frail, hardworking, Bible-thumping widow who kills—and in most hideous fashion—because she only wants the best for her son. And Bruno Fischer, whose moody, gloomy paperbacks of the 1950s always centered on lonely and confused men, here tells the story of a man who finally goes over the edge after five years of "twisting, brooding jealousy." In both cases, the cops eventually get their man, but the reader gets no peace of mind. The stories are too violent, too close to home, their endings too obviously tacked on for the sake of the genre.

Even police procedurals by some of these noted authors cut like a knife. In lesser hands the cops may have been drab or cartoonishly heroic. Here they're fully realized, lifelike, even fallible. Lawrence Treat's fictional police stories have dazzled readers since the late 1940s. In "Body in Sector R," we follow an unglamorous New York City cop on the trail of a killer in his first big murder investigation. And in very different fashion, Erle Stanley Gardner, best known as the creator of the Perry Mason books series, recounts the details of the murder of film director William Desmond Taylor. This story can only be called a procedural by default, since it's generally agreed the police never really investigated the case properly at all.

Humor was another editorial taboo. Normally, the magazines were grim and earnest, as straightlaced and straight-faced as J. Edgar Hoover. Yet humor—sometimes black, sometimes slapstick—drifts through some of the finest of these stories, and it only goes to point up man's inability to know and control his fate. Harlan Ellison's irrepressibly sardonic wit is a mainstay in his extraordinary crime novels and it turns up, too, in "Mystery Man Lucks and His Missing Bucks," the story of a con man extraordinaire "with a caravan of beautiful women any Sheik would shriek for." And Craig Rice, the first lady of hard-boiled fiction, doesn't let the odd and sordid facts in the enigmatic Wynekoop case get her down in her flawless, tragicomic treasure, "Murder in Chicago."

This is not a historical project and I've chosen to present only works that have stood the test of time. In place of brand-name writers who never mastered the form, I've included stories by some who never achieved fame for their fiction and stories by others who were once well known but whose stars have since dimmed. Among them, there is Charles Burgess, whose 1960 novel *The Other Woman* is long forgotten, but whose frightening portrait of a New Orleans man possessed by redheads merits closer inspection; D. L. Champion, who gave us some of the most unusual private eyes ever published in the pages of *Black Mask*, here writes about a hefty, turn-of-the-century black widow, a story which is bound to give you (as it did me) the chills; and Robert Faherty, author of *Swamp Babe*, writes of a man obsessed by the tango, and the misstep that led him to the scaffold. In this same light I've included "A Shot in the Dark" by Nunnally Johnson. Best known for his work as a scriptwriter and director, although he did write mysteries early in his career, his droll account of thievery among the rich and famous on Long Island deserves to be exhumed from the dust that has covered it for sixty-seven years. And, finally, one concession has been made to history, and that is S. S. Van Dine's "Germany's Mistress of Crime." Delightfully odd, this story is based on fact and is told through the eyes of Van Dine's masterfully foolish, fictional sleuth, Philo Vance.

It is unlikely most writers looked upon these works as art, but rather a quick way to turn back nervous creditors while waiting for a royalty check to come in. It is interesting to note that only two of the major authors in this collection, Jim Thompson and Lionel White, stayed with true crime for long. Most published sparingly, a handful of stories tops, before moving on to bigger, more lucrative markets.

It may have been just as well. The line between a first-rate and a cut-rate true crime story was fine. Editorial demands could often crush a fledgling writer's style as well as aid it. And the relatively easy money could lead a writer to grow stale before he hit the big time, just like the boxer who leaves his best fights in the gym and fails to show up for the main event. (That's what happened to Jack Heise. His stories from 1936 were written with uncommon energy and care. By 1940, they were strictly formula and some 52 years later, well, I'm sure you can imagine).

Whatever their intentions, one can't deny their achievements. While the genre was rigid, and editors unforgiving, the stories I have detailed, and others that you are about to read, show writers trying valiantly—and sometimes successfully—to rise above the limits of the formula without destroying it. And in the final analysis this might be the true crime pulp's greatest legacy. It asked for little, but its built-in drama provided a forum for writers to produce fresh and disturbing stories that live on to this day.

Today, *True Detective* and its sister titles survive without me. I now work for *America's Most Wanted*, where I write reenactments. They like to tell me my job is to catch criminals. I prefer to think I'm helping to keep the spirit of the pulps alive in this electronic age.

And, sadly, the magazines live on without Art Crockett, too. A heart attack claimed this man of quiet dignity on June 23, 1990. He never saw *Murder Plus*, but I know it would have brought him much happiness.

Art always had a soft spot for redheads. Redheads like this volume's covergirl and Rose Mandelsberg-Weiss—better known as the "Queen of the Dickbooks," under whose keen and watchful eyes the editorship has been entrusted. And a fine job she's doing. Thanks to her, the magazines are starting to make a wonderful comeback.

Perhaps, they will someday enjoy a second Golden Age.

I hope so.

Until then, fix yourself a stiff drink, relax, and enjoy these stories of old.

Just don't forget to lock your doors.

ROBERT BLOCH

Today, serial killers seem to be springing up across the American landscape as often as McDonald's franchises—but·Ed Gein, serial killer 1950s variety, was a pioneer in the field. Gein's grim legacy had a profound influence on many writers, including Thomas Harris, author of *Silence of the Lambs*. Harris recently acknowledged he based many of Dr. Hannibal "the Cannibal" Lechter's peculiar traits on Gein. But ROBERT BLOCH was there first. An expert in the art of terror, Bloch has written hundreds of short stories since the late 1930s, and twelve of his best, including "Fat Chance," "Frozen Fear," and "Impractical Joker," appear in *Chamber of Horrors* (Award, 1966). He's gone on to write quite a few novels, films, and TV scripts, but his blessing and his curse are that he will forever be remembered for one book based on Gein, his 1959 classic, *Psycho.*

The Shambles of Ed Gein

"Searchers after horror haunt strange, far places," wrote H. P. Lovecraft in the opening of his story, "The Picture in the House." "For them are the catacombs of Ptolemais, and the carven mausolea of the nightmare countries. They climb to the moonlit towers of ruined Rhine castles, and falter down black cobwebbed steps beneath the scattered stones of forgotten cities in Asia. The haunted wood and the desolate mountain are their shrines, and they linger around the sinister monoliths on uninhabited islands. But the true epicure in the terrible, to whom a new thrill of unutterable ghastliness is the chief end and justification of existence, esteems most of all the ancient, lonely farmhouse of backwoods New

England; for there the dark elements of strength, solitude, grotesqueness and ignorance combine to form the perfection of the hideous."

Lovecraft's tale then goes on to describe a visit to one of these "silent, sleepy, staring houses in the backwoods" inhabited by a weird eccentric whose speech and dress suggest origins in a bygone day. An increasingly horrible series of hints culminates in the revelation that the inhabitant of the house has preserved an unnatural existence for several centuries, sustaining life and vigor through the practice of cannibalism.

Of course it's "only a story."

Or—is it?

On the evening of November 16, 1957, visitors entered an ancient, lonely farmhouse—not in backwoods New England but in rural Wisconsin. Hanging in an adjacent shed was the nude, butchered body of a woman. She had been suspended by the heels and decapitated, then disemboweled like a steer. In the kitchen next to the shed, fire flickered in an old-fashioned potbellied stove. A pan set on top of it contained a human heart.

The visitors—Sheriff Art Schley and Captain Lloyd Schoephoester—were joined by other officers. There was no electricity in the darkened house and they conducted their inspection with oil lamps, lanterns, and flashlights.

The place was a shambles, in every sense of the word. The kitchen, shed, and bedroom were littered with old papers, books, magazines, tin cans, tools, utensils, musical instruments, wrapping paper cartoons, containers, and a miscellany of junk. Another bedroom and living room beyond had been nailed off; these five rooms upstairs were nailed off and deserted.

But amidst the accumulated debris of years in the three tenanted rooms, the searchers found:

two shin bones;

a pair of human lips;

four human noses;

bracelets of human skin;

four chairs, their woven cane seats replaced by strips of human skin;

a quart can, converted into a tom-tom by skin stretched over both top and bottom;

a bowl made from the inverted half of a human skull;

a purse with a handle made of skin;

four "death masks"—the well-pressed skin from the faces of women—
mounted at eye level on the walls;

five more such "masks" in plastic bags, stowed in a closet;

ten female human heads, the tops of which had been sawed off above
the eyebrows;

a pair of leggings, fashioned from skin from human legs;

a vest made from the skin stripped from a woman's torso.

The bodies of 15 different women had been mutilated to provide these
trophies. The number of hearts and other organs which had been cooked
on the stove or stored in the refrigerator will never be known. Apocryphal
tales of how the owner of the house brought gifts of "fresh liver" to certain
friends and neighbors have never been publicly substantiated, nor is there
any way of definitely establishing his own anthropophagism.

But H. P. Lovecraft's "true epicure of the terrible" could find his new
thrill of unutterable ghastliness in the real, revealed horrors of the Gein
case.

Edward Gein, the gray-haired, soft-voiced little man who may or may
not have been a cannibal and a necrophile, was—by his own admission—a
ghoul, a murderer, and a transvestite. Due process of law has also
adjudged him to be criminally insane.

Yet for decades he roamed free and unhindered, a well-known figure in
a little community of 700 people. Now small towns everywhere are
notoriously hotbeds of gossip, conjecture, and rumor, and Gein himself
joked about his "collection of shrunken heads" and laughingly admitted
that he'd been responsible for the disappearance of many women in the
area. He was known to be a recluse and never entertained visitors;
children believed his house to be "haunted." But somehow the gossip
never developed beyond the point of idle, frivolous speculation, and
nobody took Ed Gein seriously. The man who robbed fresh graves, who
murdered, decapitated, and eviscerated women when the moon was full,
who capered about his lonely farmhouse bedecked in corpse-hair, the
castor-oil-treated human skin masks made from the faces of his victims, a
vest of female breast and puttees of skin stripped from women's legs—this
man was just plain old Eddie Gein, a fellow one hired to do errands and
odd jobs. To his friends and neighbors he was only a handyman, and a
most dependable and trustworthy babysitter.

"Good old Ed, kind of a loner and maybe a little bit odd with that sense of humor of his, but just the guy to call in to sit with the kiddies when me and the old lady want to go to the show . . ."

Yes, good old Ed, slipping off his mask of human skin, stowing the warm, fresh entrails in the refrigerator, and coming over to spend the evening with the youngsters; he always brought them bubble gum. . . .

A pity Grace Metalious wasn't aware of our graying, shy little-town handyman when she wrote *Peyton Place*! But, of course, nobody would have believed her. New England or Wisconsin are hardly the proper settings for such characters; we might accept them in Transylvania, but Pennsylvania—never!

And yet, he lived. And women died.

As near as can be determined, on the basis of investigation and his own somewhat disordered recollections, Gein led a "normal" childhood as the son of a widowed mother. He and his brother, Henry, assisted in the operation of their 160-acre farm.

Mrs. Gein was a devout, religious woman with a protective attitude toward her boys and a definite conviction of sin. She discouraged them from marrying and kept them busy with farm work; Ed was already a middle-aged man when his mother suffered her first stroke in 1944. Shortly thereafter, brother Henry died, trapped while fighting a forest fire. Mrs. Gein had a second stroke from which she never recovered; she went to her grave in 1945 and Ed was left alone.

It was then that he sealed off the upstairs, the parlor, and his mother's bedroom and set up his own quarters in the remaining bedroom, kitchen, and shed of the big farmhouse. He stopped working the farm, too; a government soil-conservation program offered him subsidy, which he augmented by his work as a handyman in the area.

In his spare time he studied anatomy. First books, and then—

Then he enlisted the aid of an old friend named Gus. Gus was kind of a loner, too, and quite definitely odd—he went to the asylum a few years later. But he was Ed Gein's trusted buddy, and when Ed asked for assistance in opening a grave to secure a corpse for "medical experiments," Gus lent a hand, with a shovel in it.

That first cadaver came from a grave less than a dozen feet away from the last resting place of Gein's mother.

Gein dissected it. Wisconsin farm folk are handy at dressing-out beef, pork, and venison.

What Ed Gein didn't reveal to Gus was his own growing desire to become a woman himself; it was for this reason he'd studied anatomy, brooded about the possibilities of an "operation" which would result in the change of sex, desired to dissect a female corpse and familiarize himself with its anatomical structure.

Nor did he tell Gus about the peculiar thrill he experienced when he donned the grisly accoutrement of human skin stripped from the cadaver. At least, there's no evidence he did.

He burned the flesh bit by bit in the stove, buried the bones. And with Gus's assistance, repeated his ghoulish depredations. Sometimes he merely opened the graves and took certain parts of the bodies—perhaps just the heads and some strips of skin. Then he carefully covered up traces of his work. His collection of trophies grew, and so did the range of his experimentation and obsession.

Then Gus was taken away, and Gein turned to murder.

The first victim, in 1954, was Mary Hogan, a buxom 51-year-old divorcée who operated a tavern at Pine Grove, six miles from home. She was alone when he came to her one cold winter's evening; he shot her in the head with his .32-caliber revolver, placed her body in his pickup truck, and took her to the shed where he'd butchered pigs, dressed-out deer.

There may have been other victims in the years that followed. But nothing definite is known about Gein's murderous activities until that day in November 1957, when he shot and killed Mrs. Bernice Worden in her hardware store on Plainfield's Main Street. He used a .22 rifle from a display rack in the store itself, inserting his own bullet which he carried with him in his pocket. Locking the store on that Saturday morning, he'd taken the body home in the store truck. Gein also removed the cash register, which contained $41 in cash—not with the intention of committing robbery, he later explained in righteous indignation, but merely because he wished to study the mechanism. He wanted to see how a cash register worked, and fully intended to return it later.

Mrs. Worden's son Frank often assisted her in the store, but on this particular Saturday morning he'd gone deer hunting. On his return in later afternoon he discovered the establishment closed, his mother missing, the cash register gone. There was blood on the floor. Frank Worden served as a deputy sheriff in the area and knew what to do. He immediately alerted his superior officer, reported the circumstances, and began to check for clues. He established that the store had been closed since early that morning, but noted a record of the two sales transactions made before closing. One of them was for a half gallon of antifreeze.

Worden remembered that Ed Gein, the previous evening at closing time, had stopped by the store and said he'd be back the next morning for antifreeze. He'd also asked Worden if he intended to go hunting the next day. Worden further recalled that Gein had been in and out of the store quite frequently during the previous week.

Since the cash register was missing, it appeared as if Gein had planned a robbery after determining a time when the coast was clear.

Worden conveyed his suspicions to the sheriff, who sent officers to the farm, seven miles outside Plainfield. The house was dark and the handyman absent; acting on a hunch, they drove to a store in West Plainfield where Gein usually purchased groceries. He was there— had been visiting casually with the proprietor and his wife. In fact, he'd just eaten dinner with them.

The officers spoke of Mrs. Worden's disappearance. The 51-year-old, 140-pound little handyman joked about it in his usual offhand fashion; he was just leaving for home in his truck and was quite surprised that anyone wanted to question him. "I didn't have anything to do with it," he told them. "I just heard about it while I was eating supper." It seems someone had come in with the news.

Meanwhile, back at the farmhouse, the sheriff and the captain had driven up, entered the shed, and made their gruesome discovery.

Gein was taken into custody, and he talked.

Unfortunately for the "searchers after horror," his talk shed little illumination on the dark corners of his mind. He appeared to have only a dim recollection of his activities; he was "in a daze" much of the time during the murders. He did recall that he'd visited about 40 graves through the years, though he insisted he hadn't opened all of them, and denied he'd committed more than two murders. He named only nine women whose bodies he'd molested, but revealed he selected them after careful inspections of the death notices in the local newspapers.

There was a lie-detector test, a murder charge, an arraignment, a series of examinations at the Central State Hospital for the Criminally Insane. He remains there to this day.

The case created a sensation in the Midwest. Thousands of "epicures of the terrible"—and their snotty-nosed brats—made the devout pilgrimage to Plainfield, driving bumper-to-bumper on wintry Sunday afternoons as they gawked at the "murder farm." Until one night the residence of the "mad butcher" went up in smoke.

I was not among the epicures. At that time I resided less than fifty miles away, but had no automobile to add to the bumper crop; nor did I subscribe to a daily newspaper. Inevitably, however, I heard the mumbled mixture of gossip and rumor concerning the "fiend" and his activities. Curiously enough, there was no mention of his relationship with his mother, nor of his transvestism; the accent was entirely on proven murder and presumed cannibalism.

What interested me was this notion that a ghoulish killer with perverted appetites could flourish almost openly in a small rural community where everyone prides himself on knowing everyone else's business.

The concept proved so intriguing that I immediately set about planning a novel dealing with such a character. In order to provide him with a supply of potential victims, I decided to make him a motel operator. Then came the ticklish question of what made him tick—the matter of motivation. The Oedipus motif seemed to offer a valid answer, and the transvestite theme appeared to be a logical extension. The novel which evolved was called *Psycho*.

Both the book and a subsequent motion picture version called forth comments which are the common lot of the writer in the mystery-suspense genre. "Where do you get those perfectly dreadful ideas for your stories?"

I can only shrug and point to the map—not just a map of Wisconsin, but any map. For men like Edward Gein can be found anywhere in the world—quiet little men leading quiet little lives, smiling their quiet little smiles and dreaming their quiet little dreams.

Lovecraft's "searches after horror" do not need to haunt strange, far places or descend into catacombs or ransack mausolea. They have only to realize that the true descent into dread, the journey into realms of nightmare, is all too easy—once one understands where terror dwells.

The real chamber of horrors is the gray, twisted, pulsating, blood-flecked interior of the human mind.

CHARLES BURGESS

Beacon Books, a notorious, low-rent house that specialized in soft core sex-cum-crime novels, published CHARLES BURGESS's one book, *The Other Woman*, in 1960. Sadly, this minor masterpiece is all but forgotten today. Stylistically understated, it springs to lyrical heights in lurid sex scenes. And its intricate plot about a horny real estate agent who rediscovers the joys of marriage after a fling with a beckoning wanton pays rich dividends to the careful reader. These same talents are evidenced here—in a story about a man who couldn't live without redheads...or with them.

A Killer with Women

Joe Balli surveyed himself in the mirror and liked what he saw. A man in his middle thirties, Balli knew that women were especially attracted to him, and that pleased him. Angelina, for instance. There was a woman!

Several rooms away he could hear the raucous voice of his wife, Mary, scolding their two-year-old son, and he frowned. Life had become a steady succession of quarrels ever since they were married in Galveston, Texas, six years before. For months now he'd been trying to think of some way to ditch Mary and the kid and marry Angelina.

Thoughtfully, he slipped into a leather jacket and pulled up the zipper. He donned his cab driver's cap and straightened his tie. There was only one way to deal with people who wouldn't listen to reason, he decided. Murder.

He was surprised and pleased to find that the idea didn't shock him any more. He would need a clear head when the time came, and now he knew the time was near. He couldn't stand his wife's infernal bickering much longer. Whatever happened to her now she had coming to her, he told himself stubbornly.

Slipping quietly out the back door, he slid behind the wheel of the cab and gunned the motor. In less than ten minutes he would be with Angelina at their rendezvous on Bourbon Street.

She was waiting for him when he entered the dimly lit restaurant in the heart of New Orleans' teeming French Quarter. Winding his way carefully between the maze of white-clothed tables, he hurried to their favorite booth. She looked up, her smile held little warmth.

"Hello baby."

"Hello Joe. You're late."

Balli nodded. "Yeah. I got tied up in traffic. Forgive me?"

"I suppose so."

Balli noticed her mood, "What's the matter, Angie? You got something on your mind?"

"Yes. I've been doing a lot of thinking about you and me, Joe. How long we been going together? It's been quite a while, hasn't it?"

Balli frowned. "Oh, I don't know. Six, seven months maybe. Why?"

Angelina leaned forward, her dark eyes probing into his. "I hate to rush into things, Joe, but where are we going? What's going to happen to us?"

"What do you mean?"

Angelina sighed. "Okay, so I'll draw you a diagram. When are you going to ask me to marry you? Or are you allergic to wedding bands?"

Balli grinned and took one of her neatly gloved hands in his. "Just a little while longer, baby. I promise."

Angelina withdrew her hand. "Why the delay? You're not married, are you?" she snapped sharply.

Balli laughed. "Married? Me? Of course not! Whatever gave you that idea?"

The girl shrugged. "Nothing, I guess." Suddenly her eyes narrowed to smoldering slits of fire. "If I thought you were lying to me, Joe, I'd stomp your eyes in!"

Balli spent the next half hour and several drinks placating and assuring her of his love and fidelity. For some reason she seemed hard to convince and it worried him. Had she been checking up? He breathed easier when he saw the fire finally fade from her eyes. She didn't know—yet. But he'd have to watch his step. Angelina was a redhead and they played rough.

Balli was convinced that he had to do something and fast. Angelina wouldn't wait forever. During the next few days, a number of ideas raced through his mind, but he quickly discarded them. No hit or miss plans for him. Then suddenly, it came to him. The perfect plan. Carefully he went over it again and again. It would work, he was sure of it. He decided to kill his wife on Monday. That would give him three days to smooth over any loose ends that might crop up. . . .

Captain Joseph Sonnenberg was about to go off duty when the phone rang. Monday, April 23, 1951, had been a busy day, and he was anxious to get home and relax. The moment he picked up the receiver, however, he knew he wasn't getting any sleep that night.

"Yeah, I got the address," he said. "Eleven thirty-nine Saint Philip Street, ground floor. Okay, we'll be right out. In the meantime don't touch anything."

Ten minutes later he was standing over the body of a woman in her early 20's. The fully clothed victim lay face up on the kitchen floor. Tied around her throat in a vicious knot was a short piece of rope. An empty ice tray lay close to her left hand.

Sonnenberg looked up as a bevy of officers entered the room. Captain Dowie, a stocky, florid-faced man, was in the lead, closely followed by two members of his homicide squad, Detectives Arthur Jordan and Allen Dupre. The quartet was studying the body when Coroner Gillespie arrived.

They waited while the medical man made a cursory examination of the dead woman. Finally, he looked up. "Dead about an hour, no more," he said tersely. "As you can see, she was strangled."

"Did she put up a fight?" asked Dowie.

Dr. Gillespie examined the dead woman's hands. "There's no indication of it." He pointed to a wet spot on the floor near the ice-cube tray. "She was probably removing the tray from the Frigidaire when her murderer came up behind her and slipped the rope over her head. She didn't have a chance."

Dowie nodded. The medical man's theory made sense. "What do you know about her, Cap?" he asked, turning to Sonnenberg.

"Not much. Her name is Mrs. Mary Balli. She's 20 years old, married and has a two-year-old son, Joseph, Junior. Her husband's name is Joseph Balli. He's a cab driver."

"Where is he?"

Sonnenberg shrugged. "According to Mrs. Lena Martinez, the dead woman's sister who lives upstairs, Balli takes his cab out every morning and doesn't get home until around six P.M."

Dowie checked his watch. "It's almost six now. Maybe he can tell us what this is all about when he gets here."

Leaving Sonnenberg to look after things, Dowie climbed a short flight of carpeted stairs to question the victim's sister, Mrs. Martinez. The latter, who bore a remarkable resemblance to the dead woman, seemed stunned by the tragedy. She said that as far as she knew, her sister had no enemies. On the contrary, she was quite popular in the neighborhood.

"How did she and Mr. Balli get along?"

Mrs. Martinez hesitated. "All right, I guess. They had their spats like other married folks, but nothing serious."

"Any arguments between them lately?"

"No, not that I know of."

Mrs. Martinez explained that her sister met Balli in Galveston shortly after his divorce from his first wife in 1945. Balli was a truck driver then, working at the Navy Air Base in Hitchcock, Texas. They had moved to New Orleans five years ago, but had only been living in the murder house a month.

"Did you find the body?" inquired Dowie.

"No, a man named Robert Williams found Mary. He lives up the street."

Mrs. Martinez revealed that her sister was employed as a machine operator in a textile mill a few blocks from the house. Because work at the plant was slack, she'd said she hadn't bothered to report for duty that morning.

"How did your sister get along with the other girls?" probed Dowie.

Mrs. Martinez frowned. "Come to think of it, she did have a fight with one of the girls a while back. The other girl was let go because of it."

"What's her name?"

"I don't know her last name. Her first name's Stella."

When Mrs. Martinez promised to check her sister's things to see if anything was missing, Dowie thanked her and left. He found Williams, a personable young man in his early twenties, on the porch. Questioning him closely, Dowie learned that he had been brought to the house by two neighborhood children.

"They stopped me on the street and said something about a lady being dead, so I followed them into the house," said Williams. "When I saw they were telling the truth, I called the police."

"Was there anyone loitering around the house before you found the body?"

"No, sir."

Dowie took Williams's name and address and excused him with thanks. He then talked to the two children. They said they were playing in the hall when they noticed that the door to the Balli apartment was open. When they investigated they found Mrs. Balli's body. Like Williams, they saw no one hanging around the house prior to their finding the body.

Dowie thanked them and rejoined Sonnenberg in the kitchen. He found the precinct captain studying the short piece of rope which was used to murder Mrs. Balli.

"Make anything out of it?" inquired Dowie.

"Not much," replied Sonnenberg glumly. "It's about three and a half feet long and has been recently cut from a longer piece. However, it's ordinary clothesline rope, which practically makes it impossible to trace."

A thorough search of the premises failed to uncover any additional clues. It wasn't until they examined the hall outside the Balli apartment that they got their second lead, an odd-shaped piece of worn leather.

"It's a lift from a woman's spike heel," said Sonnenberg quickly.

"It certainly doesn't belong to Mrs. Balli," said Dowie. "She was wearing low-heeled sandals."

Nor did a check of the slain woman's wardrobe reveal a pair of high-heel shoes. Examination of Mrs. Martinez's shoe rack also proved entirely unproductive.

"Maybe a woman killed Mrs. Balli?" suggested Sonnenberg.

"It's possible," agreed Dowie. "It doesn't take much strength once you've got the rope around your victim's neck. However, we know it's got to be someone who Mrs. Balli trusted enough to turn her back on."

"Maybe she was going with some guy and his wife got sore. I've known women to kill for less."

"It's a good angle," nodded Dowie. "Suppose we talk to a few of the neighbors? They may have seen something."

They did. A woman who lived across the street from the Ballis said that she saw a pretty redhead enter the murder house about an hour or so before the police arrived.

"How long did she stay?" pressed Dowie.

"Five, ten minutes. I can't be sure."

"Can you describe her?"

"I think so. She was about five feet eight in spike-heeled shoes. She was wearing a white linen dress and carried a large patent leather handbag. She was about twenty-three years old."

The woman added that the redhaired woman appeared somewhat agitated when she left.

Another neighbor said that she was looking out the window when a taxi stopped before the house around three o'clock and Mrs. Balli got out. After talking to the driver for a few minutes the two of them went inside. He emerged five minutes later and drove off.

"Did you notice what kind of cab it was?" asked Dowie.

"Yes, it was a Red Top."

Their informant said the cabbie was about medium height and weight, somewhere in his late twenties, and good looking.

Dowie jotted down the information and left. Outside, he said: "Suspects are popping all over the place. The redheaded woman and the cabbie had good opportunities, and we mustn't overlook the husband."

"Whoever did it knew Mrs. Balli wasn't going in to work today," said Sonnenberg thoughtfully. "Which means it could be an inside job."

Back at the murder house, Dowie sought out Mrs. Martinez.

"This Stella you mentioned," said Dowie. "Do you know what color hair she has?"

"Yes, she's a redhead."

Dowie nodded thoughtfully. The trail was getting warm, he decided grimly.

When Dowie returned downstairs he found Assistant District Attorney Peter Campagno waiting for him. The homicide sleuth quickly brought him up to date on what he had learned thus far. The men were about to leave when a tall, scholarly looking man in his late fifties, entered the apartment.

"My name is John Meeker," he said. "I'd like to speak to the officer in charge."

"That's me," said Dowie. "What's on your mind?"

After explaining that he was a friend of the Balli family, Meeker said: "I met Balli a couple of days ago on Canal Street. He seemed unusually worried and I asked what was troubling him. He said that he had caught his wife fooling around with another man, a cabbie like himself. When he ordered the man out of his house, the man got very angry and threatened him."

"What kind of threats?" pressed Dowie.

"Joe didn't say, but he was obviously afraid for his life. When a neighbor told me his wife had been murdered, I hurried over to tell you about it."

"Did Balli tell you the man's name?"

"No, he didn't."

"Can you tell us anything about the Ballis?" inquired Dowie.

"I liked them very much," replied Meeker. "They seemed very much devoted to each other, and it certainly was a shock to learn that Mrs. Balli played around. Although she was an extremely good-looking woman, I somehow got the impression that she was crazy about her husband."

After Meeker left, one of the lab men announced that a score of legible fingerprints had been uncovered in the apartment, all but two of which had been made by the victim, Mrs. Balli.

"Check those two with our files," instructed Dowie. "It's very likely you'll find their mates in the license files, seeing as how Balli's a cab driver."

Meanwhile, Detectives Jordan and Dupre had learned that a redhaired woman, answering the description of the one seen leaving the murder house, had been observed boarding a Broad Street bus shortly after four o'clock. According to their informant, she was crying.

"Find out which bus it was and question the driver," ordered Dowie. "If she was as agitated as our witnesses claim, the bus driver ought to remember her."

Next, Dowie called Joe Balli's employer, the Veteran's Cab Company, and learned that Balli had not contacted the office since one o'clock that afternoon. Fearing the worst, Dowie instructed Detective Charles Wersling to get the police dispatcher to send out an all-points bulletin on the missing man.

Accompanied by Capt. Sonnenberg, Dowie drove to the textile mill where the comely victim was employed, and sought out the personnel manager.

"We're looking for a redhead whose first name is Stella and who was recently discharged for fighting," explained Dowie. "Can you help us?"

"I think so," nodded the employee. He rifled through a pile of 3 × 5 index cards until he found the one he wanted. "Her full name is Stella Marshack," he said. "She's twenty-two years old and she lives on Allen Street."

"What do you know about her run-in with Mrs. Balli?" asked Sonnenberg.

"According to what I heard, there's been bad blood between them for some time," replied the mill worker. "It seems Stella once attended a party at the Balli apartment and took a fancy to Mary's husband, Joe. Whether Joe gave her a play or not, I can't say, but I do know that Stella and Mary hated each other's guts after that."

As for the brawl that resulted in Stella Marshack's dismissal, it took place in an alley behind the plant.

"It's a lucky thing somebody interfered," he explained. "Stella had Mary on her back and was stomping her in the face. Witnesses say she would have killed Mary. When a checkup showed Stella had started it, she was fired."

Dowie and Sonnenberg drove to the address on Allen Street after leaving the plant. Inquiries revealed that Stella Marshack had a large hall bedroom on the second floor. Receiving no answer to their repeated knocking, Dowie induced the landlady to open the door. A careful inspection of the room, however, failed to yield anything that would connect the redhead with Mrs. Balli's murder.

"Her clothes are all here, so that's some consolation," mused Sonnenberg. "At least we know she hasn't skipped."

Questioning the landlady, they learned that the suspect left the house shortly after two o'clock, saying she wouldn't return until late.

"She seemed terribly upset over something," she said. "I tried to find out what was bothering her, but she won't confide in anybody."

After Dowie made arrangements to have the house watched, he returned to headquarters with Capt. Sonnenberg. Electrifying news awaited them.

"Better hop over to St. Philip and Bergundy streets right away," Chief of Detectives Harry Daniels told him. "Jordan and Dupre have located Joe Balli's cab, and there's blood splattered all over the front seat!"

Dowie and Sonnenberg sped to the spot, a run-down neighborhood several blocks from the murder house. The cab doors were open and the keys were in the ignition. A number of fresh bloodstains were visible on the cushions behind the driver's seat, the steering wheel and the dashboard. Balli's wallet, containing his personal papers but no money, lay on the back seat.

"It certainly looks as if Balli met the same fate as his wife," said Dowie glumly. "But what about the body? This is a well-populated neighborhood, which makes it practically impossible for anybody to remove a body unseen."

"Maybe Balli was knocked off elsewhere and the killer left the car here to throw us off?" Sonnenberg suggested.

"It's an idea. If he's really dead, it's a cinch his death is tied in somehow with his wife's."

"Meaning Stella Marshack?"

"Why not?" countered Dowie. "The dame is supposed to have a violent temper, and there's no telling how deeply she felt towards Balli. Let's ask some questions around here. We may come up with something."

A check of the homes nearest to the taxicab uncovered nothing, however. When it was apparent that they could learn nothing of importance in the area, Dowie and Sonnenberg returned to headquarters. A message on the former's desk informed him that Stella Marshack had returned to her room. Accompanied by Detective Jordan, Dowie hurried to the address.

The officers found the good-looking suspect in her room preparing a late supper. After they identified themselves, she waved them to chairs.

"What can I do for you guys?" she inquired.

"Mrs. Balli was murdered late this afternoon," said Dowie, watching the woman's face closely.

She turned, a look of amazement on her face. "Mary? Dead?" she exclaimed. "Why, that's impossible! I spoke to her a few minutes before five. She was all right then."

"Why did you go there when you were on bad terms?"

Stella fidgeted. "So you know about that? Well, I might as well tell you the truth. I went there to tear her limb from limb, but she wouldn't open the door when she found out who it was."

Dowie looked skeptical. "You went there looking for trouble and an hour later they found her dead," he said. "Pardon me if I don't believe you."

Stella crossed a nylon-clad leg nervously. "It's the truth, so help me!" she said anxiously. "If I'd gotten into her apartment I know I would have given her a good going over, but I didn't even see her. She spoke to me through the door. That's why I was so darn mad."

Dowie studied the woman closely. Her story sounded plausible enough. Finding the heel lift in the hall outside the apartment was a strong point in her favor, he admitted.

"What about you and Joe Balli?" he asked.

Stella shrugged. "It was just one of those things," she said. "I met Joe at a party a couple of months ago, and I kinda went for the guy. I knew he was married and had a kid, but he sure had a great line. He said he liked me because I was a redhead. His first wife was a redhead, too."

Dowie nodded. "Go on."

"There isn't much more to tell. His first wife had five kids by him and lives in Victoria, Texas. He met his second wife when she was only fourteen. He sure is a great ladies' man."

Dowie advised Stella Marshack not to leave town and returned to his office. He felt reasonably certain that she had nothing to do with the murder, despite the fact that she was there around the time it happened. He was studying the shortened length of rope used by the killer when Detective Dupre entered with a short, powerful-looking man in his early 30's. The man wore a cab driver's cap and was obviously nervous.

"This is Bob Benoit, chief," said Dupre. "He's the cabbie who took Mrs. Balli home this afternoon."

Dowie waved him to a chair. "How well do you know Mrs. Balli?" he inquired.

"I never laid eyes on her until this afternoon," maintained Benoit, twisting his cap nervously. "I was cruising along Canal Street when she hailed me. It was a fifty-cent trip, but when we got to her place on Saint Philip she had only forty cents in her bag. She told me to come inside with her and she'd give me the other dime. That's all there was to it, I swear it!"

"You were inside for at least five minutes," Dowie pointed out. "Did it take that long for her to get the money?"

"No, not exactly. After I got the dime she asked if I wanted a glass of beer. I said 'yes' and she got two cans out of the refrigerator. When I finished the drink I left."

"Did you notice anyone or a car in the vicinity when you left?"

The cabbie frowned. "No, I don't think so. There was another cab parked around the corner on Miro Street, but that was all."

Dowie straightened in his chair. "This other cab, can you remember what company owned it?"

"Yeah, it was a Veteran's Cab. The city is full of 'em."

Dowie thanked the cabbie and released him. Then he turned to Jordan and Dupre. "That other cab," he said. "Does it give you any ideas?"

Jordan rubbed his chin. "Balli drives a Veteran's Cab. You can't mean—"

"That's just what I do mean," said Dowie grimly. "It might have been a coincidence that Stella Marshack was around when the murder occurred, but we can't write off the cab as another one so easily. I want the two of you to turn Miro Street inside out for anyone who used a Veteran's Cab around three o'clock this afternoon. Hustle back here the moment you get anything."

After the officers left, the autopsy report came from Coroner Nicholas J. Chetta's office. It stated that Mrs. Balli met death by strangulation sometime between four and five o'clock that afternoon. The rope had fractured her larynx, indicating that the killer was a person of considerable strength. A second report, this time from the lab, stated that Balli's blood-type had been obtained from his family physician and had matched the bloodstains found in the abandoned car.

Dowie hurried to Campagno's office where he quickly briefed the young assistant district attorney on the latest developments.

"You figure Joe Balli killed his wife?" asked Campagno when he was finished.

"I'm sure of it," replied Dowie. "From what I can learn about him, he's crazy about redheads. His first wife was one, and so is Stella Marshack, and I'll bet a month's pay he's got another one on the string right now. He's planned this caper pretty well, but too many redheads tripped him up."

Jordan and Dupre were waiting for him when he returned to his office.

"No dice, chief," said Jordan. "Nobody around Miro Street hired a cab this afternoon."

"That settles it," snapped Dowie. "We're going back to the Balli apartment and turn it inside out. We've got to find out who that third redhead is!"

A thorough inspection of this missing man's room failed, however, to reveal the name of Balli's latest paramour. Questioning Mrs. Martinez a second time, Dowie learned that the suspect was extremely fond of fish food, and frequently patronized a certain restaurant on Bourbon Street.

With a snapshot of the suspect they drove to the restaurant. The manager nodded when he saw Balli's picture.

"Sure, he comes in here a lot," he said. "Angelina's his girl friend."

"Is Angelina a redhead?"

The man raised his eyes in ecstasy. "And what a redhead!"

They discovered that Angelina's last name was Prima, and that her father ran a tavern on Calumet Street, and lost little time in getting to the address. Papa Prima blanched when he learned that his daughter's lover was a married man wanted for the murder of his wife.

"But that can't be!" he exclaimed, horrified. "My girl and Joseph are going to be married someday."

"Don't bet on it," advised Dowie. "Where is your daughter now?"

Prima kept shaking his head. "She's with Joseph. They left for Rayne early this afternoon."

Dowie returned to his office where he put through a call to the Acadia parish authorities in Rayne. He gave them complete descriptions of the wanted pair and requested that they be picked up on sight.

He felt confident that it wouldn't be long before Balli would be in custody, and he was right. At three A.M. the next morning word came from Rayne that the couple had been apprehended.

Jordan and Dupre brought them back to New Orleans later that day. The girl was stunned when she learned of her lover's duplicity. She swore she had no idea he was married.

Meanwhile, Balli, grilled incessantly for eight hours, finally broke down and admitted his guilt.

"Yes, I killed her," he sobbed. "She and the kid were in my way. I couldn't go on living with her any more. That's why I got into the house the back way, strangled her when she wasn't looking and went back to my cab. Nobody saw me. Then I cut myself on the wrist and let blood splatter on the cushions so that you'd think I had been murdered, too."

"Didn't you know it would get into the papers and that your girl friend or her parents would read about it?" asked Dowie.

Balli grinned. "You think I'm dumb, eh? Everybody thought my name was Joe Garcia, even Angelina. It was a wonderful idea, but something musta' went wrong."

Joseph Balli was indicted ten days later on first degree murder charges and will be tried sometime during the Fall term. Meanwhile he has lots of time to rue the day he began preferring redheads to blondes or brunettes.

D. L. CHAMPION

D. L. CHAMPION contributed some of the most offbeat private-eye series ever published in *Black Mask* and *Dime Detective*. His characters included a midget investigator; a hard-nosed, legless ex-cop; a gaudily dressed Mexican PI; and "the unchallenged world's champion penny pincher." CHAMPION never made the leap to book form when the pulp market collapsed in the early 1950s. That is why he isn't better known today. He turned, instead, to true crime (it paid faster!), and he published as many as fifteen stories a month under a dizzying slew of preposterous pen names, until his death in 1968. This story about a most unlikely femme fatale is one of his best.

Madame Murder

When she was six years old, Belle Gunness underwent a searing, traumatic experience as usual as it was unnerving. Every day of the week, save Sunday, she watched her father as he neatly decapitated her mother.

Belle's parents were members of a theatrical troupe which traveled extensively through the Scandinavian countries.

Her father was a magician and the climax of his act consisted in placing his wife's head on a block and releasing a miniature guillotine—which apparently decapitated her. Synthetic blood gushed realistically all over the stage and the head appeared to fall with a delightful macabre pop into a wicker basket.

It was an extremely effective act and the audience ate it up. So did little Belle Gunness. She witnessed this execution at each matinee and enjoyed it more than any other spectator.

It wasn't too long before she invented her own play act. It was a simple game which required only a doll and a hatchet. Little Belle began chopping off the head of every doll she could get her hands on.

The world at this time was totally unaware of Sigmund Freud, and psychiatry had not yet been invented. No one knew what a psychic trauma was and no one had the slightest idea that her father's guillotine act would profoundly affect Belle Gunness's later life—and the lives of at least a dozen men and possibly as many as 50.

Belle's father died while she was still a child and her mother brought her from Norway to Chicago. It was there that she met Merrel Sorenson. Sorenson was a man of middle age and a widower. By profession he was a private detective, but whatever talents he had in his field never bothered Belle.

They had been married for a year when a fire in their Chicago home destroyed the furniture. Belle, to her delight, collected something better than $2000 in insurance. She considered this in the light of found money, and began to wonder how she could get more of it.

It occurred to her then that Sorenson carried a $3500 policy on his life.

Her first move was to persuade her unsuspecting husband to take out a second insurance policy in the amount of $5000. Her second was to negotiate for the purchase of a farm in La Porte, Indiana. Belle Gunness was not possessed of many virtues but she was by no means a fool. It seemed to her that in the event of Merrel Sorenson's dying under curious circumstances, a rural sheriff could be more easily tricked than the Chicago police department. In addition, the farm at La Porte was a bargain. Some years before an entire family, consisting of seven members, had been mysteriously slaughtered during the night. The house reputed, locally, to be thoroughly haunted—not by a single ghost but by seven.

Belle bought the place cheaply. She did not fear ghosts. By the time she left the property, however, the ghosts had excellent reason to be terrified of her.

Ninety days later, Merrel Sorenson dropped dead. In Chicago, he may have been a first-rate private detective. But in La Porte he died without ever knowing who had put arsenic in his coffee. The doctor who signed the death certificate was quite satisfied that Sorenson had died of a digestive ailment, and Belle eagerly collected the insurance, which totaled up to $8500.

Belle's next husband was Peter Gunness and it was his name by which she was generally known. Probably because with one exception, he lasted considerably longer than her other consorts.

During the two years she spent as the wife of Peter Gunness, Belle went about establishing herself as a solid citizen of the community. She became a pillar of the church and no one sang hymns more loudly, praised the Lord with more gusto. She visited the La Porte County Orphanage and adopted three infant children, two girls and a blue-eyed boy. She was active in local charities, spoke harshly of no one, and laid down saucers of milk for stray cats. It was a convincing and effective cover-up and nobody could have been more amazed than Peter Gunness on the morning that he got hit in the head with a meat cleaver.

Belle Gunness summoned the doctor who shook his head sadly and, in turn, summoned the sheriff and the coroner.

Belle, with tears streaking down her cheeks, announced in a broken voice that the meat cleaver had fallen from the kitchen shelf directly onto the balding pate of her poor husband.

The coroner looked at the dead man's skull and gave it as his opinion that the cleaver would have had to fall from the top of the Eiffel Tower in order to split Gunness's head almost down to the chin. The kitchen shelf was five feet from the floor and Gunness who had been sitting down when the accident occurred would have been a scant foot beneath it.

Belle Gunness then wanted to know how a man who called himself a Christian could make such a horrible implication before an hour-old widow.

The sheriff inquired politely if the deceased had been insured in his wife's favor.

It seemed he had—to the extent of $4000. But averred Belle Gunness, if any mean-minded member of the community thought that she would break the law, much less one of the Lord's Commandments for a measly $4000, he was badly mistaken. She had never been so insulted in all her life.

The sheriff, after hearing Belle's speech, was hesitant. But the coroner insisted that the cleaver could not have fallen on the head of the deceased; it had been wielded by an outside agency. Since Belle was the sole outside agency present when the tragedy had occurred, the sheriff took her to the county jail.

She wasn't there long. Public sentiment was outraged. Belle Gunness was a staunch churchwoman. Belle Gunness carried soup to the sick and old clothes to the poor. Belle Gunness had taken three little waifs from the orphanage into her home. How then, asked the community with more passion than logic, could she be a murderess?

The authorities yielded to public pressure. Belle Gunness was released. The insurance company sighed and handed over the $4000 without further argument.

Even though Belle Gunness was completely vindicated, she had learned a lesson. It occurred to her that if, in the future, there were to be any corpses lying about her property, it would be far better if they were kept in a place where the suspicious eye of the coroner would not fall on them.

She announced that she was going into the hog raising business, and to that end engaged a mason to erect a smokehouse.

The smokehouse, which was made of cement, was attached to the kitchen by a narrow passageway. It contained all the accessories incidental to hog butchering: meat hooks, a vat, a cutting machine, and a number of keen knives and cleavers.

In the plot of ground contiguous to the smokehouse, Belle Gunness announced she planned to plant a vegetable garden. She fenced this land in with a rabbit-wire wall which was eight feet in height. When all this was done, she acquired several hogs, sat herself down at her writing desk, chewed the end of her pen thoughtfully, then composed an advertisement which was duly inserted in a farm periodical with a large Midwest circulation: "Personal: Charming but lonesome young widow, owning a fine farm in La Porte County, Indiana, wishes to make the acquaintance of a respectable gentleman of substantial means. Object matrimony. No letter considered unless writer is willing to become personally acquainted at the earliest opportunity."

This advertisement, to say the least, was rather misleading. At this stage of her life, Belle Gunness could have been considered attractive only by the standards of a lecherous hippopotamus.

She was five feet, eight inches in height, and weighed some 230 pounds. Her hair, which had been dyed red a year before, was faded and unkempt. Her skin was weathered and tough. Her arms were thick, muscular, had the power of pile drivers. Her bosom was vast, held in check by a straining steel corset. She wore, as a rule, overalls and a man's battered felt hat.

The first respectable gentleman of substantial means to reply to Belle Gunness's advertisement was Ole Lindboe of Chicago. Lindboe was a middle-aged bachelor. He arrived at La Porte with $200 in cash, a $500 diamond ring, a costly gold watch and a light and amorous heart.

Belle apparently had little trouble in relieving Lindboe of his tangible possessions. But when he asked to marry her and, as her husband, share the profits of the farm, Belle demurred.

"I can only marry you if you really love me," Belle said. "I've already had a couple of unhappy experiences."

Lindboe inquired exactly how he could prove the depth of his affection.

"Work here for me for a while," said Belle. "If you prove worthy, I'll marry you."

Lindboe nodded assent. "All right. How much do you intend to pay me?"

Belle was shocked at this solecism. "Pay my fiancé?" she exclaimed. "I never heard of such a thing."

Lindboe finally went to work for nothing. At the end of the two months he was still a bachelor and he was still unpaid. He confronted Belle, laid down an ultimatum. Either he was to be married or paid. And that very night, too.

Belle eyed him quizzically. She said, "You've been very patient. Tonight, I'll settle with you in full. In the meantime, go out to the vegetable garden and dig a big hole. I want to bury the garbage later."

Ole Lindboe dug a great big hole. In the morning, it had been filled in—and Ole Lindboe had vanished. His skeleton was dug up, and identified by his teeth, some six years later.

Belle Gunness spent no time weeping over Ole Lindboe. She wrote a letter to the farm magazine asking them to repeat the advertisement that had run before.

This brought Mr. John Moos of Elbow Lake, Minnesota, into her life. Mr. Moos, a prosperous farmer, did not come empty handed. He brought $5000 in cash along with him.

What evidence is available indicates that John Moos surrendered his capital and became Belle's combination hired man and lover. Apparently, he was not indispensable in either capacity. Three months later he disappeared during the height of Belle's hog butchering season.

Belle announced to her neighbors that Moos had returned to Elbow Lake, and smoothed over a new vegetable patch in her garden.

It was then that Belle Gunness met Ray Lamphere, who seemed to have signed an iron-clad contract with his guardian angel at birth. As far as Belle Gunness was concerned, he led a charmed life.

They met, not through the matrimonial advertisement, but on the street in La Porte. Lamphere was a graduate of Indiana University, and he was broke. This latter fact was not destined to win over Belle Gunness, but oddly enough, she took a liking to him.

She offered him a job on her farm and she actually paid him wages. Moreover, whatever affection Belle Gunness entertained for Lamphere was reciprocated. Lamphere was genuinely fond of Belle. He importuned her to marry him. She never did. Since they soon became lovers, the wedding would have been a technicality only and Belle was of no mind to marry a man not possessed of "substantial means."

Lamphere was still working on the farm when Eric Anderson, a Swede and widower who had just collected his wife's insurance, arrived on the scene carrying a copy of the farm journal, which at Belle's instructions had just printed her luring advertisement for the third time.

Ray Lamphere resented Anderson's presence, but Belle quickly relieved her new suitor of what cash he had brought with him and tenderly promised her hand in marriage. Lamphere, despondent, took to drink.

He frequented the town's saloons during the time that Eric Anderson was presumably pressing his wedding suit. However, upon his return home one evening, Belle Gunness gave him to understand that things between them were as they had been before.

"What about Anderson?" asked Lamphere, amazed.

"He's gone. He jilted me. Decided to marry a girl in Chicago, instead."

Lamphere frowned, "How come he knows a girl in Chicago? He told me once that he'd never been in the state of Illinois."

Belle shrugged her ample shoulders. "What's the difference? We'll never hear from him again. Forget it."

Lamphere forgot it—for the moment.

Between 1903 and 1906, Belle Gunness's matrimonial proposition was printed several times in various rural periodicals. And during that time there were half a dozen applicants for her ponderous hand. In spite of the fact that she married none of them, their presence invariably aroused Ray Lamphere's jealousy. He never knew if he was to sleep in the main bedroom or in the cubicle off the kitchen which was assigned to the hired man.

However, Lamphere's fear of losing his mistress to another always vanished at the same time as did his rival. If he ever wondered that Belle Gunness was busy in her smokehouse both in and out of hog butchering season, he said nothing. If he was ever curious as to what she did with the sacks of quicklime she ordered from Indianapolis, he held his peace.

The only man, apparently, to escape from Belle Gunness's lethal embrace was George Anderson of Tarkio, Missouri. He had read Belle's advertisement with interest. He was a widower with a neat bank account and he was lonely. He packed his bags, bought a book of travelers' checks and took the cars to La Porte and the "charming but lonesome young widow."

It was Belle Gunness's first experience with travelers' checks. When she learned that each check must be signed by Anderson she was keenly disappointed. This, obviously, complicated matters.

After serving Anderson an ample supper on the night of his arrival, she said, "You know, it would be a good idea if you signed those checks before you went to bed."

George Anderson, by no means as naive as some of Belle's suitors had been, lifted his eyebrows and said, "Sign them before I go to bed? For goodness sake, why?"

Belle shrugged. "Something might happen to you during the night."

"If anything happens to me there's no reason to endorse the checks. The money will eventually go to my heirs." He paused, had an afterthought. "Besides, what could possibly happen to me?"

Belle shrugged her power-packed shoulders. "You never can tell. Lots of persons die in their sleep, you know."

Anderson frowned and looked at Belle sharply. He was still frowning when he bedded down on the couch in the living room.

He was awakened in the middle of the night by a slight, shuffling sound. He opened his eyes to see Belle Gunness clad in a capacious nightgown, staring at him. In one hand she held a lighted candle. In the other, a meat cleaver.

Anderson sprang from the couch as if it was afire. He said, "What are you doing here?"

"Oh," said Belle blandly, "I couldn't sleep. I remembered that some of my butchering tools needed sharpening so I figured I might as well do the job now. I stopped by here to make sure that you were comfortable."

There may have been moments in George Anderson's life when he was more uncomfortable than he was at the moment but they did not come immediately to his mind.

He dressed with the speed of a volunteer fireman and departed La Porte forever, taking his unsigned travelers' checks and the memory of Belle's meat cleaver along with him.

Early in 1907 John Alden arrived at the La Porte farm via the same lovelorn route as had the others. He avoided the cleaver for two whole weeks.

At the end of that period, Belle Gunness dispatched Lamphere on an errand which guaranteed his absence for at least three hours. Then she invited Alden into her smokehouse and gave her attention to more serious matters.

Lamphere, however, did not carry out Belle's instructions. He went instead to a La Porte tavern. He enjoyed only three glasses of beer, since the bartender refused to grant him any credit. Then Lamphere returned home.

He arrived at a most inauspicious moment. He strode into the smoke-house just as Belle had laid the corpse of John Alden on a chopping block and was honing the edge of the cleaver. She turned red.

Lamphere's face turned gray. It was doubtless true that he had suspected dirty work was going on. But actually to see his mistress calmly readying to chop up a suitor was something else.

"My God," he said, "what are you doing?"

"I'm cutting him up," said Belle coolly. "The quicklime will work better that way. Then I'm going to bury him in the vegetable garden."

"You mean," gasped the horrified Lamphere, "that you murdered him?"

"Self-defense," said burly Belle. "He tried to trick me. Goodness knows what sort of girl he thought I was. I've never been so insulted in my life."

Lamphere, through either desperate love or desperate fear of his own life, kept his mouth shut.

Shortly after John Alden had been run through the sausage grinder, Ole Budsberg, powerful, blond painter, brought himself and $200 in cash to La Porte. He was, in a short time, relieved of both his wallet and his life. The vegetable garden was growing in size.

The last suitor of record to pay court to Belle Gunness was one Andrew C. Helgelin of Aberdeen, South Dakota. He had replied to Belle's provocative advertisement and had received, in return, a burning love letter.

Helgelin withdrew some money from the bank, packed his clothes and headed for Indiana. He only lived a week but he proved to be the biggest bonanza of all.

For some reason or other he failed to observe that Belle Gunness in no wise resembled the "charming widow" who had written of herself 'for publication. He was immediately smitten. He was all for an instantaneous marriage, but the obese object of his affection wasn't having any. What sort of girl did he think she was?

When Belle requested her customary proof of genuine love, Andrew Helgelin daringly slapped his wallet on the table and offered her the entire contents. Since this obviously did not move the 230-pound bulk of his beloved, he vowed that he would get in touch with his bank back in Aberdeen, instructing them to convert his securities to cash and wire the funds to Belle.

This struck Belle as a capital idea. It took exactly a week to complete the transaction. And in exactly a week, Belle invited Helgelin on an inspection tour of her modern smokehouse. He did so, and finished the trip in the adjacent vegetable garden.

Back in South Dakota, Alex Helgelin, brother to Andrew, became worried. He knew Belle's address, since Andrew had told him where he was going. He communicated with Belle, asking, anxiously, for news of his brother. This disconcerted Belle no whit. She answered promptly. Andrew, she wrote, left the farm a week after his arrival. She loved him and was as interested as Alex in his whereabouts. She suggested that Alex come at once to La Porte, bringing an adequate amount of cash with him. They would use the money to search for the missing Andrew. She was certain that with some cash she could bring the brothers together.

Alex, however, never made the trip.

At this period, in early April of 1908, Belle Gunness's position became shaky for the first time. She heard from a sheriff's deputy that Ray Lamphere, while drunk, had told a group of fellow drinkers that if anything ever happened to him at the farm, they were to request the sheriff to investigate. He had hinted darkly at horrendous doings at Belle's place.

Belle Gunness's reaction was characteristic. She didn't defend herself. She attacked.

Vowing that she had never been so insulted in all her life, she showed up at the county courthouse and announced that Lamphere had threatened her life on several occasions. She swore out a warrant for his arrest. However, after a private session with him in his cell, during which no one knows what compromise was reached, Belle withdrew the charge and Lamphere was freed.

But Belle remained uneasy. Perhaps, the little racket of running gentlemen possessed of substantial means through the sausage grinder was petering out. Perhaps, the time had come for a "twenty-three, skiddo," which in those days meant to take it on the lam.

Late in the evening of April 27th, 1908, the Gunness farm was suddenly ablaze. No one gave the alarm until it was too late, and the buildings were burned to the ground.

On the following morning, the charred ruins were carefully searched. Four blackened bodies were found. One was that of a woman. The other three were bodies of children—two girls and a boy. The inference was obvious. Belle Gunness and her three children had been destroyed by the flames. Moreover, there was a natural suspect for the sheriff—Ray Lamphere, who curiously enough had not slept at the farm that night. Too, it was a matter of record at the courthouse that Belle had sworn he had often threatened her life.

Ray Lamphere was arrested, tossed in jail and charged with murder, arson and everything else that the prosecutor was able to think of at the moment. The charred corpses were sent to the morgue. There, the coroner, who Belle Gunness rightly had considered a most suspicious man, viewed them. He conceded that the smaller bodies were those of Belle's adopted children.

. He announced flatly that the adult corpse was not that of Belle Gunness.

"It was three inches shorter," he stated. "It is eighty pounds lighter, Belle Gunness was possessed of good, sound teeth. This cadaver is wearing an ill-fitting plate."

By this time Ray Lamphere, in order to demonstrate his own innocence, was talking like a radio announcer trying to beat the clock. He told the sheriff of the death of John Alden and of the mysterious disappearance of Belle's other suitors. The sheriff promptly armed his deputies with shovels and sent them out to the farm.

By dusk they had dug up the remains of what were twelve recognizable skeletons. In addition, they had discovered four cartons full of miscellaneous bones. Helgelin and John Anderson had not entirely decomposed, thus they were identifiable.

Further examination by the coroner revealed that the children had not died by fire. They had been neatly cracked on the skull before the blaze had started. It was evident now that Belle had committed murder and arson to hide her own tracks. Exactly where she had obtained the woman's body which she hoped would be taken for her own was never known.

That isn't all which was never known. The State of Indiana offered a large reward for her apprehension. Every police headquarters in the United States was notified. But Belle made her 230 pounds hard to find. During the years the search spread into Australia, Canada, England, Europe, both Americas and Africa. But no one ever wittingly laid an eye on Belle Gunness.

If "Madame Murder"—Belle Gunness—still lives, she will be about 80 years old. Most officials are inclined to believe that she is dead, that she died quietly and respectfully in a feather bed—not while being run through a sausage machine.

HARLAN ELLISON

It is an honor to present this exposé by the one and only HARLAN ELLISON. I was a teen when I first read Ellison's *Gentleman Junkie and Other Stories of the Hung-Up Generation*, his remarkable collection of stories from the 1950s and 1960s. Most of the subjects were far from my dreary suburban diet of "Brady Bunch" reruns, but his voice spoke to me, awakened something in me. For the first time I was aware of the presence of the author in the creation of a literary text. I've often returned to his books over the years—*Gentleman Junkie; I Have No Mouth & Must Scream; No Doors, No Windows; Angry Candy*. Now a better, wisely mature reader, I've come to appreciate even more his remarkable gifts: his ability to mix and match genres, to turn on a dime from comedy to tragedy, the land mines he sets up, unforeseen till it's too late. And I am not alone in my belief that Ellison has singularly revolutionized the detective story, brought both its content and form into the modern age. It is asking a lot of Ellison to be able to instill a minor historical-criminal footnote like "Mystery Man Lucks and His Missing Bucks" with this kind of power. Maybe too much. But even here, *very* early in Ellison's career, when he was writing as Ellis Hart, one hears his sly wit and unique voice, as he brings to life the death of con man Al Lucks.

Mystery Man Lucks and
His Missing Bucks

There are a good many ways to make a million dollars: you can save Eagle stamps for fifty years, or you can rob a bank, or you can marry a millionairess, or you can figure a foolproof method for beating the Irish Sweepstakes. There are all kinds of ways.

Then there was the method employed by Allen M. Lucks. Simply stated, it ran about like this:

A stunning, long-legged redhead, accompanied by a shorter, but no less gorgeous brunette, walked up to an apartment door in Paris' swank George V hotel. Idly patting her expensive coiffure into place, the redhead rang the buzzer.

Had anyone familiar with Paris night-life been strolling down the corridor at that moment, he might have wondered why two of the more well-known Folies Bergère showgirls were unaccompanied that early in the evening, and what they were doing ringing the bell of that apartment.

The passerby would have been totally floored had he seen the squat, florid, slightly balding man, with an excess in the tummy category, who opened the door. The man looked pleasantly surprised. "Yes?" he inquired.

"Monsieur Lucks sent us," the redhead answered, smiling prettily. "He told us to tell you we are at your disposal, for as long as you are in Paris, Monsieur."

The fat little man's eyes lit up. He remembered Lucks from dinner the night before. The fellow had said he was a go-between for some people who wanted to sell war surplus. The fat man had smiled at Lucks—that was his business, buying war surplus. And Paris, this June of 1952, was abounding in quick-change artists wanting to unload war supplies.

Now this. He looked at the girls more appreciatively as Lucks' words ran through his head.

"Tomorrow at 7 P.M.," Lucks had said, "there will be a knock at your door and two girls will walk in. Ask no questions, pay no money, enjoy yourself and tell them when to report back."

As the fat little man ushered the girls inside, bolted the door, and prepared for a night of *vive la France*, he made a mental note to get in touch with Lucks the very next day to thank him. Have to throw some business the way of a fellow who'd do anything as nice as this.

And that, dear reader, is how mystery man Allen M. Lucks went about making several hundred millions of dollars for himself and clients...millions which no one can find! November 27, 1955, was an important day for 53-year-old bachelor Al Lucks. He died that day. And all his relatives are currently weeping sad, dark tears. No one can say how sorry they are to see good old Al go, but they *are* moaning because Lucks' vast uncountable fortune is nowhere in sight.

For Allen Lucks died as mysteriously as he lived—an international figure on first-name terms with some of the most influential crooks and influence-peddlers in the world. He died so mysteriously, in fact, that from November 27 to March 2 of this year, not the slightest hint was voiced that he had even died!

Now the big scramble is on. The Lucks fortunes are nowhere in sight. Where are they? That's what the deceased's surviving relations would like to know. They suspect the money is scattered across three continents, in numerous banks under phony names, and in safe deposit boxes too numerous to mention. Al Lucks trusted no one. He had a fear of stocks and bonds, and a glowing admiration for the personal sanctuary a safe deposit box offers.

Some of that money is in a Swiss bank—and Swiss banks being notoriously discrete about releasing information—it may mean years of dickering before a penny of that money sees the light of day.

Right now, a European liaison man of prominent Scranton, Pennsylvania, lawyer Jerome Myers, is frantically scurrying through the capitals of Europe, trying to locate a fortune so large, no one feels capable of estimating its size.

This isn't a strange ending to the career of mystery playboy Al Lucks. It is fitting, somehow. That's the way he lived—with little notoriety, with much money, and with a caravan of beautiful women any Sheik would shriek for!

What's that? You say you never heard of multimillionaire Lucks? You ask what the big pitch is with him, and why all the interest? You wanna know who he was and where all this dough came from that no one can find? All right, tell you what I'm gonna do—I'm gonna tell you the whole story of Fast-Bucks Lucks from start to finish, with a punch-line that'll knock you dead.

It should. It killed Al Lucks!

*   *   *

Lucks made his entrance the same way Abe Lincoln did; of poor but honest parents. However, it didn't take our boy Al long to find out that what was good for Mr. Lincoln was not necessarily good for Mama Lucks' little boy Allen.

In 1903, the Lucks family, merchants of Hazelton, Penna., a rugged hard-coal town, rejoiced at the birth of their son. Their joy was compounded in 1923 when Al graduated from Syracuse University. When he obtained his law degree from Georgetown Law School in 1926, with an enviable record as a superlative student, the family knew they had a real *mensche* (Big Man) in the family. Oh, Al was smart, all right.

He practiced for a while in Washington, with a noticeable lack of success. Finally, Al returned to Scranton and started looking around for business. It seemed almost providential that Al should strike upon the biggest money in law available at that time. During this period—the late twenties—there was a lot of liquor bootlegging in the coal regions, and, logically enough, a good many bootleggers needed a mouthpiece when the long arm of the law beckoned angrily toward court.

In short order Al Lucks became well known in the courtroom of Federal Judge Albert M. Johnson (who was driven from the bench in 1946 under threat of impeachment from the House of Representatives). Al Lucks suddenly came into affluence. In a very short time Lucks became known as the man to see if you needed a fast way out.

Then in 1943 the smell of all the loose money drew Lucks to greener pastures . . . Washington, where he began a palm-greasing stint unparalleled in the D. of C.'s unpleasant annals.

Lucks tossed girlie parties for deserving bigwigs at the drop of a G-string, and it paid off in big tips about big sales that resulted in big contracts with big profits for Lucks.

Lucks got in on the ground floor of war surplus after World War II, outshrewding some of the shrewdest fast-buck men in the country. That ground floor was so big, covered so much territory, that Lucks hied himself overseas to Paris where he operated out of the George V, while maintaining a full-time suite in Frankfurt, Germany, which is U.S. Army headquarters in Europe.

Employing the same natural cunning that made him a wheel in the bootlegging rackets, Lucks shortly became middleman in dozens of multi-million-dollar transactions, never risking his own money, yet reaping fantastic profits merely by knowing whom to call and when. He began living high, to the tune of $100,000 a year for fun and games. The money he made over that was clear net profit, securely secreted away.

Everything from women to influence he bought and used. The women particularly. Lucks had more than an eye for the dolls. He had a pair of eyes, plus 20-20 binoculars in case something might get past him.

The only pictures available of mystery man Lucks—who correctly judged the best way of staying out of the reach of investigating committees was to stay out of the public limelight—are those he took with his female companions, of whom there were many.

One of the many was Diane (Golden Girl) Harris, a young roundheels with a penchant for soft money and running down hotel corridors sans clothing. Lucks was quoted as saying:

"I've never seen a finer lady than Diane. If you can't say nice things about a lady, don't say anything. Diane is a full lady. I don't believe anything else that is said about her."

Which is a nice bit of philosophy from the guy who was about to be sued in 1954 on charges of paternity. Ex-chorine Harriette Levi wound up with a juicy out-of-court settlement in that case—after Allen admitted the siring—and disappeared from sight with her ten-year-old son.

The women came and went like the autumn breezes, an endless stream of easy-virtue gals, marching in and out of Fast-Bucks Lucks' fabulous George V suite.

At the height of his fantastic career, Lucks met and dealt with such notorious fortune-hunters as Washington's top influence-peddler John Maragon, English ex-con George Dawson who made over $100,000,000 in a deal where he sold the U.S. Army 14,000 of their own trucks, and even the late Senator Kenneth McKellar, big boy in the infamous Crump machine of Tennessee.

All these men, and more—from junk dealers to cabinet members—were intimates of Lucks and his lovely entourage. All of them were ready to dance when he pulled their strings. For all of them made fortunes as Lucks' career progressed.

By 1950 Al Lucks was operating almost full-time out of Paris, and showing a great deal of reluctance to go back to the U.S. Probably because there were half a dozen men back there, waiting to either sue or stab.

At this time, the rumors had it that Lucks had made a fantastic killing in Argentina. The rumors told of a vast supply of automobile parts, assembled in Canada, and sold to the Argentine government, with profits being split by Lucks, dictator Juan Peron, and Peron's economics minister.

The beauty of the whole transaction was that the parts were never delivered!

Then came 1951, a bad year for Lucks. Newspaper stories began appearing about him. First there was the New York Supreme Court suit by Alvin Reiss of the Lehigh Trading Co. Reiss claimed to have bought $1,109,760 worth of surplus trucks and shipped them to Lucks in Europe for a promised 15% commission—which he never got paid. The case dragged on and on, never resolving itself, because Lucks was too shy to return to the Land of the Free.

When he *did* enter the country, his trips were infrequent and secretive. He would stop at New York's Essex House or the Mayflower in Washington, transact his business hurriedly, drop in on his relatives in Scranton, and be back in Europe before anyone realized he'd even been around.

But from there on out, Lucks' star began to wane. First the Reiss suit, then charges from other American agencies, then the Jelke trial investigations where the Lucks name figured prominently. Then the suit by Harriette Levi.

As if he didn't have enough burdens to shoulder, Lucks was being blackmailed by several parties and for several different reasons. Things were starting to turn. His fortunes were decreasing. He was still living at his $100,000 a year clip, still treating the girlies to the best, and still maintaining his exclusive apartments.

But it was the beginning of the end for Allen Lucks.

On November 25, 1955, late, late in the wee hours, the switchboard of the George V buzzed alarmingly. The operator picked up her phones and heard a girl's frantic voice from the Lucks suite moaning that "Monsieur Lucks, 'ee eez dead!"

It wasn't quite true, but when they raced upstairs, they found Al Lucks on the way out as the result of a stroke. He was raced to the French Clinic in Paris, and two days later he died. The medical report stated he had died from a cerebral hemorrhage—induced by overexertion.

The two girls who were found in his apartment with him were turned back onto the streets, where they quickly disappeared, with the awed stares of police following them.

Then began the crazy game of "bucks, bucks, who's got the Lucks bucks?" The scramble was on, and in the ensuing hustle, the whole sordid story of Lucks's influence-selling, his procuring, his shady dealings on both sides of the Iron Curtain, came out.

Where his money now reposes, how much he had cached away—all these are mysteries . . . just a few more mysteries surrounding a man who clothed himself for years in secrecy.

Even so, all of Al Lucks's deals pale into insignificance at his latest, current transaction. No matter how much money he has hidden away in the bank vaults of Europe, what Al is doing *now* is his biggest business deal.

He's handling the Lucks concession in Eternity, trying to buy his way into Heaven! You can lay your bets with Pete, the angel on the gate. The odds are Terrific!

ROBERT FAHERTY

To call ROBERT FAHERTY "a master of detective fiction" might be stretching things just a bit. He left behind only one novel, *Swamp Babe*. In 1958, Crest Books, a Fawcett imprint, published this backwoods crime adventure about "a teenage temptress wild and beautiful as the untamed swamp that spawned her." It is enjoyable, and eminently readable, yet it would be hard to make a case that it rises above scores of other paperbacks that clamored for attention on bookstore shelves during the 1950s. Faherty's true crime output was considerably more substantial and, for my money, more satisfying. He had a knack for spotting odd crimes with outrageous characters and bizarre motives. He knew how to plot, and he had an eye for the incongruous detail, just the right detail to capture time and place. Such is the case with the story you are about to read, one of my favorites, about a turn-of-the-century dance fan who paid the ultimate price because he was "unable to resist the lure of the fascinating rhythm of the seductive tango."

The Dancing Beauty and the Fatal Trap

The diffused glare of the locomotive's headlight illumined vaguely the clumps of small trees and the shadowy forms of bushes in the lowland.

Engineer Robert Rohel, guiding the Elgin, Joliet & Eastern freight train west from Chicago, saw the two straight-line gleams of the rails as he peered out from the cab. Then—one of the lines was broken. Too late to stop, the horrified engineer saw a dark object on one rail.

As Rohel set the brakes and threw over the throttle, the great wheels of the engine passed over the object. The train jolted to a stop and he rushed back.

"A woman on the tracks!" he exclaimed to his fireman as they held their lanterns over a crumpled form beside the rail. "I couldn't save her. This is awful...the first time it's happened to me."

Rohel gently touched the body, turned it over. There was nothing he could do.

Stars shone in a clear sky. The lonely area was dark except for the distant glow of the train's lamp, and, farther ahead, little points of light marking a station in the town of Wayne, Illinois. It was a warm night—September 26th.

In the morning, Coroner William A. Hopf examined the body in a morgue in West Chicago.

"Might have been an accident," he said. "She may have fainted or fallen there and struck her head. Although it is strange that she should be walking in that lonely spot. Then," he continued, "there's a possibility she committed suicide. Might have picked that spot purposely."

The coroner saw a face of considerable attractiveness, framed by rich, abundant brown hair. Though the body was broken, the facial features were virtually unmarred. The woman's dark dress was of fine quality silk. A small gold watch, probably of little value, was pinned to the dress and intact despite the violence of the train's impact.

"I guess there's little I can do except write a report and hold a routine inquest," he said. "The trainman cannot be blamed, of course."

But Coroner Hopf was thorough. He touched the face and found the skin broken near the mouth. There seemed to be a round hole in the left cheek. He studied the head. There was a hole in the posterior skull.

"A bullet wound!" he exclaimed. "This woman was shot!"

A bullet—probably of .32 caliber—had passed through the mouth, the palate, and then gone out through the back of the head.

"I don't believe the wound in the cheek was caused by a gun placed very near it. There're no powder burns," the coroner reasoned. "Most likely the gun was held a few feet away. Probably the killer expected that at the moment the train struck the body his crime would be concealed forever—and, certainly, it nearly worked out that way."

Since it was established that the woman had been murdered, Sheriff
A. A. Kuhn hurried with deputies to the railroad tracks.

There was not a trace of the gun near the scene. Determined not to
overlook any clues, however, Kuhn got down on hands and knees and
searched the grass. Before long he found a broken bracelet of gold. It was
inscribed: "From W.H.A. to M.A." As he was examining it closely, a
deputy came running with a woman's purse, turned inside out, which he
had found thirty feet away.

"She must have been robbed," he said. "There's nothing in or on the
purse to tell who she was."

That question seemed to be answered a few minutes later. A white card
was found in the grass. It bore a printed name, "Mildred Allison." Kuhn
turned it over. On the back, faintly penciled, was: "Felecita Club."

Another deputy found scraps of torn paper, which the sheriff held
carefully and took to the office.

The scraps were pieced together and revealed the embossed name of a
downtown Chicago hotel. Some fragments were missing, but the others
formed words. A cryptic message!

"Dear... gang... girls... Dunham   farm... money... $14... $500...
you can have what you want."

Like the other words, a signature was written in ink: "A. Harron."

Dunham farm was near the intersection of the tracks of the Elgin, Joliet
& Eastern and the Chicago, Aurora & Elgin Railroads, near the place
where the train had struck the body. Kuhn hurried there with the pasted
fragments of the note.

The manager's wife said she had never seen the note and had no idea of
the meaning of the message. Told about the girl on the tracks, she
recalled an incident confirming the murder theory:

"After I left the Aurora & Elgin electric train at 8 o'clock last night, I
noticed a man and a woman who apparently had come from Chicago on
the same train. They walked near me, together, and talked in a friendly
way. The woman joked about being 'out in the country' at night.

"Then they walked, arm-in-arm, along the Wayne road. That would
have led them near the point at which the two railroads meet, close to the
place where the train hit the woman."

Thanking the woman, the sheriff mapped three immediate moves: a
check to learn positively whether the described couple had come from

Chicago, a hunt for the mysterious "Harron" of the note, and an inquiry at the Felecita Club to establish the identification of the victim if possible.

He telephoned a complete report of the case to Captain John J. Halpin, in charge of Chicago detectives. Halpin promised complete and prompt cooperation to solve the crime.

Kuhn questioned the guards of the electric train which had reached Wayne at 8 o'clock. One remembered a couple answering to the description as having boarded the train at the Chicago terminal at Fifth Avenue. He said the woman had had a small suitcase and the man, no baggage. They had seemed on the best of terms, and had chatted and joked.

To Kuhn, this meant that the crime had not been the result of a chance encounter ending in a holdup!

Halpin's first move was to send detectives to the downtown hotel on Michigan Avenue in search of Harron. They found that a man of that name had registered there but had left, saying he expected to return there in a few days.

Then the captain hurried with his men to the Felecita Club, a dance academy on Thirty-third Street near Cottage Grove Avenue.

The manager, Frank Oleson, said he knew Mildred Allison. His description of her was the same as that of the girl in the West Chicago morgue.

"Miss Allison was a beautiful girl and one of the best tango dancers in Chicago," he said. "She has been at my club many times, and has been a great favorite since the popularity of the tango developed. I don't know why anyone would want to harm her!"

Oleson went to West Chicago and definitely established the victim's identity.

Kuhn and Halpin went to Chicago with Oleson and questioned him at length about every known detail of the girl's life.

She had been married twice, he knew, and her first husband lived in Chicago. Her full name was Mildred Allison Rexroat, but she used only "Allison." She was the mother of two young children by her first husband, Allison. Mildred had had many admirers at the dancing academy and some had been very attentive. But Oleson said he did not know of anyone who might have had a motive to kill her.

The officers showed him the fragments of the mystery note.

Oleson could offer no help on that.

"I want to talk to both the men who have been married to her," Halpin said. "First, I want to search her living quarters. We may have to dig deeply into a woman's life to find the point at which the killer entered it."

Oleson directed the police to a home on Eggleston Avenue where the dancer had had a room.

There among a miscellany of clothing and toilet articles, Halpin found papers, letters and pictures. There were letters from both husbands, some in tender vein, others hinting of quarrels. Addresses were given: Allison, the first husband, lived on the South Side. Rexroat, the second, lived at Macomb, Illinois.

Halpin made telephone calls until he located both men, and received assurance that they would undergo questioning. He decided the best place for the conference would be in the morgue, with Mildred Allison Rexroat, a silent, lifeless witness.

Under the vigilant eyes of Halpin and Kuhn, the two men walked into the dimly lighted chamber of death and looked upon the face of the woman they had loved. State's Attorney C. W. Hadley of DuPage County followed them in.

"I haven't the slightest idea of who killed her or why she was killed," Rexroat said quickly, as he turned away and faced Hadley.

Allison seemed deeply moved and continued to gaze at the still form.

"Mildred—" he said. "I loved her, and, I wanted to keep her. But she drifted away from me, found new companions. Then she divorced me."

"Where were you on the night of September 26th?" Hadley asked.

"At home, on the South Side. I can prove that by a number of people. I was in the house and in the neighborhood all evening."

Rexroat spoke.

"I was in my father's farmhouse at Macomb."

The officers made an immediate checkup of their alibis and found that both were true.

Everett Rexroat then told a story tinged with sadness and bitterness:

"I met Mildred at a dance club on the South Side and I fell in love at first sight. I couldn't stay away from her. I went to see her every night. Within a few weeks I asked her to marry me. She didn't believe I meant it at first, but I convinced her I loved her, and she consented.

"We were married and I brought my bride home to the farm at Macomb. We were happy as ever any married couple had been—at least, I was happy. Then Mildred began to grow tired of country life, and talked about the city and the bright lights. I told her I must stay on the farm, but she became more dissatisfied every day. One night when I came into the house after a hard day's work I learned she had packed her bag and had gone away.

"That broke me up for a long time, but I knew it was useless to try to follow her and persuade her to come back. I never saw her again—until now!"

After establishing that Rexroat and his father and two neighbors had spent the evening of September 26th in the farm house, Halpin sent detectives to search Allison's home. They found a trunk marked with Mildred's name and containing her personal effects. Apparently it had been brought there very recently.

Halpin was interested in that peculiar circumstance and searched the trunk thoroughly. He found many letters, some in German, some voicing vague threats against the dancer. But the captain vainly sought a name and address that would give him a lead.

Other loose ends of the investigation had to be picked up. He sent a squad to the Michigan Avenue hotel in a new quest for the writer of the mysterious note found near the railroad tracks.

The detectives found Harron.

"Mildred Allison?" the man said. "I know nothing about her, except what I have read in newspapers."

The pasted note was shown to him.

"I can explain that easily. I wrote that note to a friend of mine who lives at Wayne, alluding to an attempt of some swindlers to get me in on a scheme which, I am sure, would have defrauded both of us. It just happens that he tore the note up out there."

The statement was verified quickly by the police. Another promising lead had failed, and the killer, still unnamed, remained at large.

While Captain Halpin went to the Eggleston Avenue house to locate and question the woman from whom Mildred Allison had rented her room, a strange physical clue was discovered.

A hair switch, of the type used in that day to give woman's crowning glory a more abundant appearance, was found in the freight yards of the Burlington Railroad, south of downtown Chicago.

The switch was taken to Captain Halpin as he was questioning the victim's landlady. "That is Mildred's. I'm sure," the woman said. "It is made of her hair! That is exactly the shade of hers."

She stared at the grim reminder of the dead dancer.

"Mildred put that into her rattan suitcase when she left here that evening. She said she was going to Wheaton to arrange about forming a tango class there." Wheaton was only a few miles away from Wayne, the scene of the crime.

"She had talked with a man, often, about the class," the landlady continued. "I think she was to meet him that night. Did you find her diamond ring? She had a valuable one."

"That was not either of her husbands?"

"No, he was a young fellow she met recently when dancing, probably at Felecita. I think it was Mr. Spencer."

"Tell me all you know about this Spencer," Halpin asked.

"I saw him one evening when he came to call for Mildred. I think he may have been the man who telephoned to her the afternoon before she started for Wheaton. The voice was like Mr. Spencer's, a low drawl."

"Do you think that was his real name?"

"I don't know that he ever used another. He was rather short and stocky. He had strong, thick shoulders. I would say he was between twenty-eight and thirty-two years old. His hair was brown and he had blue eyes, and his face was ruddy. He wore gold eyeglasses. His clothes were like a minister's—black suit and high collar."

"His weight and height?"

"About five feet, six inches tall, I think, and he must have weighed about a hundred and forty-five pounds."

The description fitted a man who Oleson said had danced the tango with Mildred at the Felecita!

Sheriff Kuhn received the report at Wheaton and sought sponsors of a tango class there. Hours of inquiry resulted only in word that no one had heard of plans for such a class.

But there were two men named Spencer in Wheaton!

Kuhn hurried to one, a merchant. He did not answer the description of the mystery man, and he promptly accounted for all his movements on the night of September 26th.

The second, a younger man, denied he had ever been interested in the tango or in any dancer. Mildred's landlady looked at him and said he was not the admirer of Mildred.

The merchant then recalled that a salesman named Spencer often came to Wheaton on business. Detectives rushed eagerly to the salesman's employers in Chicago.

That young man, records and correspondence proved, had been in southern Illinois the night of the crime. While the detectives were in the office the salesman came in. He did not fit the description of the hunted man given by the victim's landlady.

"Three Spencers!" Halpin groaned, "and not the man we want. I hope we don't have to sift out all the Spencers in Illinois."

Halpin rechecked the descriptions given of the man who had been seen on the train.

The train attendants and the farm manager's wife agreed that he had been stocky, short and brown-haired, and had worn a dark suit.

Sheriff Kuhn telephoned his report to Halpin then. He had ordered with results, a wide search of the area along the Elgin, Joliet & Eastern tracks. A deputy had found, hidden in a marshy spot near the tracks, a heavy hammer wrapped in a towel, and a newspaper dated September 23rd. The hammer bore the imprint of a Chicago hardware dealer. It weighed three pounds.

Halpin dispatched detectives to the store. It was hard to figure out what part the hammer had played in the case. The dancer had been shot and, apparently, had not been struck on the head. Had the killer planned the murder long in advance, planned to kill with the hammer—and secreted it there on September 23rd?

Halpin was eager for the report from the store. But the new clue failed. The store had sold many such hammers to mechanics, and there were no records kept of such sales.

"This murderer has all Chicago to hide in," Halpin told his men. "But we've got to dig him out, quick. It's an even chance he thinks that he is safe and that the city is the best place for him to keep under cover. Maybe he has used the name of Spencer only in his contacts with the girl he killed. He may think he's perfectly safe under another name.

"But I have a hunch this fellow will show up again around the dance halls. I don't believe he will stay away from girls very long. We're going to cover such places, and we're going to get a lead on him, or find him, in one of them."

*   *   *

Halpin mapped an amazing campaign of vigilance over dance halls, schools and clubs, concentrating on those of the South Side. District captains were instructed to have plainclothes on the watch for the mysterious Spencer, described fully in communications to the captains. And Halpin sent his best men to the halls to mingle with the dancers, to be attentive to the girls, and to talk about the tango murder case with them, while watching always for the appearance of a short, thick-shouldered man wearing gold eyeglasses.

Surely, Halpin reasoned, the slayer would come forth from wherever he had been hiding, harassed mentally by his guilt to find a measure of relief in the satisfaction of his craving for companionship with women. The tango, newly imported from the Latin countries, had won many to its seductive grace. Perhaps the man of gun and hammer was an addict and would be unable to resist the lure of the Spanish music and the exhilaration of embraces of young girls to its fascinating rhythm.

Three nights passed without result. Halpin sent new instructions to his captains, to insure that police on post would watch every report carefully.

"The fellow has got to come out into the open," Halpin said. "He's got to try to forget that scene on the railroad tracks. He'll go looking for girls—and he may betray himself in doing it."

The next night a detective phoned Halpin.

"I've got something," he said. "I've met a girl in a hall who says she knew a guy that looked like Spencer and was tango-crazy. A few nights ago he danced with her, and he invited her to have a drink at a party at his house. She went out with him, but found that the house was just a rooming place and that there was no party. She left him. She said he mentioned having known Mildred Allison. The fellow was nervous and excited, she said. The house is near the Felecita Club."

Halpin rushed to the address with half-a-dozen detectives. While front and rear were guarded, the captain and two men entered and found the landlady. They described the man, and she indicated a room at the head of the stairs.

The room was dark, it seemed. Halpin tired the door. It was locked. He rapped. There was no sound within. The three men put their shoulders to it and broke the door open.

The room was empty, but the bed was rumpled as if recently occupied.

The frightened landlady said she had made it up early that afternoon.

"What was this fellow's name?" Halpin demanded.

"He wouldn't give a name," she said. "He paid for a week, four days ago. But he had a suitcase, and it's gone. It looks like he's moved out."

She described the tenant fully. The picture tallied exactly with that of Spencer, but she had not seen gold eyeglasses.

"He had a funny suitcase," she said. "It was that wood stuff—rattan they call it."

Mildred Allison's suitcase had been of rattan!

"He's our man," Halpin said, "and we have had a tough break. Missed him by a couple of hours! But he'll turn up again in this part of town. I'm betting."

Again, while Spanish rhythms were played in the South Side dance halls and young men and girls and old men and girls swayed and pirouetted in the gyrations of the tango, detectives watched.

Halpin then got a report that a man resembling Spencer had been seen in a cheap dancing resort of unsavory reputation near Twenty-second and State streets. He sent more detectives into the area.

That night a woman told a uniformed patrolman that she had been threatened by a man who had taken a room in her house two days before.

The patrolman told one of Halpin's detectives. The sleuth had been thinking only in terms of "Mr. Spencer," and he considered this new development only in that light. He questioned this woman.

"Is the fellow short, brown-haired, with bulky shoulders?"

"Yes. How did you know?"

"Is he in your house now?"

"No, he went out. I meant to tell him he must vacate the room, but I was afraid to, after he threatened me during an argument because there wasn't a lock on the door of his room."

The detective hurried to the house and into the room. A high collar was on the dresser. Under a paper in a small drawer of a dresser he found a loaded .32-caliber pistol. In a corner of the room was a pair of shoes caked with mud.

"Maybe he was a thief. He had a woman's diamond ring. He showed it to me," the landlady said.

The detective looked into a clothes closet, and saw a small rattan suitcase.

He rushed to telephone and told Captain Halpin:

"I've located Spencer, sure!"

The captain arrived in ten minutes with an automobile load of heavily armed detectives. Quickly he posted his men, one at the rear door, another in a doorway forty feet from the house, two in doorways across the street, out of sight. One took a position in a dark corner of the living room. Halpin and one sleuth stayed in the man's room.

At midnight the front door downstairs slammed, and a man hurried up the stairs with heavy steps. Halpin heard the doorknob turn. He took one step forward quietly, with his .38 ready. The door swung open and Halpin thrust his gun forward.

There was a gasp and a scuffle. Halpin and his man hurled the newcomer to the floor, and handcuffs were snapped on his wrists.

In the light of the downstairs hall the detectives studied their prisoner. He was short, with thick neck and heavy shoulders. He wore a high collar and a black suit. Brown hair, blue eyes. Halpin fished a pair of gold eyeglasses from the prisoner's vest pocket and put them on his nose.

"Just like a preacher," Halpin said. "You could pass for a Madison Street evangelist."

"Say, you dicks have the wrong man," the prisoner whimpered. The voice was a drawl, low and soft.

"We've got the man who killed Mildred Allison Rexroat, and that's the one we've been looking for!"

At the detective bureau that night Oleson and Mildred's landlady identified the prisoner as the mysterious Mr. Spencer; and the suitcase was identified as the one carried by Mildred Allison Rexroat on her journey to death.

Then Spencer talked.

"Sure, I killed her."

"You planned it all long before, didn't you?"

"Sure, I did. I used to dance with the girl, and, believe me, I sure could do the tango with her. I liked her at first and soon fell head over heels in love with her. I asked her not to dance with other fellows and go around with them. I wanted her for my own. She didn't mind me, and I got mad about it. I figured if I couldn't have her I would put her away, and while I was doing it I would get her money and her ring.

"You know, I heard about that place out in the country. Remember, about a year ago, a woman was killed out there with a rock by somebody and they never got a line on the guy that did it? I picked that spot, I like a hammer for that kind of work, so I got a big one and went out there and put it where I could have it handy.

"I made a date with Millie and kidded her along about some people in Wheaton wanting to learn the tango. I said we had to go to Wayne to meet one of them on a farm, and she might need some money to rent a hall and make other arrangements.

"Millie fell for it. On the train I made love to her and promised her a lot, and she believed me. Women are soft for me!

"When we got off the train I said we had to walk along a dark road near the tracks. Millie didn't mind. She said it was a fine night for a walk in the country. I tried to lead her along to the spot where I had the hammer hidden, but she didn't want to go there, so I decided I wouldn't make her suspicious. I didn't want her to yell for help. I like a hammer; it's quiet.

"I stopped near the tracks, anyway, and decided to do the work right there. I put my arm around her and held her close while I pulled out my gun. Then I stepped back a little and gave it to her, right in the face.

"She fell right over without saying a word, and I grabbed her purse and her ring. I didn't take the bracelet. I didn't think I could sell it for much.

"I had this train idea all figured out. I dragged Millie onto the rail and dropped her there. I figured people would say it was just another train accident. I thought for sure the train would hit her head. It was a tough break for me that I didn't make sure her head was on the rail."

Halpin listened grimly to the horrifying story.

As the day for the trial at Wheaton drew near, Spencer obtained a lawyer and said he would fight the charge. Meanwhile he revealed that his real name was Henry Spencer and that he had served a ten-year term at Joliet Prison for burglary.

The trial was one of the most amazing spectacles seen in an Illinois courtroom. State's Attorney Hadley led the state's fight to get a swift verdict and a death sentence.

Among the spectators in the crowded courtroom were the two men who had loved and married the murdered tango dancer.

Spencer lighted a cigar as he sat at the defense table, a red ribbon in the lapel of his coat.

The judge rapped his gavel and ordered him to stop smoking.

"I won't," he said, and continued puffing until a balliff took the cigar from him.

When a lawyer began a plea, talking of "irresponsibility" and "mental weakness," Spencer stood and shouted:

"Cut out all this red tape! Get twelve men to say I killed my pal Millie and then take me out and hang me. Don't waste all this time. Send somebody out to build a scaffold. String me up!"

He gripped his throat to illustrate the hanging.

Spencer was a prophet. Twelve men did rule that he killed Mildred Allison Rexroat, and that he was guilty of murder in the first degree.

"I'll appeal," his lawyer said.

"Cut out the appeals," yelled Spencer. "Let's get this rope party over!"

He turned to the spectators and said:

"I hope you people all enjoyed this trial, and got what you came for. I want you all to come and see me swing!"

The judge decreed that Spencer must hang on December 21st.

Defense counsel appealed to the Supreme Court, and there was a reprieve after Wheaton officials objected to a hanging during Christmas week.

Hanging was scheduled for January 22nd, but a new delay was granted for review of the evidence. Then the Supreme Court ruled that Spencer must die for his crime.

On July 31st, 1914, Spencer stood on the scaffold, a red flower pinned to his shirt. The white cap was fitted over his head and the noose adjusted.

He was dead a minute later, his body on the ground—a few miles from the place where he shot Mildred Allison Rexroat and placed her body on the railroad track.

BRUNO FISCHER

From the late 1940s until about 1960, publicity-shy BRUNO FISCHER was one of the most successful mystery writers in the field. Along with top-shelf talent like Jim Thompson, Lionel White, Day Keene, Harry Whittington, Gil Brewer, Charles Williams, James M. Cain, John D. McDonald, and David Goodis, Fischer's books were a mainstay in the Fawcett Gold Medal paperback line, his stories a fixture in *Manhunt*, the finest of the postwar crime fiction digests. And he was good. Read *More Deaths than One*, *Her Flesh Was Cold*, or *The Girl Between*, and you'll know what I mean. Today, one must search dusty shelves at secondhand bookstores and flea markets to find his books. But the effort is worth it. His lean, pared-down writing style, his somber, often-brutal observations about small-town America, and inventive storytelling techniques (check out his 1947 *More Deaths than One*, a novel presented through the eyes of seven people: six suspects and a detective) make for powerful reading indeed. This little lost gem is from earlier in his career. It is about a radio singer's mysterious death—and the clues detectives pieced together to bring her unlikely killer to justice.

The Footprint in the Snow

Dawn was trickling through the frosted bedroom windows when the persistent jangling of the telephone awoke Chief of Police Edward K. Herrick. His wife stirred, muttered, "Who can that be at this hour?" and snuggled deeper under the covers. Reluctantly Herrick left the warmth of his bed and groped his way drowsily downstairs to the telephone.

Patrolman Michael Rossi, who was on duty, said excitedly, "Chief, there's been a murder."

Abruptly Herrick was wide awake. For nine years he had been Chief of
Police of Marvin Center, an incorporated village of Long Island, New
York, and during that period the nearest thing to a homicide had resulted
from automobile accidents. He had, as a matter of fact, never in his life
been on a murder case.

"Did you identify the body, Mike?" Herrick asked.

"No trouble about that, Chief. She was found right outside her house.
Did you know Vivian Lahey, the radio singer?"

The picture of the bright-eyed brunette with a charming, heart-shaped
face leaped up in Herrick's mind. In a place the size of Marvin Center,
there weren't many of the older families he didn't know. He had never
spoken a word to Vivian Lahey, but he had been casually acquainted with
her father before he had died several years previously, and he had heard
her voice on the radio.

"Will Hitch, the milkman, found the body about fifteen minutes ago,"
Rossi was saying. "She was struck over the head by an empty milk bottle
and—"

"Not by Hitch!" Herrick broke in.

"No, no," Rossi said. "Miss Lahey lived with her sister and brother-in-
law, George Engleberry, at 37 Oak Lane. Hitch found the body near the
back door when he was delivering milk. What do I do now, Chief?"

"Keep Hitch there. See that nobody touches the body or goes anywhere
near it. And get somebody to call the rest of the force. I want every man
there."

As Herrick hung up, he felt a sense of inadequacy. Every man on the
Marvin Center police force meant exactly five men, including himself. Up
until now, that many had sufficed to uphold law and order and enforce
traffic regulations in the placid community fifty miles from New York
City. But this was murder. He could count on the full cooperation of
Arthur Simms, the District Attorney, and the State Police, but crime in
Marvin Center was essentially his responsibility.

Mrs. Herrick was wide awake and curious when he returned to the
bedroom. As he dressed, he told her of the murder.

"Vivian Lahey!" she exclaimed. "Well, I'm not surprised!"

With one sock dangling from his hand, Herrick turned sharply to his
wife. "What's that?"

She bit her lip, as in regret over her outburst. "That was a foolish thing for me to say. But when an attractive girl like that runs around with a married man like John Shanken—"

"Shanken?" The Chief frowned. "You can't mean the haberdasher on Division Street?"

"All I know is what I've heard. Of course it may be only idle gossip, and even if it isn't, it probably doesn't mean anything." She added somewhat contritely, "I suppose in a terrible thing like murder it's unfair to get anybody in trouble by repeating rumor."

"You never can tell," Herrick said slowly.

Daylight was complete when he took his car out of the garage. It was a bitingly cold morning. A thin sheet of ice had formed over the five inches of snow that had fallen two days before.

Oak Lane was a two-block-long street consisting of neat gray-brick suburban houses, each detached from the other by a driveway which ran between them. Patrolman Michael Rossi's bulk was planted solidly at the head of the driveway between Numbers 37 and 39; he kept back the gawking crowd which, in spite of the early hour, had already gathered. Herrick spoke briefly to Rossi and started up the driveway.

"Watch where you walk, Chief!" a voice shouted in warning.

Sergeant Raymond Sperling had arrived a few minutes before. He leaned against the far corner of the house, and then ducked back. Herrick looked down at his feet. His galoshes made deep imprints in the snow, but many feet had come and gone along the driveway in the last two days, in addition to the two icy ruts that the car had formed. Gingerly he walked the rest of the way in one of the car ruts.

When he turned the corner of the house, he saw the dead girl. She wore a fur coat, and at first sight that huddle of fur gave the appearance of an animal lying in the snow. But arms and legs protruded from the coat. Somebody, probably Rossi, had placed a towel over her head.

Sergeant Sperling was down on his knees, scooping pieces of a broken milk bottle onto a cardboard. Beside him stood the big valise that contained the police kit—all the scientific equipment the Marvin Center force possessed. Sperling was a bright, rosy-cheeked young man who had attended the New York City Police Academy and read voluminously on the latest methods of detection.

"Watch those footprints, Chief," he warned again, looking over his shoulder. "The murderer must have come and gone this way."

"How can we tell which prints are his?" Herrick muttered. He brooded over the thick curves of broken glass Sperling had gathered on the cardboard. "It was very cold last night. Chances are the murderer was wearing gloves. The only fingerprints you'll probably find are those of the people in the house who had a right to handle the milk bottle."

"All the same, you want me to be thorough, don't you?"

"Of course."

Vivian Lahey's body lay within three or four feet of the back door. The snow had not been shoveled from the stoop or the walk, but, since the snowfall, feet had beaten out an icy path. On either side of the path there were occasional indentations in the snow where a foot had strayed. And in a small area around the body drops and streaks of frozen blood were scattered on the white snow.

Careful not to tread on any of the blood, Herrick went to the body and lifted the towel. Half the girl's face was buried in the snow; the visible half was as lovely as that of a wax figure. A black fascinator was still over her hair, and blood had seeped through the material and had frozen.

Herrick replaced the towel and straightened up. "Coroner Ames will be here soon. I called him before I came."

"I wonder if anybody heard anything," Sperling mused, "though my idea is that the blow killed her, or at least knocked her out, before she could make a sound. It had to be a terrific blow to break a milk bottle." He pointed a finger. "She didn't stagger or anything or the snow would be messed up. She just keeled over, scattering blood on the way."

The Chief raised his eyes to the back stoop. Two empty milk bottles stood on the top step. Three must have been put out last night. He shivered in his overcoat. He had never before realized what a deadly weapon a prosaic milk bottle could be.

"Concentrate on this area," he told Sperling, and returned to the street.

The two remaining members of the Marvin Center force, Patrolmen Irving Byron and Joseph O'Connell, had arrived. Herrick dispatched them to question the immediate neighbors.

Will Hitch, the milkman, stepped forward. He had telephoned his company, and another man had been sent to continue his route. His story was brief. At around six-twenty he had walked up the driveway to leave the usual order of two quarts of milk and one bottle of cream at the back door. His flashlight had picked out the furry shape in the snow.

"When I bent over her, I saw all that blood," Hitch said, "but even then I wasn't sure she was dead. I took off my glove and touched her cheek, and her skin was as cold as ice. Then I went up to the door and rang the bell. Mr. Engleberry stuck his head out of the window and I told him. He came outside and so did his wife, both of them hardly dressed, though it was freezing cold. Engleberry took one look and shoved his wife back into the house. I went in with them and phoned Police Head-quarters. Guess that's all I can tell you. Want me any more?"

"You can go," Herrick said, and went up the porch steps to the house.

Engleberry must have been watching from the window, for he opened the door before the Chief could ring the bell. He wore a faded bathrobe over his pajamas and slippers on his feet. He was a tall, thin man in his early thirties, with a narrow face and deep-set, brooding eyes.

"I'm Vivian Lahey's brother-in-law, George Engleberry," he introduced himself. "My wife is upstairs in the bedroom. Naturally she is terribly upset over the death of her sister. Is it necessary to—ah—bother her now?"

"I'm afraid so," Herrick said. "But first I'd like some information from you."

In response to the Chief's questions, Engleberry revealed that he had come to Marvin Center six years before to take a job as linotype operator with the Marvin Center Press on South and Division streets. A year later he had married Rose Lahey, and had rented this house. Rose's sister, Vivian, had moved in with them and shared expenses. He and his wife had no children.

"Was Vivian Lahey ever married?" Herrick asked.

"No."

"I suppose a good-looking girl like she was had quite a few men friends?"

The brother-in-law shrugged. "I guess she did. But she spent most of her time in New York, especially when she was working. She'd stay at a hotel and not come home for days at a time. I guess her dates were mostly New York men and she'd meet them there to go out with them."

"No man in particular?"

Engleberry glowered. "Vivian liked to run around. I thought I was sort of responsible for her, she being a single girl and living with us, but she never paid any attention to me."

"What about local men?" the Chief persisted.

"Well, she didn't bring any to the house." Engleberry hesitated, then added, "All I know is that she did have a date last night. At least I imagine she did because she left the house at around nine-thirty last night, and wasn't home when I went to bed."

"Any idea who she was with?"

"No. She received another phone call before she went out, but she didn't tell us who called."

"May I see your wife now?" Herrick asked.

Reluctantly Engleberry led the Chief into a bedroom. Rose Engleberry was lying on one of the twin beds. Like her husband, she wore a robe over her night clothes. At the sight of Herrick, she sat up. She was a plump woman in her early thirties. Her eyes were red with weeping and her hair straggled down her face.

She told Herrick that she didn't know whom her sister had been out with the previous night. Vivian was rather secretive about her men friends. One thing, however, was certain: The date had been made at the very last minute, when somebody had phoned her after nine, because at seven o'clock Dwight Braun had phoned Vivian and she had told him she was going to spend the evening at home.

"Who's Dwight Braun?" Herrick asked.

"He was Vivian's agent," Mrs. Engleberry said. "George and I didn't approve of him. Vivian had plenty of talent, but except for a few spots now and then on one of the big networks, the only singing jobs she could get were small stations with bands nobody ever heard of."

"Then she couldn't have been making much money?"

Engleberry answered that one. "Very little left after expenses and agent fees and all that. That's the chief reason she stayed on in Marvin Center with us instead of moving near the studios in New York. It always seemed to me that she could have done better if she hadn't been tied up with this agent, Dwight Braun. His agency is very small; he hasn't even got a real office. I told her what she needed was a big-shot agent.

"Well, last week she decided to break off with Braun. Last night at seven he called up and asked if he could come out and see her. I guess he wanted to talk her into staying with him. Vivian said she'd be home, but at about nine-thirty she got that second phone call. She put on her coat and said she'd be right back, and that's the last we saw of her."

"Did Braun show up?"

"At around ten, I guess," Engleberry said. "He waited around for a whole hour and got sore and left. I don't blame him for being sore. Here he had come all the way from New York and Vivian hadn't even waited for him."

"Did you hear her come home? A car pull up or her walking up the driveway or anything like that?"

They shook their heads.

Mrs. Engleberry put her handkerchief up to her eyes and muttered, "Mr. Braun was angry when he left. Vivian might have been coming home just as he left the house and they met outside."

"Rose!" her husband exclaimed. "Do you realize you're accusing a man of murder when you know nothing about it?"

She looked at him in surprise. "Why, I said no such thing, George."

"Another thing," Herrick injected quietly. "What was Miss Lahey doing around the back of the house? Had she driven a car into the garage?"

"Vivian couldn't drive," Engleberry replied. "She came around to the back door because she'd lost her key to the front door. I was planning to have another one made, but I didn't get around to it."

The Chief recalled the bit of town gossip his wife had told him. "What about John Shanken?"

There was a brief silence. Engleberry and his wife looked at each other. Then the husband said, "You mean the Shanken who has the men's store? What about him?"

"George, there's no sense trying to protect anybody," Mrs. Engleberry said.

"Vivian's dead!" he objected angrily. "Why let her name be dragged in the mud?"

"Don't you want her murderer caught?" Herrick asked softly.

Mrs. Engleberry blew her nose noisily and started to sob. Her husband raged. "Vivian was as fine and decent a girl as you could find. I don't know who killed her. It could have been a thief or a madman. Did you think of that?"

Herrick excused himself and descended the stairs. Sergeant Sperling was in the hall.

"I think I've got something, Chief. Come on outside."

They left through the back door. Near the corner of the house, beyond the girl's body and a little to the right of the path, Herrick saw an inverted cardboard box resting in the snow. Tenderly Sperling lifted the box and revealed a footprint in the snow.

"Look at this," he said excitedly.

Herrick squatted. A foot had crushed through the top layer of ice and pressed down the snow beneath. At the heel of the print there was a ragged smear of blood and another at the instep.

"Somebody made this after Miss Lahey was murdered," Sperling explained, "after her blood had been spilled on the snow. See how the blood is everywhere else. It lies on top of the ice in globules and it froze that way. But the shoe came down here and spread and pressed the blood. The toe points to the driveway. Here's part of another print—see this rubber heel?—and then he turned around the corner of the house and walked down the driveway along one of the car ruts. I looked, but I haven't found another print of a rubber-heeled shoe."

Herrick nodded. "It's that rubber heel that interests me more than the blood. With all the snow and ice these last few days, nobody would leave the house without something over his shoes." He glanced at the dead girl's feet. "She's wearing galoshes. So am I. You're wearing rubber and the milkman wore boots. I'd say that this footprint was made by somebody who went out in a car and didn't expect to do much walking. Or somebody who came from New York where the snow has been cleared from the streets. Well, it's a lead."

Sperling beamed happily. "It's more than a lead, Chief. It can be evidence. I can make a plaster cast of this footprint. All I need is some talcum powder to shake over it and some fine shellac to spray with a Flit gun. I repeat that a couple of times and then I get some very fine plaster of Paris from a dentist and make a cast. If we can find the shoe, we can take it and the cast to the police laboratory in Brooklyn and have them matched up. It's as good as a fingerprint."

"If we find the shoe," Herrick observed dryly.

A black cloth handbag lay near one of the dead girl's gloved hands. Herrick looked through it. He found a wallet containing eighteen dollars. Obviously the motive for her murder hadn't been robbery.

Patrolman Byron came up the driveway with the information that the woman next door, in Number 39, had heard two people fighting outside during the night. Herrick felt his shoulders lighten a little. Here, at last, was a witness. He hurried to the house next door.

Mrs. Tracy M. Anderson, a fading middle-aged blonde, wearing a cloth coat over her house dress, was watching the crowd that was gathering by the minute in front of Number 37.

"Well, I'm not sure it was exactly a fight," she said. "But the voices sounded like a quarrel."

"Did you recognize the voices?" Herrick asked.

"Well, one was Vivian Lahey's, I suppose, but all I can be sure of is that it was a woman's voice. You see, I was in bed, more than half asleep, when those voices woke me up. The bedroom is on that side of the house, right next to the Engleberry driveway. I heard a kind of muttering at first, then the voices rose but I can't tell you who the man was, even if I'd ever heard his voice before."

"Did you hear what was said?"

"No. Just voices. Then I fell asleep. I told that other policeman who was here that I didn't hear anything else—no cry or anything like that. I just fell asleep in the middle, I guess. And I can't tell you what time it was. All I know is it was night."

"What time did you go to bed?"

"A little before twelve," Mrs. Anderson replied. "Me and my husband both. The children were in bed since ten. But Tracy—that's my husband—he didn't hear a thing. He sleeps like a log."

"Where's your husband now?"

"He left for work a little while ago. But he didn't hear anything. We talked about it when we heard poor Vivian Lahey was murdered. That was when I remembered hearing those voices. I said to Tracy—"

Mrs. Anderson went on talking, but she had no more to contribute. Herrick was satisfied that she had given him vital information. Vivian Lahey had quarreled with the man who had murdered her, which meant that she had known him well. And likely the murder hadn't been planned, but had resulted from the quarrel. A milk bottle was the sort of weapon one would snatch up in a fit of overpowering rage.

John Shanken scowled when the Chief entered his haberdashery store.

The clerk stepped up to Herrick, "What can I do for you, sir?" But before the Chief could reply, Shanken waved the clerk aside and beckoned Herrick into the back room of the store.

Shanken was an athletic-looking man in his late thirties. He dressed like a fashion-plate, as befitted a man who sold men's wear, and sported a sleek mustache. Herrick recalled that Shanken, in spite of a wife and three children, was considered quite a lady killer.

The Chief asked casually, "Have you heard what happened to Vivian Lahey?"

"The news is all over town." Shanken had trouble finding a place to rest his gaze. He shuddered. "Terrible tragedy! She was such a fine girl."

"A friend of yours, I hear."

The haberdasher shrugged. "Oh, well, I knew Miss Lahey as a good customer. She bought all her Christmas and birthday presents for male relatives and friends in my store."

Through narrowed eyes, the Chief studied the man. There was no doubt that he was badly frightened. He hazarded a guess. "Where did you go with Miss Lahey last night?"

It worked. Shanken's head jerked up; the fear in his eyes was plain. "I didn't kill her! I swear—"

"Where did you go with her last night?" Herrick repeated.

Shanken dropped limply into a chair. "I was going to tell you. I'd just heard of the murder and I was about to go to the police station when you came in."

"Were you?" Herrick grunted skeptically. "All right, tell me now."

"She—I—well, we've been seeing each other. Secretly. Look, Herrick, there's nothing to be gained by letting my wife know."

Herrick felt an unpleasant taste in his mouth. "I can't promise you anything. It depends on whether you're innocent and how completely honest you are with me."

"I've nothing to hide from the police," the man insisted. "But if my wife should find out—well, the scandal—" He shook himself and went on, "Vivian hasn't let me see her for three weeks. I went almost crazy. She is—she was a very lovely girl. Last night I phoned her."

"At what time?"

"Around nine. A little after."

"As late as nine-thirty?"

"It may have been. I told Vivian that if she didn't at least come out and talk to me for a few minutes, I'd barge into her house. She gave in grudgingly and I picked her up in my car on the corner of Oak Lane and Lanning Place. We drove and parked and drove some more while I kept arguing with her."

"How long?"

"What? Oh, hours."

"In the cold?"

"I've a heater in my car," Shanken replied. "Vivian said that people were talking about us and that we mustn't see each other again. I couldn't give her up. She was in my blood. I argued and argued. I—" He broke off and hunched his shoulders. "It was no use, so after a while I drove her home."

"What time was that?"

"I don't know. Around midnight."

"Can you fix the time closer than that?"

Shanken was thoughtful, and then shook his head. "I'm afraid not. I was very upset. I didn't bother to look at the time. I'm sure it was at least twelve. Maybe a few minutes later."

Herrick was ready to spring a trap. He asked with apparent indifference, "What happened when you walked to the back door of the house with her?"

"I—" Shanken took a deep breath, "I didn't get out of the car with her. By that time we were both pretty sore at each other. When I pulled up in front of Vivian's house, she got out of the car and slammed the door. I drove home."

"Just like that?" Herrick said grimly.

"I tell you I did. I wouldn't hurt a hair of her head."

"You said you were sore at her."

"But not enough to kill her. Why would I want to kill her? That would be crazy."

"Crazy," the Chief muttered. "By the way, did you wear rubbers or galoshes last night?"

"I never wear galoshes. They look frightful. Rubbers sometimes, but—" He frowned up at Herrick. "I don't understand the question."

"All the same, I want an answer. What did you wear on your feet last night?"

"Just my shoes. The garage is under my house. I didn't have to walk in the street."

At any rate, that was Shanken's story and he stuck to it. Herrick debated with himself whether to take him to Headquarters for further questioning, and decided not to. He hadn't enough on the man to hold him and would only succeed in putting him on his guard. In a place the size of Marvin Center, where Shanken was a businessman of considerable importance, it was necessary for the police to feel their way carefully.

As the day wore on, the responsibility of the case piled on Herrick's shoulders. He knew that the whole town—indeed, the whole county—was watching him. This was the first big test in his nine years as Chief of Police.

In the late afternoon Arthur Simms, the District Attorney, and Dr. Everett J. Ames, County Coroner, came to his office for a conference.

Dr. Ames had his preliminary report. He agreed that Vivian Lahey had probably died between midnight and 1 A.M., but he could not give a definite statement until he had completed the post-mortem, which would be some time the following day. He had no doubt, however, that the blow with the milk bottle had killed her almost instantly.

"Sergeant Sperling went over the broken pieces of the bottle for finger-prints," Herrick reported. "He found about what we expected—the prints of Mr. and Mrs. Engleberry and one of the milkman, Will Hitch. On a night as cold as last night, practically everybody wore gloves."

"How about the New York City end?" District Attorney Simms inquired. "Miss Lahey worked there and most of the people she knew, it seems, live there."

Herrick nodded. "I spoke to the New York Homicide Bureau on the phone. They promised full cooperation. All the men she's known in New York are being investigated." He sighed. "But I hardly expect anything to come of that. I am convinced that the murderer did not come all this way to murder her. The crime shows all the marks of having been impulsive, unpremeditated."

"And Shanken admitted he had been out with Miss Lahey last night," Simms rubbed his lean jaw. "He's our man."

For brief moments they sat about the desk in silence. Then Herrick said glumly, "You're the District Attorney. Can you prove Shanken guilty in court? Have you even enough to indict?"

"Well, no," Simms admitted. "Not yet, at any rate."

Shortly after the District Attorney and the Coroner departed, Sergeant Sperling entered the office with a cardboard box under his arm. Within the box, the white plaster cast of the footprint was carefully protected by excelsior.

"The casts are finished," Sperling announced. "I made three. I'm sending Mike Rossi to New York with one. Now what shoes do we look at?"

Herrick had not mentioned the cast to the District Attorney. He was afraid it wouldn't be taken seriously; he wasn't sure himself whether or not to take it seriously. But Sperling believed in what he was doing, and there was nothing to be lost by following through.

"Try Shanken first," the Chief told him.

It was almost time to knock off for supper when a dumpy little man walked into Police Headquarters and introduced himself to Herrick as Dwight Braun, the radio agent.

"Say, what's the idea of sending the cops after me?" he demanded. "I'm minding my own business when a couple of detectives barge in on me and ask all kinds of questions about Vivian Lahey's murder. That was the first I heard of it. They acted as if I'd killed her."

Herrick grunted with satisfaction. The New York police were wasting no time.

"Did you kill her?" he asked softly.

"Don't be a sap!" Braun spread his plump body on a chair and set fire to a cigarette. "The minute those cops left, I drove out here to let you know what happened last night." And he told substantially the same story as the Engleberrys.

"Did you drive out to Marvin Center in your car last night?" Herrick wanted to know.

"Sure. The train connections out of this place are terrible, especially at night."

"Let me get this straight," Herrick said. "Miss Lahey was in New York more than she was here. Yet you took this trip late at night, when you could as easily have seen her in the city?"

"Who says so? The point is, Vivian decided to get another agent after all I'd done for her, and then she wouldn't even discuss it with me. Maybe she wasn't a top-notch singer and maybe she would never have been, but the ten percent commission I made on her was worth spending an evening on."

"And after having come all this distance you left without seeing her."

"I was sore, I'd phoned Vivian beforehand and she'd said she'd be home, and then she left before I arrived and hadn't returned by eleven. She wasn't enough of a big-shot for me to take that from her."

Herrick toyed with his pencil. "Did you wear rubber shoes last night?"

"Huh? What for? The sidewalks were clean. At least in New York they were."

The Chief went out and returned with the third plaster cast of the footprint. While Braun watched in bewilderment and flung questions at Herrick, the latter got down on his knees and carefully placed the agent's shoe in the cast. Braun's foot was almost womanish in its smallness; there was a good inch to spare at the toes. The Chief didn't have to compare the heel markings to know that Braun's foot had never made that print.

As Herrick clambered back to his feet, he saw Sperling standing in the doorway with the cardboard box under his arm and an amused smile on his lips. "That man's foot is too small, Chief. I could've told you without measuring."

Herrick gave the Sergeant an annoyed look and retreated behind his desk. "You can go," he told Braun wearily.

"Does that mean I won't be bothered any more?" the agent demanded.

"It means you can go now," the Chief said snappishly. He was annoyed with himself at discovering that his nerves were on edge.

When Braun had gone, Sperling advanced into the office and placed the boxed plaster cast on the desk. "I drew a blank myself, Chief. John Shanken's shoes weren't the right size either. I went to his store and he made no fuss while I matched his shoe. His foot is too big by at least a size, so I didn't bother going to his house to look at his other shoes."

Herrick studied his fingernails. "You know more about these scientific methods than I do, Ray. How much confidence have you that footprint means anything?"

Sperling hesitated before answering. "If the murderer made that footprint, then Shanken is out."

"If!" Herrick echoed. "That's the trouble. You may be able to show that that footprint was made after the murder and not before. But you can't prove to a jury's satisfaction that it's the murderer's."

"Well, Chief—" Sperling obviously did not want to put himself out on a limb. "If Shanken had made that footprint, it would at least prove that he had gone to the back door with Miss Lahey."

"But it doesn't prove that he didn't," Herrick muttered. He stood up in sudden decision. "Come with me, Ray. And bring that cast."

They drove to 37 Oak Lane. Rose Engleberry was home alone. Evidently she had not dressed all day, for she still wore her nightgown and a robe and slippers. In ten hours she seemed to have aged ten years.

"When do you expect your husband home?" Herrick asked her.

"Usually he gets home a little after six, unless he works overtime," she replied listlessly. "Do you want to wait for him?"

"You'll do just as well. I'd like to get the events of last night clearer in my mind. You say you went to bed at about eleven?"

Her plump shoulders shrugged. "Around then. I'm not certain of the time, except that it was right after Dwight Braun left."

"And your husband went to bed with you?"

She sat back in the corner of the couch and looked curiously at the Chief. "Why do you ask that question?"

"I'm anxious to pin down the time of the murder. I imagine it was after Mr. Engleberry went to bed or he would have heard something."

"As a matter of fact, George stayed up a little while longer. He wanted to finish reading his paper."

"Did you hear him go to bed?"

"No. I fell asleep practically at once. And as we have twin beds—" She stopped. A shadow crossed her face. "Why don't you ask George?"

"I will," Herrick said dryly. "Now, Mrs. Engleberry, I have a favor to ask. We found a footprint outside in the snow. If it belongs to Mr. Engleberry, whose footprints would naturally be all around the house, then we can eliminate it from consideration. May we see your husband's shoes?"

She took some time to consider the request, then said doubtfully, "George, of course, is wearing a pair of his shoes. Hadn't you better wait till he comes home?"

"We're in a hurry. All we want to do is measure any of his shoes for size."

"Well, all right." She rose slowly. Herrick and Sperling followed her up the stairs.

In the bedroom, she rummaged in a closet and came out with a pair of heavy brogues. "Will these do?"

Sperling placed his box on the floor, untied the string and opened the lid. He scowled at the heavy shoes and solid leather heels and tried one for size. It seemed too wide.

He looked at Herrick and shrugged and then said to Mrs. Engleberry, "Are those the only extra shoes he has? What I need are a pair of dress oxfords with rubber heels."

"He has only one good pair and he wears them to work. But there's an old pair somewhere. Just a minute." She dug into the closet again and this time came out empty-handed. "They're not here. George may have thrown them out or perhaps they're at the shoemaker's."

"When was the last time you saw them?" the Chief inquired.

Again the shadow crossed her face. She chewed on her lower lip. "Why don't you ask George those questions? Anyway, it seems to me that all this bother about shoes is ridiculous."

Sperling tied up his box. Herrick thanked Mrs. Engleberry for her cooperation and the two men left the house.

"Well Chief?" Sperling said when they were in the car. "He seems to wear the same size, but you can't tell exactly from those heavy shoes. And we need more than size. We need positive identification. That wouldn't be legal evidence even then, but it would be a lead. Should we drive over to the print shop where he works?"

The Chief closed his eyes in frustration. He had the thought that all day he had been running in circles.

"We might as well try it," he said almost indifferently.

When they reached the Marvin Center Press on Division Street, they learned that George Engleberry had left five minutes before. Sperling said, "We must have passed him on the way. Should we go back to his house?"

"Why not?"

More lights were on in Number 37 than there had been ten minutes before. A cream-colored sedan was parked in the driveway. The door was again opened by Mrs. Engleberry. She started at the sight of the two policemen.

"Why are you back?"

Herrick said placatingly, "We still want to ask your husband those questions and we noticed his car outside."

His manner seemed to reassure her. "He's down in the cellar tending the furnace." She raised her voice. "George, come up here."

"Who is it?" a voice came hollowly.

"Please come up."

"Just a minute."

As Herrick waited in the hall with Sperling and Mrs. Engleberry, an urgent feeling that he should be doing something came over him. Almost without thought, he started down the hall toward the kitchen.

He was in the kitchen when Engleberry appeared through the cellar door. The man drew back as if from a blow. His deep-set eyes were wild, his cheeks pinched.

"What do you want?" he asked hoarsely.

Herrick's gaze was drawn down to Engleberry's feet—to the worn, split shoes. They didn't go with the clean neatness of the rest of his clothes, and his wife said he wore good shoes to work.

"Are those the shoes you wore all day?" the Chief demanded.

"I—" Engleberry's eyes dropped to his feet. He started to shake. "Sure, I wore those shoes to work. They're comfortable." His voice rose stridently. "What's the matter—can't I wear any shoes I want?"

Herrick snapped, "Keep your eyes on him, Ray," and pushed past Engleberry and rushed down the cellar steps. Behind him he heard Mrs. Engleberry utter a choked cry.

When the Chief reached the cellar, he paused in indecision. Engleberry's manner had been that of a man very badly frightened, but how much did that mean? And if it did mean anything, how sure could he be that there was anything to be found here in the cellar?

His eyes fell on the coal furnace. He was hardly breathing as he pulled the door open. A little sigh escaped him at what he saw on the glowing coals. Quickly he snatched up a shovel and a poker.

The smell of burning leather and rubber was acrid in his nostrils as he carried the smoldering shoes upstairs on a shovel. The three others were still in the kitchen.

Engleberry had dropped down on a chair beside the porcelain-topped kitchen table, and his face was in his hands. Dully he looked up when Herrick entered with what was left of the shoes.

"I didn't want to hurt her!" Engleberry moaned. "I didn't know what I was doing. I didn't mean it!"

Later that night, he made a complete confession to Herrick and District Attorney Simms.

He said that all along it had been Vivian Lahey whom he had loved. Years ago he had asked her to marry him, and when she would not have him, he had married her sister Rose. But through the five years of his married life Vivian lived in the same house, and her constant presence kept his passion for her alive. He insisted that he had never made an indecent proposal to her or approached her in any way, but he admitted that he had been jealous of the other men she had gone with.

Her affair with Shanken had affected him most. Because Shanken was a married man with children, it had seemed to Engleberry that she was degrading herself. Once or twice he had spoken to her about it. Her retort had been that her personal life was none of his business.

The night of the murder, he had remained up reading after his wife had gone to bed. He had heard a car pull up, and through the living-room window he had seen Vivian get out. He had recognized the car as Shanken's. At that, the twisting, brooding jealousy that had tormented him for five years had caused something to break inside him. He had gone to the back door, and there, standing outside the stoop without hat or coat, he had abused her.

Again Vivian had told him that it was none of his business what she did. He lost his head completely. In the grip of insane rage, he had snatched up a milk bottle and struck her.

When he had seen her lying dead in the snow, some measure of self-control had returned to him. He had stepped to the corner of the house and glanced down the driveway to make sure that nobody had heard or seen anything. Then he had returned into the house and undressed in the bathroom. Because he and his wife slept in twin beds, she had not heard him slip into his bed.

Next day his nerves steadily deteriorated, especially when he had observed Sergeant Sperling making a cast of a footprint in the snow. He hadn't been sure what that had meant, but he had been afraid it was evidence against him. He had hidden the shoes he had worn the night before in the cellar.

When he had returned from work, his wife had told him that the police had been there to look at his shoes. Panic seized him. He had rushed down to the cellar to burn the shoes. And when Herrick had retrieved them from the furnace, it had not occurred to Engleberry that that smoldering mass of leather and rubber was probably worthless as evidence. He had been too far gone, at the end of his rope. His nerves hadn't been able to take more.

Six weeks later, on January 29th, 1945, George Engleberry was tried for murder in the second degree. His defense attorney tried to prove temporary insanity, but the jury thought otherwise. He was found guilty and given a sentence of twenty years.

LESLIE FORD

Leslie Ford was really Mrs. Zenith Jones Brown, who also wrote under the pen name David Frome. Beginning in the early 1930s, Brown simultaneously juggled two impressive detective series. The first, using her Frome pseudonym, was set in London and the provincial United Kingdom, and it featured the little Welshman Mr. Pinkerton and his trusty friend Inspector Bull. Mystery historian Howard Haycraft named the first Mr. Pinkerton Book, *The Hammersmith Murders* (1930), to his list of "cornerstones" of the detective story, a major honor. Zenith Brown's second series appeared under her Ford byline, and in this one her hero shuttled across the United States cracking cases. Here, it was Colonel John Primrose, "a straight-backed, courtly, bronze-skinned" amateur detective who took center stage. Despite their differences in setting, what the two series share in common is excellent research. Mrs. Brown loved to travel, and her books faithfully and painstakingly captured any given locale. Unfortunately, what they also have in common, to my ear at least, is heavy-handed, unwieldly prose which sometimes obscures her ingenious, well-thought-out narratives. One cannot register this complaint about this lively "lost" story as told to Ford by James L. Carrol, Former Assistant Detective Chief, Buffalo, N.Y.

The Scar-Faced Fugitive and the Murdered Maid

Eyes wide in growing horror, the young housewife approached the bed on which sprawled the limp form of her pretty maid, Pauline Soko-lowska.

Even by the waning light of the March afternoon, she could see deadly, crimson stains that crept from beneath the girl's dark, disheveled hair. One arm dangled loosely over the side of the bed. The fixed eyes stared in a look of astonishment. Her mouth was half-open as if death had stopped a scream.

Slowly, the woman pulled back a bloodstained quilt with trembling fingers. She saw that the girl's dress was pulled up, exposing silk-stockinged thighs. But what her gaze fastened on was a scarlet ring darkening the garment over the right breast.

Scant seconds later, a telephone operator at Buffalo, N.Y., police headquarters heard the frightened plea:

"There's been a murder! Please come quickly . . ."

It was 5:45 o'clock. Before 6 o'clock, a score of detectives and uniformed men led by Austin J. Roche, chief of detectives, had arrived at the two-family home on Sterling Avenue, Buffalo.

Hardly had we launched our search for clues when the first newspaper extras were shouting the news. A sex fiend had bludgeoned, then shot the attractive young girl, the headlines screamed.

Quickly, the girl's employer told us what she could about her maid and the events of that afternoon. She had hired the East Side school girl just a week before, she said, to help with the housework and in caring for her four-year-old son.

When she arrived home that day from a downtown shopping trip, she found the youngster playing in the kitchen. He usually came home from kindergarten about 4 o'clock. There was no sign of the maid or any indication that dinner had been started.

A glance into the bedroom told her why.

The home was subjected to a minute examination. Flecks of blood were on the kitchen floor. A cabinet edge bore a few hairs and a bloodstain. The wash bowl in the bathroom was damp with crimsoned water globules. Someone with bloody hands had washed there, we decided. Probably the killer. Discarded in the tub was a blood-soaked wash cloth.

Medical examiner Earl G. Danser hurried in while detectives were examining the home. Sizing up the situation, he grunted as he observed the disarray of the victim's dress.

"Sex case?" he asked.

"Looks like it," admitted Chief Roche.

Dr. Danser pulled aside the garment, revealing a small dark wound an inch to the left and below the center of her right breast. He examined the head wound.

"Nasty rap. Offhand I'd say her skull was fractured," he said. "But the bullet probably killed her. Find the gun?"

Roche shook his head. "Not yet."

"Know who did it?" queried the doctor, looking up from the body.

Roche shook his head again.

"I'll post the body immediately then. Call me in a couple of hours and I'll let you know what I find."

"Thanks," Roche replied briefly.

Presently an undertaker's hearse was bearing the body to the county morgue. Detectives resumed their examination of the house. Even the yard was subjected to close scrutiny but no weapon was found. Then the neighbors were questioned.

This line of investigation soon proved valuable. A woman across the street said she had seen Pauline working at a sewing machine a few minutes before 3 o'clock. A window from the neighbor's home gave her a view into that part of the house.

Another neighbor provided a lead. About mid-afternoon, she said, she had looked from a window when she heard the screech of brakes. She was in time to see a truck bearing the name of a large downtown hardware company grind to a halt several doors up the street.

The truck, narrated the neighbor, backed up and halted in front of the house. The driver jumped out bearing a small package. He disappeared up the driveway. At this juncture the neighbor had left the window. She heard the truck pull away later, she said, but did not know just how many minutes had elapsed.

Another neighbor told substantially the same story. Detectives hurried back across the street to check this information with the family.

Had they ordered anything from the hardware store? They said no. Occupants of the upper flat, who had not been home at the time of the murder, also were interrogated in like vein. They, too, said they had bought nothing from the hardware company.

Why then had the truck driver gone into the home, we asked ourselves. Had he discovered the girl home alone, made advances and then slain her in murderous passion? It would bear checking.

The line of interrogation so far had seemed to establish one thing fairly definitely—that the murder probably had taken place between 3 and 4 o'clock that afternoon of March 29, 1926. Fanning out, detectives asked countless questions of excited neighbors. Another lead developed. A silk stocking salesman had made a house-to-house canvass in the neighborhood that afternoon.

The salesman had visited the house, we discovered. A card bearing his name and a notation to the effect he would return at a later date had been left at the side door. He lived on Crescent Avenue not more than a mile from the murder scene and was located at dinner.

Any suspicions we had that he might have been the man we sought were dispelled after a few minutes' conversation. He told a straightforward story. Yes, he had called at every home in the vicinity of the murder. He had left his card at the murder house when he had been unable to get any reply to the buzzer. That was approximately at 3:30 o'clock.

It seemed certain then that Pauline had been dead at that time. Perhaps the killer had been in the house when the hosiery salesman rang the buzzer. At any rate our time was narrowed down to 30 fateful minutes. What had gone on in them?

Another thing the salesman told us seemed important. While he was walking at Tacoma and Sterling avenues, he said, he had seen a man hurrying along with blood dripping from his face.

"Dripping?" he was asked.

"Well," he replied, "there were several good sized drops. He really did have bad scratches on the right cheek. Anybody would have noticed it."

From neighbors we also gleaned another clue. It was of the fantastic variety but it had to be checked. A peculiar incident had taken place near the house about the time of the murder. Three men, apparently of foreign birth, had been observed walking down the street. Two were delivering handbills. A third followed, carrying on one hand several razor strops. He was talking excitedly in his native tongue and the three paused occasionally to engage in heated verbal tiffs. But had they any connection with the murder? We began looking for the handbills.

In the interim we were checking the hardware company driver. Armed with the address given us by his superiors, we went to a modest Elm Street home. He was not known there! Thinking that perhaps we had the wrong address, we doubled back to the store, checked its employees' list and made certain we had the right address. That was peculiar. Did it mean the driver was our man?

We looked over our files of wanted persons. The driver's name did not appear in them. We checked our arrest lists. So far as we knew he had never been picked up. But he was going to be, if we had our way. But we had no clue as to his whereabouts. That meant we would have to wait until morning and see if he reported for work. If he did not know he was being sought, perhaps he would report as usual. Time enough to worry if he didn't. There was other work to be done.

We turned to the investigation of the man with the blood-smeared face, the handbill distributors, and their strop-carrying acquaintance. With regard to the former, hours of work brought no results. But a check of the handbills left at North Park homes showed they were advertising a sale. We sped to the store, checked the list of distributors and later came up with two frightened men.

They had, they admitted, been in the vicinity of the murder house, but they protested they had no knowledge of the crime. And their assertions served also to clear their strop-carrying friend. He had been making a canvass of barbershops with his wares. They had been with him about the time of the killing and could establish an alibi for him. The distributors shook their heads in answer to our query as to whether they had seen a man with a scratched and blood-smeared face.

It was at this juncture that Dr. Danser called with his report. It made us forget our previous failures for it placed an entirely different light on the situation. The girl, said the medical examiner, had died, as he thought from the first, from the bullet wound. Entering her right breast, the bullet hit a rib, veered and pierced her heart.

The medical examiner's next statement startled us. Pauline Sokolowska was not criminally assaulted. She died a virgin!

That placed an entirely different complexion on the case. At a stroke it ruled out the whole foundation of our original investigation. We were seeking a sex criminal but there had been no sex crime. Dr. Danser said there was no evidence on the body of any attempt at a criminal assault. Obviously it was not a case of death during an attempted rape.

We sat down to consider what the news of the medical examiner meant. Here we were in the midst of an intensive check, trying to form a list of sex criminals who either might know the Sokolowska girl, or who might live in the neighborhood. Now that was out.

We went to interview the dead girl's grief-stricken mother. She was a widow and, sobbing, told us how happy she had been when Pauline found work. Her wages, though small, meant much to the family. We tried to glean from our conversation whether she knew of anyone who might have wanted to harm the girl. But she did not.

Still we pressed on. What about an incipient romance? Was there a chance a jealous boy friend might have been the killer? After more questions, we at last located the girl who apparently had been Pauline's closest confidante.

She blushed when we asked if Pauline had ever had any trouble with boys. Had any ever got fresh? Well, she answered, Pauline had slapped a boy's face a week or two before. That incident had taken place on an automobile ride. The boy had tried to steal a kiss and received a resounding slap on the face. After that he had been ultra penitent and decorous.

Just on a chance we hunted him out. But it was evident from the start that he was not our quarry. A ruddy-faced youth, he seemed genuinely shaken at the girl's death. Questioned about the face-slapping incident, he shamefacedly admitted it was true.

"Sure, she slapped my face and I guess I deserved it," he said. "But I wouldn't have harmed a hair on her head. She was swell."

Next morning we raced to the hardware company on receiving a call that the driver we wanted had reported for work. He was a lanky, raw-boned fellow.

After telling him we were policemen, we questioned him about the erroneous address. But he was not perturbed.

"Oh, that," he said. "Well, I used to board with some people there. But when they moved I did, too. Been bunking with a friend and never thought to tell the company."

That blasted the theory that he might have been a criminal seeking to get by on a phony address. But it did not clear him of suspicion of murder. As to his presence at the house around the time Pauline was killed, he had a ready explanation.

"I had a package for that street number but it was not for Sterling Avenue," he said, explaining that he had made a wrong turn and got into the wrong street. Not until he visited the house and saw the name on the door did he realize he was on the wrong street, he said.

It took only a few minutes to verify his story. After a bit more questioning we returned empty-handed to headquarters. We were thoroughly irritated. Twenty of us were working on the case and we knew exactly nothing about the killer. It was at this juncture that Police Commissioner James W. Higgins called me into his office.

"Jim," he said, "this is a tough nut to crack, and it appears to me as though two or three men will get farther than a mob."

I nodded, waiting for him to go on. He continued:

"I'm assigning you, Detective Sergeant George Maloney and Sergeant Charles Sheehan to the job. You've got carte blanche. Get to it, and good luck."

That put the three of us squarely in the middle. From our past experience with Commissioner Higgins, we knew that he was a good boss. And he expected results!

We went back into a huddle over a cup of coffee. Methodically, Maloney, Sheehan and I went back over every known angle of the case, debating each point in hopes of shedding new light on the mystery.

One, two, three hours sped by. Reluctantly, we came to the conclusion that the entire investigation thus far had been off the correct track.

It was not until then that light began to dawn. If the killer had not been a sadist or a revenge murderer, then he must had some other reason for going to the house. And that reason might very well not have been murder!

In an instant my mind had grasped the significance of the thought. That was it. The murder was not paramount. It was a side issue! Why then had the killer gone to the house?

It was at this point that an incident which had occurred a few weeks previously correlated itself with the problem at hand. The wife of a well known Buffalo attorney had returned to her home in North Buffalo one afternoon and surprised a husky, good-looking young man in the act of ransacking the place. He threatened her with a pearl-handled revolver and fled.

A daylight burglar! It clicked. Maloney, I knew, had been checking on such a criminal. There had been a wave of daylight lootings and all were in the general vicinity of the murder house. How foolish not to have thought of that before! But was it the right answer? The burglar only entered homes where no one was present, and Pauline had not left the place. That seemed a flaw.

Maloney wrinkled his brow when the matter was put up to him.

"I have been trying to get a line on a daylight burglar all right, Jim," he said, "but he always works in places where everyone's out."

I told him that had occurred to me, that I could not shake off the conviction that this was the right trail. Sheehan listened and made notes.

"You may be right," he agreed, "at least we should check it."

Maloney brought out his notebook and recounted to us his investigation into the depredations of the daylight marauder. He had visited the home of every victimized householder. The attorney's wife was the only one who had seen the man. She had described him as rugged and good looking. From her story we knew the thief carried a revolver. And Pauline Sokolowska had been killed by a revolver bullet.

The thief, Maloney continued, stole money exclusively. Valuable gems he disregarded, even if the cash totaled only a few cents. One of his most recent jobs he had been in a Colvin Avenue home not a dozen blocks from the murder house. There the burglar had entered, either by means of a duplicate key, or through an unlocked door. He had extracted $17.50 from an envelope addressed to a missionary society and departed leaving everything else unmolested.

But where was the connection between the daylight burglary and the Sokolowska murder? The thing preyed on my mind. I dragged the other two back to the murder house again. Once again we went over the place. It was then that I noticed a thing that had been mentioned in our description of the place at the time of the killing but which otherwise had gone unheeded.

A book Pauline had been reading had been found beside a couch in the parlor. It lay open, pages facedown on the rug as though someone lying on the sofa might have dropped it there when overcome by drowsiness. Was this part of the answer?

My mind raced and we argued the matter excitedly. Suppose Pauline had been lying down reading when the burglar had entered. Maybe the girl was dozing and did not hear him come in but then awoke. A tussle followed. She had fought desperately, we knew, for in his report the medical examiner said there was skin under her nails. She must have scratched her attacker.

We were more hopeful. Our job now was to find a burglar with a revolver and probably a scratched face.

"What about it, George?" I asked Maloney. "Have you any ideas as to who the daylight burglar might be?"

He rubbed his chin reflectively. "I'll tell you, boys," he answered. "I haven't been able to shake off the thought it's somebody from the neighborhood. Else how would he know when the people would be out?"

"The attorney's wife didn't recognize him," Sheehan pointed out.

"True," admitted Maloney, "but the chances are he knows more about the people in the neighborhood than the people in the neighborhood know about him. He cases his jobs mighty well. There's never been anybody home—before."

"Well," observed Sheehan, "what do we do now, make a house-to-house canvass?"

I shook my head. That sounded too much like an impossible task. "Why not check our burglar file?"

The suggestion met with approval and the next hour found us in the bureau of identification deep in photos and records of burglars who had exhibited efficiency in casing their jobs, who worked by day, and who lived in the general vicinity of the murder house.

It was a tedious job and one that we were often tempted to drop. Only the conviction that we were on the right track kept us at it. We learned that day that patience truly has its rewards. In the midst of our checking we suddenly came upon one name that stuck out from the rest like a sore thumb.

"James Lewis Venneman," I read.

We exchanged glances. In that instant each of us knew what was revolving in the other's mind. Venneman was known to us. He lived on Colvin Avenue not a great distance from the murder house, and right smack in the neighborhood where the daylight burglar had been working.

We needed no folder to remind us of Venneman's reputation. At seventeen he had been sent to the Elmira reformatory after an altercation in a West Side poolroom. Surrounded by a gang of young men, Venneman had drawn a revolver and threatened to shoot.

Subsequently police had found in his possession a list of houses many of which had been entered by a thief who specialized in stealing money. And after the listing of each home was a brief descriptive paragraph, such as "Two-story; porch; windows unlocked, man and woman away all day."

All told there were 50 such notations. Sixteen were crossed off. Investigation revealed those 16 places had been entered.

We knew further that Venneman now was employed in an auto agency which was located in the general vicinity of the murder scene. We needed to talk to Venneman. In a few minutes we were headed for the auto agency. But we did not find our man there.

"He didn't come in today," said his boss.

"Is he in the habit of laying off?" Sheehan asked.

"No, he isn't. It's the first time it's happened."

"When did you see him last?" inquired Maloney.

"Yesterday afternoon. He was out making calls and he came in before he knocked off."

"Did he have any trouble that you know of?"

We asked the question carefully. Venneman's employer's face clouded at the words. "Well his face was scratched. He said . . ."

"His face scratched!" We could not help interrupting.

"Yes," he continued. "Said he got into a fight with some chaps who almost hit him with their car at Delaware and Amherst streets."

"Did he say what it was all about?"

"Nothing except that they had an argument and one of them dug at him with his nails when Lou tried to pull him out of the car."

We had learned enough. A visit to Venneman's house was not unproductive. His parents were worried because he had not been home the previous night. But where he was his parents did not know.

When a check of his haunts had been made without uncovering any trace of Venneman, we sat down to compile a list of everything we knew about him. He was an excellent athlete and once had tried out but failed to make the grade with the Cleveland Indians. His prowess as a pitcher had earned for him release on parole from Elmira reformatory. He had written to the head of a roofing concern which had a good semi-pro ball club and had asked for a job, drawing attention to his athletic ability. Given the job, he had been paroled, and had worked one day—enough to comply with the law so as to escape resentence for parole violation—then had quit.

A quick checkup revealed that Venneman was keeping company with a young woman whose home was on the West Side. She was employed in a restaurant in Tonawanda, a Buffalo suburb. Venneman was in the habit of calling for her when she finished work in the afternoon. We learned that the night of the murder he had called for her as usual and after dinner had taken her to a theater.

In questioning the young woman we came across an interesting fact. It was with regard to the scratches on his face. He had told her, she said, they were caused in a fight with some men in a car but he had said it happened at a different point than the one he had mentioned to his employer.

We had an ever-growing conviction that Venneman was the man we wanted.

But where was he? After leaving the theater he had been seen to glance at an early edition of a morning newspaper. Shortly afterward he had dropped from sight. That edition had announced that police were seeking a man with a scratched face in the Sokolowska killing.

A routine bit of checking gave us a lead as to what had happened to Venneman. Questioning a ticket agent who had been on duty in the railroad station the night Venneman disappeared we learned that a man answering his description had purchased a ticket for Pontiac, Michigan. The scratched face was the point which stood out in the ticket-seller's mind and he readily identified a photo of Venneman.

Further questioning brought to light the fact Venneman had an uncle living on a farm in South Township near Pontiac. Maloney hopped a train for Michigan and early the next morning we received a wire. He had Venneman under arrest.

Venneman had been taken without trouble. Confronted with the evidence we had compiled, he confessed that he had shot Pauline during a burglary of the home. But he contended, the shooting was accidental. And then it was that we learned details of how he had burglarized homes when the householders were out. He simply telephoned first. If he got an answer he hung up. If he got no answer, he concluded that no one was home and proceeded to do a quick job of entering the place and stealing what money he could find.

"Where I made my mistake," he said bitterly, "was when I telephoned this home. The phone was upstairs and when I got no answer I figured everybody was out. The back door was open and I walked in. The girl had been reading on a couch and was asleep. I ransacked the back part of the house and was ready to leave when she woke up and saw me."

It was not hard to picture what had transpired next. The girl had screamed and tussled with Venneman, scratching his face. Fighting her off, he gave her a blow that sent her reeling. Her head hit the edge of a cabinet. She slumped unconscious to the floor.

Venneman said he carried her into the bathroom and washed off her face and head, accounting for the blood we had seen in the bowl. Then he took her into the bedroom in which we later found the body. But, said Venneman, in laying her down, the gun, which he was carrying under his coat, slipped out and discharged, the bullet piercing the girl's body, killing her on the spot. Then, Venneman related, he fled from the house and decided to leave town when he saw newspaper accounts of the police search for a man with a scratched face.

Venneman said in answer to our queries about the death weapon that he had taken it out into a sparsely settled part of Kenmore, a suburb immediately to the north of Buffalo, where he tossed it away in marshy land. Donning rubber boots, Maloney, Sheehan and I spent several afternoons at the scene with the prisoner before I finally was fortunate enough to come across the revolver.

On April 5, Venneman was indicted on a charge of first degree murder. His trial was begun on June 14, and two days later, after the state had entered its evidence, Venneman was permitted to plead guilty to the reduced charge of second degree murder. On June 18, he was sentenced to from 20 years to life.

ERLE STANLEY GARDNER

Over the years many of the most distinguished crime writers, of both fact and fiction, have attempted to crack the William Desmond Taylor case. Taylor was a big-time film director, and his 1922 murder remains one of Hollywood's great unsolved mysteries. Some have implicated comedienne Mabel Normand, others have pointed the finger at Mary Miles Minter, a twenty-year-old rising starlet, or Taylor's secretary, or Charlotte Shelby, Minter's domineering mother. Enter ERLE STANLEY GARDNER, an author uniquely suited to judiciously weigh the bizarre facts of this case. Gardner was a thriving attorney in Southern California for twenty years before embarking on a full-time literary career. His first stories appeared in *Black Mask* in 1923. The year 1932 saw the publication of his first Perry Mason book, *The Case of the Velvet Claw*, the beginning of a series that would become so big that by the time of his death in 1969, there were more than 100 million Mason books in print. If Gardner has never received the critical acclaim he deserves, it might in large measure be because of his books' popularity. This is unfortunate. Not all but many, especially the early ones, were the perfect companion for bus or train, gripping, gritty, and action packed. Between novels, Gardner used to report on some of the most notorious murder cases of his day for the popular men's adventure magazine *True*. That is where he published this account of the Taylor murder, and it remains to this day one of the finest and most even handed. His judgment? You'll just have to keep reading to find out.

The Case of the Movie Murder

To those who are familiar with the psychology of Southern California, it will come as no surprise that when this section came to make its contribution to classic murder mysteries, it should bring forth a case which Hollywood itself could only label "super-colossal."

The William Desmond Taylor case runs true to form throughout. Not only is the main thread of the plot so weird and bizarre as to challenge the credulity of the reader, but it is to be noted that it had its inception at a time when at least one of the witnesses described the weather as "unusual."

On the night of February 1, 1922, William Desmond Taylor was seated in a rather modest, two-story, bungalow-court residence eating dinner. The hour was approximately 6:30.

At this particular time, there was much in vogue in Los Angeles the type of construction known as the "bungalow court." Bungalows were constructed side by side, not fronting on the street but on a walk or driveway which ran the length of a deep lot. In this way it was possible to crowd productive rentals on every inch of a relatively deep lot.

The bungalows in the court where William Desmond Taylor lived had been largely rented by people who were connected with the motion-picture industry. While newspaper accounts present some conflict as to the exact location of some of the neighboring tenants, it would seem from a reading at this late date that Taylor's bungalow was a double, and in the other side of this bungalow lived Edna Purviance, at the time Charlie Chaplin's leading lady. The bungalow opposite was occupied by Mr. and Mrs. Douglas MacLean.

It was a period of transition in the picture industry. The early days, when pictures floundered around with train robbers and bandits, had given way to the adaptation of drama. It was the era of increasing salaries, of the silent film with its dramatic subtitles. One of those most frequently used at the time has become immortalized, "Came the Dawn of a New Day." This subtitle was usually shown with a background of drifting clouds, gradually lighting up, and accompanied by appropriate inspirational music on piano or organ.

William Desmond Taylor, while an important director, was working for what would today be considered a mere stipend in the industry; but at that time, he was in the big-money group.

The income tax of the period was at the rate of four percent and there were, even then, mumblings and grumblings on the manner in which the tax hogs were gathering around the trough in an orgy of wasteful spending. The point is mentioned because it appears that Taylor was in the process of performing a very disagreeable task. He was making out his income tax for the year 1921. His partially finished statement showed an income of $37,000.

Henry Peavey, Taylor's colored houseman, announced that dinner was served, and the motion-picture director left his income-tax work to go to the table where a simple meal was served to a lonely bachelor.

This was the period in Hollywood's development when it was unnecessary for the famous to stroll into the night spots and be photographed by reporters for the fan magazines.

Here was an important director dining alone at 6:30 in a relatively small bungalow court. The furnishings, however, were in exquisite taste. The bookcases were filled with books which were well chosen and well read. Such art objects as were in the room were those which could only have been selected by a connoisseur. These surroundings give us a clue to the man's character. They indicate a modest, simple man with a large income living a simple, unassuming life.

So far there has been nothing to indicate that the life of this man is other than an open book. His associates see in him a grave, dignified, thoughtful executive. Yet he has vision and imagination. His face lights up with a kindly smile. He is a practical philosopher with something big-brotherly in his grave manner.

Adela Rogers St. John, one of the most articulate of the associates of film celebrities, and a famous writer in her own right, was later to say of him: "William D. Taylor was the sort of man that revived your faith in the sex. . . . He was so steady, so consistent, so sure in his judgments, that he couldn't turn out a bad piece of work. . . . He had a breadth of vision and a businesslike understanding of what the screen needed."

So here is a dignified, magnetic executive sitting down to dinner on this cold February night, his income-tax statement on his desk, his mind occupied with the destiny of the screen.

At about 6:45, Mabel Normand was driven up to the court by her chauffeur.

Mabel Normand was one of the most glamorous, colorful figures of the silent screen. It needs only a glance at the publicity given her to realize something of her dynamic character. For instance, it was mentioned at a somewhat later date that she simply couldn't be bothered to set her watch backward and forward when, on a transcontinental train trip, she passed from one time zone to another. So she carried several watches with her, presumably set according to the different time zones. When she passed from one time zone into another, she disposed of the watch which was no longer accurate by the simple expedient of tossing it out of the window.

Under cold and careful appraisal, this story bears the unmistakable stamp of the press agent. Mabel Normand certainly was not traveling by day coach. Pullman windows of the period were double and of heavy glass. This was before air conditioning on the trains and, while the windows were frequently raised a few inches at the bottom, there were permanent, heavy, close-meshed screens to keep out as much of the dust as possible. But this watch-throwing episode is indicative of the period, of the thinking of the people, and of the star. The mere fact that this would have been considered good publicity at the time is interesting. Nowadays, if a star had the habit of tossing watches out of a train window merely because she couldn't be bothered to set the hands forward or back, her public relations men would tear their hair in agony lest the idiosyncrasy be discovered and publicized. But in those days this was all a part of the temperament which one associated with a great actress.

On this night of February 1, 1922, Mabel Normand had been sitting in the back of her chauffeur-driven car eating peanuts and dropping the shells on the floor. As she left the car to call on Taylor, she instructed her chauffeur to clean up the car. Then she hurried through the cold chill of the early evening to the rear of the court and the bungalow occupied by the director.

Taylor was engaged in talking over the telephone when Mabel Normand was admitted by the houseman.

Mabel Normand visited with Taylor while the houseman served dessert to the director. Then apparently the houseman went out to visit with Miss Norman's chauffeur, perhaps helping him to clean up the peanuts. His recollection is that he left around 7:30 and when he left, Miss Normand and Taylor were drinking cocktails.

There is an almost pastoral simplicity about the scene. The motion-picture director, having had his dessert served at around seven o'clock, is now engaged in drinking cocktails with Mabel Normand, who apparently must have dined before she arrived. Therefore the Normand stomach must have contained dinner, peanuts, and cocktail, ingested in that order. William Desmond Taylor, progressing from dinner to cocktails was spared the ordeal of the peanuts.

Now it appears that Taylor was very anxious that Mabel Normand should read a book. In some unaccountable manner an impression seems to have been created that this book was by Freud. There were, it seems, two books that Taylor was very anxious Miss Normand should read, and he had sent one of them over to her house that day. But the other was one for which he had asked her to call in person. On February 11th the newspapers were to contain a statement by Mabel Normand that this book was *Rosmundy* by Ethel M. Dell, and she is at a loss to understand how a rumor started that this was a book of Freud's.

Did Miss Normand and Taylor discuss this book while they were chatting in the bungalow? It is worthy of note that while Taylor had sent one book over to Mabel Normand's apartment that day, he had asked her to call for this book in person. Why?

And it was to develop, moreover, that when she left him at 7:45 it was understood he was to telephone her at nine o'clock and find out how she liked the book. Again, why?

Be that as it may, at 7:45 Mabel Normand says she left Taylor alone in his bungalow, and it is to be noted that according to the statements of both Mabel Normand and her chauffeur, Taylor escorted Miss Normand out to her car, a gallant gesture on the part of the director which may have cost him his life; for one of the police theories was that he left the door of his bungalow open while he was escorting Miss Normand and that a shadowy figure who had been lurking in the alley took advantage of this opportunity to slip into Taylor's little bungalow.

Taylor, blissfully unconscious of what was so soon to happen, stood at the curb, watched the car drive away, turned and walked back to keep his appointment with death.

On the morning of February 2, 1922, Henry Peavey, the houseman, came to the house at 7:30 A.M. ready to begin his day's work.

He opened the door and stood petrified at what he saw. The body of William Desmond Taylor lay stretched out on the floor, lying on its back with the feet toward the door. Over the legs was a chair which had overturned.

Henry Peavey ran out of the door, screaming that Mr. Taylor was dead. In his own words, "I turned and run out and yelled. And then I yelled some more."

E. C. Jessurum, the proprietor of the bungalow court, responded to the alarm.

What happened after that is very much of a blur. Apparently, from the first newspaper reports, the police were promptly notified and immediately took charge in a routine manner. A physician appeared and diagnosed the death as from natural causes—apparently a hemorrhage of the stomach. The coroner's office put in an appearance, and it was then found that Taylor had been shot by a .38 caliber revolver. The bullet, of ancient vintage and obsolete design, had entered the left side at about the place where the left elbow would have rested if the hands were hung normally at the side. The bullet had traveled upward until it lodged in the right-hand side of the neck just below the skin.

Later on, two peculiar points were noticed. One, that the body was lying neatly "laid out," the limbs stretched out straight, the tie, collar, cuffs unrumpled—what was, apparently, a most unusual position for a corpse. There never was any explanation of this, if we can discount the statement of one of the officers, who said the deceased may have done this "in his death struggles."

The second point, which developed a little later, was that the holes made by the bullet in the coat and vest did not match up. With the arms at the sides, the hole in the coat was considerably lower than the holes in the vest; and it was only when the left elbow was raised that the bullet holes came into juxtaposition.

It was because of this fact that the police promptly advanced the theory which, for the most part, they seem to have stuck with through thick and thin, that there was something in the nature of a holdup connected with the crime and preliminary to it, and that Taylor was standing with his hands up at the time he was shot.

Apparently the bullet was fired from a weapon held within a very few inches of the body.

Searching Taylor's body, police found jewelry and money of over two thousand dollars in value. There were seventy-eight dollars in cash in his pocket, a two-carat diamond ring on his finger, and a platinum watch on his body. The watch had stopped at 7:21; and nearly three weeks after the murder, the police suddenly decided this might be a clue. On February 21st they rushed the watch to a jeweler to find out whether it had run down or had stopped because of the concussion of the fall of the body. The newspapers blazoned the shrewd but somewhat tardy idea of the police to the public.

On the twenty-second they carried the answer. The watch had run down.

On the desk was an open checkbook. Nearby was a pen. Also there was the half-completed income-tax blank previously mentioned.

Edna Purviance, Charlie Chaplin's leading lady, and apparently a close friend of Mabel Normand's, stated that while she knew William Desmond Taylor, the acquaintance was a casual, nodding acquaintance and that was all. She had noticed that there was light on in the Taylor side of the bungalow when she returned home somewhere around midnight on the night of the murder.

At sometime between 8:00 and 8:15 that evening Douglas MacLean, who occupied bungalow 406-B (Taylor occupied 404-B), noticing the "unusual" cold, went upstairs to get an electric stove. While there, he heard what he refers to as a "shattering report," muffled, yet penetrating to every corner of the room.

His wife went to the door of 406-B and was just in time to see a figure emerge into the light from the Taylor bungalow. This figure paused on the porch, turned back toward the oblong of light from the half-opened door and stepped inside briefly, as though to say some word of farewell. He was smiling. Then he stepped back to the porch, quietly and normally closed the door, walked directly toward Mrs. MacLean for a few steps until he came to the opening between the houses, then turned, walked down between the two houses and vanished into the night.

In her first statement, Mrs. MacLean described this figure as being that of a man with a cap, and a muffler around his neck. She couldn't be absolutely certain whether the man did or did not wear an overcoat. She was, however, sure of the cap. Then later on, she said that the figure might have been that of a woman instead of a man. A woman dressed in man's clothing.

At approximately 7:55 P.M., however, Howard Fellows, who was driving Taylor's automobile and who had been told to get in touch with Mr. Taylor that evening, called him on the telephone and received no answer. At 8:15 he went to the Taylor bungalow, rang the doorbell, and got no response. On the other hand, he stated that he had telephoned Taylor two or three times before 7:30 in the evening and had received no reply.

He put up Taylor's automobile for the night and walked home. He was wearing a cap and a raincoat, and so far as he is concerned, he is satisfied he is the man Mrs. MacLean saw. But apparently he did not open the door nor was the door open when he was standing on the porch.

So, if he was the man Mrs. MacLean saw, then she must be mistaken in her recollection of what the man did. Incidentally, it is to be noted that Mrs. MacLean apparently is not the type to be hypnotized by her own recollection. It was exceedingly cold and there is probably no doubt but what the figure wore an overcoat. A less scrupulous witness would have said she saw an overcoat. A less painstaking one would have visualized the fact that the man must have worn an overcoat, and so gradually built up the conviction that he was wearing one. Not so Mrs. MacLean. She is sure of the cap, she is fairly sure of the muffler, and there she stops being sure. A most commendable sign. But bear in mind that she is certain that she saw this figure on the porch step back to the lighted doorway. She saw him step out and "quietly and normally" close the door.

There were the usual stories of puzzling clues. Mysterious figures slithered through the pages of the newspapers. A streetcar conductor said a man who answered the description given by Mrs. MacLean had boarded a car on Maryland Street, at either 7:54 or 8:27 the night of the murder. He was about five feet ten inches, fairly well dressed, weighed about a hundred and sixty-five, had a cap of light color, and the conductor remembered that he wore something tan. He can't remember where the man left the car. There was also a man who insisted that shortly before the murder he had been stopped on the street by someone who asked first for a fictitious address and then asked to know where William Desmond Taylor lived. The information was given. There were two men at a service station who remembered that shortly before six o'clock a man answering the description of the man seen by Mrs. Douglas MacLean had stopped at the service station and inquired where W. D. Taylor lived. The man was described as about twenty-six or twenty-seven, a hundred and sixty-five pounds, with dark suit and a light hat or cap. They directed him to the bungalow court and this was the last they saw of him.

A Mrs. C. F. Reddick, a neighbor, stated she was awakened by a shot or a backfire between one and two o'clock in the morning. Police fixed the time of death as between 7:40 and 8:15 P.M., Wednesday, February first.

At nine o'clock Mabel Normand had been lying in bed with her book, waiting in vain for William Desmond Taylor to call.

He had then been dead for approximately an hour.

It is to be noted that in the room where the body was found were three framed pictures of Mabel Normand. On February 18th there was publicity given to a locket with a photograph of Mabel Normand and bearing the inscription, "To my dearest."

For a while the investigation followed routine lines. There was some indication that a mysterious man had stood back of Taylor bungalow waiting for an opportunity to slip in through the door. He was apparently someone who had reason to believe that by waiting in that position an opportunity would present itself—perhaps someone who knew that Taylor had or was going to have a woman visitor and that he would quite probably escort this woman out to her automobile. In any event, there was a litter of cigarette stubs indicating that someone had stood there waiting for some little time.

It is reported that there was a mysterious handkerchief bearing the letter "S" lying near the body. One of the police detectives picked this up and rather casually left it lying on a table. When he looked for it again, it had disappeared, and apparently has never been heard of since.

This ushers in the now-you-see-it-now-you-don't phase of the case. With bland, disarming casualness, "authorities" and others toss off statements which make the reader dizzy.

We may as well begin with the Mabel Normand letters. Apparently Mabel Normand's first knowledge of what happened was when Edna Purviance (who, it will be remembered, occupied the other side of the William Desmond Taylor bungalow) telephoned her on the morning of February second and told her that Taylor was dead. Miss Normand seems to have gone directly to the bungalow and asked for certain letters and telegrams which she had sent to Taylor. She was very anxious to have them returned to her and said that she knew exactly where they were.

From a study of the newspapers it is not always easy to reconstruct exactly what happened and the order in which it happened. In the *Los Angeles Examiner* of February 10, 1922, it is stated that when Peavey found Taylor's body, the first person he telephoned was Charles Eyton, manager of the Lasky Studios. Eyton and other picture people seem to have been on the scene nearly an hour before the police arrived. Some eight days after the murder a writer was to state boldly in the press, "The mad effort being made by the powers in the Hollywood motion picture colony to block the investigation will avail them nothing now that Woolwine has assumed command." Woolwine, it is to be noted, was at the time the district attorney.

The day before that statement, a newspaper had printed that, "It is suspected that both of them [picture actresses] are revealing only half truths because the complete disclosure might affect their professional interests. And it also is suspected that pressure has been brought to bear on them from others in the industry not to make disclosures which would injuriously affect the sales value of their pictures."

It is therefore understandable that against such a background we will find rumors and contradictions, naive explanations which fail to explain. Facts are to be glossed over with a smear of whitewash, evidence will vanish from under our noses.

But piecing together the facts solely from what the public was able to read in the press, we proceed to consider the rather remarkable history of these Normand letters.

In an interview on February 5th, Mabel Normand stated to a reporter, according to the published account, "I sought those letters and hoped to get them before they reached the scrutiny of others. I admit this, but it was for only one purpose—to prevent terms of affection from being misconstrued."

However, on February 7th we find a published quotation from Miss Normand to this effect: "There have been insinuations made that I went to Mr. Taylor's house after the inquest Saturday to seek some of my letters to him. That is grossly erroneous. I went to the bungalow at the request of the detectives and in their company and solely for the purpose of showing to them the exact location of the furniture as it was placed in the room before I left. It was to show how disordered the place had become after the intrusion of the murderer."

In any event, it seems that Miss Normand arrived at the house and made a request for her letters and was given permission to take them. It is not clear from whom she made this request, exactly when it was made, or who gave her the permission. But she is reported to have said that she knew where they were and to have gone immediately to the top drawer in Taylor's dresser in his upstairs bedroom.

The letters weren't there.

Under date of February 7th it was stated in the press that it is believed a man of high position and influence in the motion-picture world may have taken the Mabel Normand letters, and perhaps others too, in order to protect the fortunes of actresses in whom he had a business interest.

Public Administrator Frank Bryson claims that when his representatives arrived at the Taylor home Thursday morning, the room was filled with detectives, motion-picture people, and reporters, and the premises were swarming with them.

The *Examiner* of February 9, 1922, contains the following: " 'It is very evident,' one of the officers said, 'that someone who entered the house shortly after Taylor's body was found made a thorough search and took all letters which Taylor had received from women, or men, which might aid in solving the mystery of his death.' "

Now then, surprise, surprise! On February 10th, Frank Bryson, the Public Administrator, stated that he had found the Normand letters concealed in Taylor's apartment, "under a double lock." Where were these letters between February 1st and February 9th? Is it possible that the officers searching the house did so in such a slipshod manner that these important letters, "under double lock," were not discovered for a period of more than a week? "Under double lock" is slightly reminiscent of the subtitles of the period. Figuratively it is an expression which hints at impenetrable security. Taken literally it means two locks. There is no specific interpretation given of how it was used in the quoted statement.

On February 11th Mabel Normand's attitude toward these letters discovered "under double lock" seems to have been almost casual. She is quoted as saying, "My letters to him—I would gladly set them before the world if the authorities care to do that. I have nothing to conceal. . . . I have been charged with trying to recover those letters; with trying to conceal them. That is silly. If those letters are printed you will see that they are most of them casual. . . ."

And on February 10, 1922, the district attorney, Thomas Lee Woolwine, stated that the Normand letters contained nothing helpful in the investigation. Another official who had read them said that they were not the burning missives which they had been imagined to be. Apparently these letters were returned to Miss Normand. On February 14th Miss Normand admitted that she now had the letters.

There seems to be no explanation as to why letters which had been "under double lock" in Taylor's residence had been overlooked for a period of some eight days.

In fact, the William Desmond Taylor murder case as reported in the press has some of the Alice-in-Wonderland qualities which leave the thoughtful reader rubbing his eyes.

There is yet another letter to figure in the investigation. Police opening a book in the library some time after the murder noticed that a letter fell out. The letter had the crest of M.M.M. and read: "Dearest, I love you. I love you. I love you," followed by several cross marks and one big cross mark and signed, "Yours always, Mary."

On August 14, 1923, the press stated that Mary Miles Minter, declaring that the time had come to reveal the true relationship that existed between William Desmond Taylor and herself, had announced they were engaged at the time of Taylor's death. She is also reported to have set forth her reasons why the engagement had not been disclosed immediately after the murder.

In fact one of the peculiar developments of this case is the manner in which important facts are to be published for the first time years later. In the press of March 26, 1926, four years after the crime, the public learned, apparently for the first time, that two "strands of blonde hair" found on the body of William Desmond Taylor were being safeguarded by the district attorney's office and were forming the basis of a new probe for the slayer. And it is in May of 1936 that we find Captain Winn in a newspaper interview disclosing that in the toe of one of William Desmond Taylor's riding boots were found a dozen fervent love letters written in a simple code, all signed "Mary." These letters were described as the outpouring of a young girl's heart to the man she obviously loved.

But this is no ordinary murder mystery. Probably no other murder case has existed in history where every feature was so touched with bizarre mystery.

William Desmond Taylor, the simple, kindly motion-picture director as Hollywood knew him, had managed to preserve the secret of his identity. But now that he had been murdered and an investigation was started into his background, it was disclosed that the famous director had a complex past filled with checkerboard patches of mystery that would have done credit to one of the movie plots of the period.

William Desmond Taylor, it developed, was really William Cunningham Deane Tanner. In 1908 William Deane Tanner had, it seemed, carried on a business in New York from which his share of the profits amounted to a cool twenty-five thousand dollars a year, and in those days that was a very considerable sum of money—particularly when one remembers that the income tax had not as yet been discovered and applied to our economic life.

For some undisclosed motive William Cunningham Deane Tanner, after having attended the Vanderbilt Cup Race in the fall of 1908, returned to New York, sent a message to a hotel where he evidently maintained a room asking to have clothing sent to him, drew five hundred dollars from his business, and vanished.

One minute here was a prosperous businessman with wealth at his fingertips and influential friends and connections. He had a charming wife, a beautiful daughter, an established business, a rosy future. The next moment he had vanished into thin air.

There follows a hiatus which has never been satisfactorily filled. There are rumors of this and that. Apparently he was in Alaska for a while. And it is certain that sometime along in 1917 he drifted into Hollywood where he became William Desmond Taylor and rapidly climbed the ladder of fame and influence.

But prior to that time, in 1912, his brother, Dennis Deane Tanner, also suddenly vanished into thin air, leaving a wife and two children.

The wife of this brother subsequently secured a divorce. She moved to Southern California and while there saw a motion picture of some of the screen notables. Watching those flickering figures on the silver screen, she suddenly gripped the arms of her chair, leaned forward, and stared incredulously. The picture of William Cunningham Deane Tanner, her long-missing brother-in-law, was before her startled eyes. She saw the man's familiar figure, his gestures, his smile. And the man was William Desmond Taylor, the noted motion-picture director who was fast winning wealth and fame in the world's motion-picture capital!

She immediately notified her sister-in-law, telling her what she had seen, and was calmly advised that this was no news as her sister-in-law knew it already. Yet apparently there had been no attempt made by Mrs. William Cunningham Deane Tanner to communicate with her husband.

Thereafter, to complicate the situation, the ex-Mrs. Dennis Deane Tanner went to William Desmond Taylor and accused him of being William Cunningham Deane Tanner who had disappeared in 1908. And the man who was her brother-in-law blandly asserted that the woman was suffering from a case of mistaken identity. Yet apparently he kept an eye on her and when her health broke down, he sent her every month an allowance which she received regularly up to the time of his murder—all of the time, however, insisting that this woman was a total stranger to him.

Nor is this all. As William Desmond Taylor had hurried through the chill of that early February evening to keep his appointment with death, he had in his pocket an assortment of keys which fitted no doors the police were ever able to discover. Moreover, in his bungalow, if we are to believe the testimony of his houseman, was a mysterious pink silk nightgown which was to figure prominently in the murder case.

No less an expert than Arthur B. Reeve, famous author of mystery stories of the time, is authority for the statement that Taylor's employee (referring perhaps to Taylor's former secretary, Edward F. Sands), doing a bit of amateur sleuthing on his own, made it a habit to take this silk nightgown from the bureau drawer where it was neatly folded, fold it over again and in a certain distinctive manner, then return it to the drawer. The next morning he would find that the folds of the nightgown had been changed, indicating that it had been worn and refolded. The amateur detective would unfold it, fold it once more in his distinctive manner, only to find that the next morning it had been used and refolded. Later on, everyone concerned is to minimize the importance of this nightgown. The houseman is to say he paid no attention to it; police are to push it out of the case as of no importance. Arthur Reeve doesn't say where he got his information, and the press is to be very coy about the initials which may or may not have been embroidered on the garment.

There was much gossip around Hollywood as to those initials, and we find Miss Normand referring to the nightgown in the press as having initials on it. But the issue is confused by the manner in which the authorities shrug the matter off. As one of the papers said: "Little importance was attached to the pink silk nightgown found in the director's apartments. This, it was learned, had been laundered only once or twice and bore no initials or other marks by which its ownership might be determined."

Despite the fact that William Desmond Taylor was drawing an excellent salary, his money seemed to disappear into thin air. His bank accounts melted away as by magic.

On January 31st he is asserted to have gone to the bank and drawn $2500 in cash. And then the following day, the day of his death, he had reappeared at the bank and deposited $2500 in cash. No explanations offered, no subsequent reason found by police. Apparently on January 31st he had felt he would need $2500 in cash. The next day the need had passed and the money was returned to the bank. However, later on, after this withdrawal and deposit have been accepted as a fact of the case (and apparently the report originated from the public administrator who had taken charge of Taylor's property after his death and certainly should have known), we are to find a sudden flurry of explanations and alibis. Taylor, it seems, was going to buy some diamonds. So, quite naturally, he went to the bank and withdrew this money. Then he changed his mind about the diamonds and so redeposited the money. Simple, just like that. Then, some two week after the murder, there is another puzzling statement to account for this mysterious withdrawal and deposit. This one really should win a prize. On February 15th the newspapers blandly asserted that although it had been stated that Taylor withdrew $2500 from the First National Bank on January 31st and made a deposit of that sum, or of $2350, on February 1st, it had been disclosed the day before (evidently February 14th) that he had not withdrawn any large sum from the bank within the last two weeks before his death.

Now you see it and now you don't. These peculiar "reports" and the charming naiveté of the police—a whole two weeks. Tut, tut!

On February 6th, Miss Normand is reported as having said that when she visited Taylor on the night of the murder, Peavey answered her ring at the doorbell and told her Mr. Taylor was telephoning. Not wanting to interrupt, Mabel Normand waited outside. When Taylor heard her voice, however, he hurriedly cut off his phone call and rushed to her.

Now notice what Miss Normand is reported to have said at that time about that telephone conversation. "If there is a possibility that the jealousy of another woman enters into the mystery, I feel certain that the phone call which he was receiving as I entered his apartment had something to do with it. Whoever it was calling him seemed intensely absorbed in what he had to say."

Naturally the question arises, How did Mabel Normand know this person had called Taylor instead of Taylor having been the one to place the call? How could Mabel Normand, entering the room, and seeing Taylor hastily terminating a telephone conversation, know that the person at the other end of the line was intensely absorbed in what Taylor had to say?

Did Taylor tell her about this call during the visit which followed when he and Miss Normand were sitting there alone? Did Miss Normand's naive statement show that she knew a great deal more about that call than she told police? It is an interesting field for speculation.

Let us digress at this point for just a moment to mention an article which appeared in the February 1, 1929, issue of *Liberty* in which Mr. Sidney Sutherland, the author, states that he had talked with Mabel Normand the year before (apparently 1928) about the Taylor murder. And at the time of this conversation she is reported to have said, "When I reached Bill's open door, I heard a voice inside; he was using the telephone. So I walked around the flower beds for a few minutes until he had quit talking and hung up. Then I rang his bell. He came to the door, smiled, and held out both hands. 'Hello, Mabel darling,' he said. 'I know what you've come for—two books I've just got for you.'"

Sometime after that fatal night, one of Taylor's friends was to express it as his opinion that he was the one with whom Taylor was talking on the telephone at the time Mabel Normand arrived. But a cautious reader, thinking over those several statements of Miss Normand's, will wonder what Taylor said to her about that telephone conversation during the period when they were seated side by side on the davenport sipping their cocktails. And why did Miss Normand apparently try to point out to the police the possible significance of that telephone conversation?

Moreover, William Desmond Taylor had been the victim of mysterious burglaries. In fact, only some two weeks before his death his place had been burglarized and someone had stolen some jewelry, also a large number of specially made cigarettes which the director had had tailored to his individual taste. Then pawn tickets *in the name of William Dean Tanner* had been placed in an envelope and mailed to William Desmond Taylor so that he could, by using his right name and paying the amount of the loan, redeem the jewelry which had been stolen from him.

Some six months or so prior to his death, Taylor had returned from a trip abroad and had accused his secretary, a man by the name of E. F. Sands, of forgery. Apparently the charge was that while Taylor was abroad, Sands had forged checks, charged bills for expensive lingerie and women's clothing and had generally looted the apartment. At about this time Sands disappeared, vanishing into thin air, and has never since been located by the police although every effort has been made to find him.

Keep this man, Sands, in mind. On February 10th, newspapers asserted that a Denver man who "asked that his name be withheld" declared that Sands was none other than Taylor's brother! This man was reported to have known both brothers well. Sands, it seems, was engaged to a beautiful girl and the older brother won the love of that girl. Years later the younger brother entered the office of this mysterious informant and tried to find out about the whereabouts of the older brother. This mysterious informant is reported to have said, "I will stake my life that when Sands is caught the mystery of Taylor's murder will be cleared up and a number of events and elements in the man's life which now seem obscure will be made plain. Revenge is the motive behind the murder of William Desmond Taylor."

Mabel Normand's testimony at the inquest, as reported in the *Los Angeles Times* of February 3rd, and which purports to give the gist of her statement, is that a certain "Edward Knoblock had Mr. Taylor's house while Mr. Taylor was in Europe last summer, and that Mr. Taylor had Mr. Knoblock's London house. Sands apparently stayed right along in Mr. Taylor's service in Los Angeles, and also assisted Mr. Knoblock. Two or three days before Mr. Taylor was to arrive from London, Sands told Mr. Knoblock that he thought he would take two or three days leave of absence, but would be back again Sunday. He never showed up again. When Mr. Taylor arrived from London, he said he found that Sands had stolen everything, had forged his name to checks and had gone to Hamburgers and bought lingerie. . . . A few weeks ago Mr. Taylor's house was robbed again. Then from Stockton he kept getting anonymous letters, and he received a pawnbroker's ticket, showing that things had been pawned in the name of a Mrs. Tennant, who is Mr. Taylor's sister-in-law. The way Mr. Taylor knew it was really Sands was because he had always spelled Mrs. Tennant's name wrong, and the wrong spelling was on the ticket. Mr. Taylor knew that Sands wasn't out of California by this fact."

Apparently there is some confusion about the name on these pawn tickets. This may have been due to the fact that there were several pawn tickets and more than one burglary. In the 1936 interview previously referred to, Captain Winn is authority for the statement that at Fresno on the record of a pawnshop where the names of all borrowers were kept, there appeared "in handwriting that was readily identified by experts as that of Edward Sands, the name of 'William Deane Tanner.' "

There is evidence that William Desmond Taylor felt very bitter toward his former secretary. Apparently when Taylor was asked by the police whether he would be willing to go to the trouble of having Sands extradited from another state, Taylor replied, "I would go to any trouble or expense to extradite him not only from a neighboring state but from any country in the world. All I want is five minutes alone with him."

In the *Examiner* of February 4th, Claire Windsor recalled a conversation she had had with Mr. Taylor about a week before his death. Apparently that was only about a week after the mysterious burglary of Taylor's house. And according to Miss Windsor, Taylor had said, "If I ever lay my hands on Sands I will kill him."

There were, of course, the usual reports and rumors. Sands was reported to have been arrested in various parts of the country; he was called upon by the officials to appear and establish his innocence. He was even offered immunity by the district attorney if he would establish his innocence of the murder of William Desmond Taylor and furnish information which would assist the authorities in locating the actual murderer.

Sands made no move.

Since we have previously mentioned this 1936 newspaper story about Captain Winn's impression of the case, we may as well incorporate some other things which were in that interview. For instance, Captain Winn's statement, "From another source, a source that even now I do not wish to reveal, we learned that Sands, within twenty-four hours of the time of Taylor's murder, had made the statement: 'I came back to town to get that — — — Taylor.' The same person who heard Sands make this rash threat emphatically declared that he again saw Sands—he could not be mistaken in his identification—within a block of the Alvarado court less than an hour before the fatal shot was fired."

In this interview Captain Winn also takes up the claim that Edward Sands was none other than Dennis Gage Deane Tanner, the mysterious missing brother. "Clear, distinguishable photographs of Sands were virtually nonexistent," Winn is reported to have declared. "Pictures of Dennis Deane Tanner were even scarcer, one faded print of the man being the only likeness ever turned up. It was hard to say that a similarity existed between the pictures of Sands and the faded print of Dennis Deane Tanner. But it was as hard to say they were dissimilar. . . . Our investigation revealed that William Deane Tanner had made no less than three trips to Alaska in quest of gold, and that, on at least one of these trips, his brother, Dennis, accompanied him."

A peculiar conflict developed in connection with the testimony of William Davis, Mabel Normand's chauffeur. A moving-picture machinist, George F. Arto, insisted that either on the night of the murder or on the preceding night he saw Peavey talking to some man in the alley back of Taylor's house. Two days after that statement, Arto was reported to have said that on the night of the murder a man other than Davis was talking with Peavey in front of the court where Taylor lived. Davis, Arto is reported to have said, was sitting in his (presumably Mabel Normand's) car at the time. Davis and Peavey both denied this. For a time newspapers mentioned this conflict in the stories of witnesses, then seem to have let it drift into oblivion.

This was during a period of relative normalcy as far as the case is concerned. For a few days one could read the newspaper reports and forget that he was dealing with anything other than the usual mysterious murder. The Alice-in-Wonderland quality was apparently all finished.

Then of a sudden the whole case skyrocketed once more into fantasy.

There entered into the picture a motion-picture executive who told a story that could well have graced one of the pictures of the time.

It seems this person had employed Taylor some years before, and that during that time Taylor had told him of having been imprisoned in England for three years. Taylor was perfectly blameless. He had, it seems, been arrested while holding money in his hand which he wanted a woman to put back in the safe. The husband of this woman unexpectedly appeared upon the scene and accused Taylor of theft; and Taylor, like a gallant gentleman, had kept silent, protecting the good name of the woman at the expense of three years in jail.

There are elaborations of this story, some of them going to the extent of putting together a plot containing a wicked gambler, a scheming husband, a betrayed woman, the gallant Taylor, and at the dramatic moment, Taylor stepping forward to stand between the woman and disgrace, bowing his head in silence and going to jail for three years rather than do anything which would cast a reflection upon the character of the woman. It was typical of the silent drama of the time.

On the 24th, one Tom Green, as assistant United States Attorney, disclosed that Taylor had wanted him to "clean out" a certain place. Taylor, it seems, was protecting a woman from drugs. She was a woman who was paying two thousand dollars a week for dope.

The newspaper gravely published this story, with no explanation as to why no disclosure had been made earlier.

Two thousand dollars a week is a lot of dope.

Then suddenly came the weirdest development of all. A rancher living near Santa Ana, some forty-five miles from Los Angeles, announced that he had picked up two hitchhikers, rough characters, who confided to him that they had been in the Canadian Army where they had suffered under the harsh discipline of a captain whom they referred to as "Bill."

It as at least intimated that this "Bill" had been responsible for one of these men being "sent up." Both hitchhikers avowed their intention of "getting" Captain Bill who was living in Los Angeles whither, apparently, they were making their way on a mission of vengeance. One of the hitchhikers happened to drop a gun. The Santa Ana rancher saw that it was a .38 caliber revolver.

To add to the importance of this clue, police now disclosed that they had received a letter from a former Army officer in London who stated that sometime after the Armistice was signed he was dining with Captain Taylor in a London hotel. As a stranger in the uniform of the Canadian Army crossed the dining hall, Taylor suddenly exclaimed, "There goes a man who is going to get me if it takes a thousand years to do it." Taylor then went on to explain that he had reported and court-martialed this man for the theft of Army property. A description was contained in this letter to the police which tallied exactly with that given by the Santa Ana rancher of one of the hitchhikers, a man called "Spike."

Apparently police had some reason to believe that these hitchhikers might be found at resorts near the Mexican border, and they immediately proceeded to comb Tijuana which is south of San Diego, and Mexicali, which is just south of Calexico in the Imperial Valley.

Fortuitously enough, they located a man in a bar in Mexicali who was named Walter Kirby and who, at the time of his arrest, was reported to have been wearing a cap similar to that worn by the figure seen by Mrs. MacLean leaving the Taylor bungalow. Moreover, this Kirby was reported to have been "positively identified" by the rancher who had picked up the hitchhikers as one of the men to whom he had given the ride. It was also reported that when Kirby's room was searched, a pair of Army breeches was found with leggings to match and several .38 caliber bullets. It was asserted he had admitted serving in a Canadian regiment in which William Desmond Taylor was serving as captain. Moreover, detectives are reported to have said they recognized Kirby as a chauffeur known in Los Angeles as "Slim" and "Whitey" Kirby. Then it is asserted that he had worked for Taylor for one day and was acquainted with him.

A pretty good case one would say.

Twenty-four hours later, Kirby, questioned by police, seems to have produced an air-tight alibi. And then comes the most interesting and amusing sequence of all. The Santa Ana rancher, solemnly asserted the newspaper, "could not identify him positively as the man to whom he had given a ride in his car. . . . He also said that the man arrested was many years younger than the one who had ridden in his car, as well as several inches shorter."

This man Kirby, promptly released from custody however, seems destined to add another page to this chapter in the mystery. Early in May of 1922, two small boys who were out rabbit hunting in the swamp bottoms of New River, west of Calexico in the Imperial Valley, discovered Walter Kirby's body.

This time the identification was positive.

Newspapers reported that shortly before his death Kirby had confided to a friend in Mexicali that someone was after him and would "end him quick." Under a dateline of May 2, 1922, the newspapers posed the questions whether Kirby died of an overdose of drug, exposure and lack of food, "or was he killed by means only known to the underworld of the border?"

It is to be noted in passing that it was asserted that Kirby was a drug addict. Habitual drug addicts, as any reader of mystery fiction well knows, are peculiarly vulnerable to murderous machinations. The drugs of underworld commerce are greatly diluted. It becomes only necessary to deliver to an habitual drug user a dose of "the pure quill" and the man, thinking he has his usual diluted dose, is conveniently removed from the scene of operations.

However, there is too much more to be written about the Taylor case to permit ourselves to be diverted over the death of Walter Kirby.

Incredible as it may seem to the reader, the fact seems to be clearly established that by the sixth of March, 1922, more than three hundred people in the United States alone had confessed to the murder of William Desmond Taylor, and there was one confession from Paris and one from England. These confessions were for the most part embellished with the most astounding detail, ranging from the plausible to the ridiculous. One person who swore he was a friend of a certain motion-picture actress is reported as stating that he passed the Taylor bungalow on the night of the murder where he observed the director and this actress in a heated argument. Slipping into the house, he saw that Taylor had a gun, struggled with him to get possession of the gun and in the course of that struggle, shot him.

In addition to these confessions, there were solemn statements by "witnesses." One convict "confessed" that he entered the Taylor bungalow for the purpose of burglarizing it; surprised by the unexpected appearance of Taylor, he hid in the only place which was available, to wit, behind the piano. And while he was hiding there, he witnesses a quarrel between Taylor and a woman who was dressed like a man, the quarrel culminating in the shooting of the director.

It is, indeed, some murder case which bring in confessions at the rate of virtually ten a day for thirty days.

But don't think you've seen anything yet. These are just the preliminaries. The Taylor case was not allowed to die.

Seven years later, in December of 1929, Friend W. Richardson, ex-governor of the state of California, exploded a bombshell by announcing that he knew who had killed William Desmond Taylor, that he had positive proof that a motion-picture actress had committed the crime and that Asa Keyes, Los Angeles district attorney, had blocked the case. Asa Keyes, the ex-district attorney, promptly issued a denial and demanded to know, among other things, why the governor had not disclosed his information sooner. Richardson retorted that he had approached the Los Angeles grand jury and had been advised that there was nothing he could do because "Keyes would never prosecute the case."

Inasmuch as these disclosures came during the heat of a political campaign, it is easy to imagine the commotion which was aroused in the press.

Pressed for an amplification of his statement, ex-governor Richardson is reported to have said that he received his information from a Folsom convict now paroled, whose name he had "forgotten, and wouldn't tell if he did remember it, because it would mean the man's death."

Newspaper reporters were not so reticent. They promptly decided that the source of the governor's information was one Otis Hefner.

On January 13, 1930, one of the Los Angeles papers which seems to have been rather unsympathetic politically toward ex-governor Richardson has this to say: "Mr. Hefner is the resourceful young man whose twice-told tales of what he knew about the murder of the Hollywood director created a big stew when former governor Friend W. Richardson threw it into the political pot several weeks ago. He did most of his talking in 1926, and was rewarded with a parole from Folsom. Now that he has been uprooted from his job and attempts to stage a comeback and support his little family, he would just as soon be left alone. But if Mr. Fitts must have the facts, here is what Hefner says he will tell the Los Angeles district attorney: That most, if not all, he ever said about the case was hearsay with him; that he never stated to anybody he could identify a woman he once said he saw leave the Taylor bungalow on the night of the murder; that he does not know where Edward F. Sands, Taylor's old valet, and now suspect in the case, is at the present time, and that the story he told Governor Richardson and saw published in San Francisco newspapers in the last few days is the old tale which the Los Angeles authorities discarded as unworthy of consideration."

With interest in the murder thus revived, newspapers reporters instituted a search for Peavey and finally located him in Northern California. What happened next is reported in the press of January 8, 1930, as follows: "Two long statements were forthcoming from Peavey during the day. As usual, they contradicted one another."

"In the first he declared flatly that a famous film actress killed the equally famous director—the same actress named by Hefner in this story Monday. He added that he would welcome a return to Los Angeles and an appearance before the grand jury, and that he had been silenced by the authorities and told 'to get out of town' shortly after the murder.

"But in his second statement, Peavey was not so certain. Later in the day, he declared that he had forgotten most of the details of the killing. He believed he knew who did the killing, but even of this he was not then altogether certain. And he didn't desire a return to this city and least of all a call to appear before the grand jury.

"In both statements, however, he fixed the time of the murder at about 7:30 P.M. Peavey, found in the Negro quarters at Sacramento, explained that the case was 'getting on my nerves' and that he couldn't remember distinctly that far back. A few hours earlier, however, he seemed to remember everything."

The name of the motion-picture actress apparently referred to by Hefner and Peavey never found its way specifically into the columns of the press but was, perhaps, intended to be a political bombshell if one can judge from the reports of the time, and failed to have sufficient explosive force to cause the case to be reopened.

Down through the years, the red thread of mystery in the William

Desmond Taylor murder case has wound its way in and out of the press. Various circumstances have "recalled the Taylor murder case." And now and again incidental sidelights have appeared in the newspapers.

During the time when Asa Keyes was district attorney, there was a flare-up over two diaries which had apparently been taken from a safe-deposit box and found their way into the possession of the district attorney. There was quite a bit of newspaper comment about these diaries but the young woman who had authored them retained shrewd counsel who advised the district attorney that if any hint of their contents became public property, the district attorney would be held strictly accountable. Apparently the threat served as a sobering influence and while the newspapers hinted a bit here and there, no quotations, excerpts, or purported summary of the contents were ever published.

Those diaries, in connection with other things, caused Keyes to rush around the country making an investigation. Once more people were interrogated—and then the thing died down again.

As 1923 went out and 1924 was ushered in with a blare of noise and the usual celebrations, Mabel Normand and Edna Purviance were at a New Year's party.

Trying to unscramble all that happened at that party is like trying to follow the directions given by a well meaning, you-can't-miss-it friend for finding some house in a strange countryside.

Suffice it to say that one of the men at the party was shot by Mabel Normand's chauffeur (not the same one she had employed at the time of the Taylor murder). For a while it was expected the victim would die. Then he recovered physically although the newspaper reported that his memory was "still sick." The preliminary hearing on this case was scheduled to open on March 9, 1924. On March 17th newspapers mentioned that Miss Normand had left the day before for New York. On April 16th the district attorney's office announced that it would not go to trial on a shooting charge against Miss Normand's chauffeur without the presence of Mabel Normand. The trial was continued until June 16th. On June 15th, the newspapers stated that the grand jury was making an investigation, trying to find out how it happened that the victim of the shooting had succeeded in leaving the jurisdiction of the California courts and also taking with him the $5000 that he had put up as security that he would be on hand to testify.

The chauffeur was acquitted.

All in all, Hollywood's contribution to murder mysteries at a time when the silent film was at the zenith of its popularity, is fully in keeping with what one might expect—a murder mystery which is "super-colossal."

At this late date it is impossible to "solve" the William Desmond Taylor murder case from the facts as presented by the press. It is, however, interesting to speculate upon lines which the police inquiry could have taken some years ago. In the first place, it seems to me that the police theory of a "stick-up" has several very big holes in it.

Let us suppose a man did slip through the door and commanded Taylor to raise his hands. The movie director complied—then why shoot him? If a man is perpetrating a robbery and the victim raises his hands, the next move is for the robber to go through his clothes and take his personal possessions. The use of firearms is resorted to when the victim refuses to comply with the order to stick up his hands. Moreover, apparently robbery was not the motive because of the money and jewelry found on the director's body.

It occurs to me that the police have either overlooked or deliberately failed to emphasize a far more logical theory than this stick-up hypothesis.

There was a checkbook on the desk, a fountain pen, also the income-tax statement. When a person is writing, if he is right-handed, he rests his left elbow on the desk and slightly turns his body. That would have the effect of raising the coat just about the amount that would be required to match up the bullet holes in Taylor's coat and vest.

Let us assume, therefore, that Taylor was writing at the time he was shot.

What was he writing?

Obviously it was not a check. He may have offered to write a check, but the person who shot him didn't want a check. He wanted something else in writing.

If William Desmond Taylor had refused to write a check, the check-book wouldn't have been there on the desk with the fountain pen nearby. If he had written a check, then it was to the interest of the person receiving that check to see that Taylor lived long enough for the check to be cashed. A man's checking account is frozen by his bank immediately upon notification of his death.

It seems to me, therefore, that some person wanted, and quite probably obtained, a written statement from Taylor. Once that statement had been properly written out and signed, the person had no further use for Taylor and probably through a desire for vengeance, or else with the idea of sealing his lips, pulled the trigger of a gun which had been surreptitiously placed against the side of the director's body.

It is interesting to speculate whether some woman may not have been concealed in the upstairs portion of the house at the time the shot was fired. The presence of a pink silk nightgown indicates that at some time previously women, or at any rate one woman, had been there.

Notice the manner in which the body had been "laid out."

If the person in an upstairs bedroom had heard voices below, followed by the sound of a shot, and then the noise made by a body falling to the floor, then the opening and closing of a door. . . . Perhaps, after ten or fifteen minutes of agonized waiting this person tiptoed down the stairs and found the body of the director sprawled on the floor. It is quite possible that this woman, before slipping out into the concealment of the night, would have bent over the lifeless body, wept a few tears, and arranged the clothing as neatly as possible.

The most interesting lead of all was offered by Mabel Normand in her comments about the telephone conversation. Quite obviously she was trying to impress upon the police that in her opinion this telephone conversation had some probable bearing upon the death of the director. It is almost certain that this was no mere casual conversation and that Taylor discussed it with her while they were talking together. How else could Mabel Normand have known that the person had called Taylor, not vice versa? How did she know that the person at the other end of the wire was very interested in what Taylor was saying? And why was her subsequent recollection of the telephone conversation so widely at variance with her original statements to the press?

Is it possible the police failed to appreciate the significance of Miss Normand's statement, or did Miss Normand, after thinking things over, decide that she had gone too far and that it would be better to forget all she might have been told about that telephone conversation?

It is to be borne in mind that the police were undoubtedly subjected to great pressure at the time. They were also confused by confessions which were arriving at the rate of ten a day for a period of thirty days. That's an average of better than one an hour for each hour of the working day.

One thing is certain, no dyed-in-the-wool mystery fan would have let Miss Normand's significant statement about the telephone conversation pass unnoticed. And I think most really intelligent mystery readers would have given an interpretation other than the stick-up hypothesis to the fact that the course of the bullet indicated the left shoulder had been raised at the time of death.

As time passes, it becomes less possible that the case will ever be solved by the police. Yet there is an interesting field for speculation in the fact that police have fingerprints of Edward Sands. It is becoming more and more common nowadays for all classes of people to be fingerprinted and the prints passed on to the F.B.I. Imagine what a furor there will be if some day the F.B.I., making a routine check of some fingerprint, comes upon that of the missing secretary of the murdered motion-picture director. That is a very distinct possibility, one which may once more bring the case into the limelight. So one can hardly write the murder of William Desmond Taylor off the books—not yet.

BRETT HALLIDAY—who was really David Dresser—is best known as the creator of one of the most famous fictional private eyes, the two-fisted, tough-talking redhead from Miami, Michael Shayne. Rivaling only Hammett's Sam Spade and Chandler's Phillip Marlowe in popularity, Halliday's Shayne made his debut in 1939 in *Dividend on Death.* In the years that followed, he appeared in 12 movies, with Lloyd Nolan and later Hugh Beaumont in the title role, on radio starring Jeff Chandler, and on television with Richard Denning. Despite the favor Shayne won with fans, as a literary stylist Halliday was no match for his predecessors. Both Hammett and Chandler were capable of dazzling turns of phrase, lavish description and detail, and pitch-perfect dialogue. Stylistically understated, what distinguished Halliday's writing over the course of more than sixty Shayne novels was his ability to tell a good story. Not a talent that makes critics gush with praise, but an undervalued talent to be sure. Underappreciated, too, is the fact that Halliday was also a top-notch true crime reporter. See for yourself in this story about a grisly slaying in a small Colorado town, one of many compelling tales Halliday published in *Master Detective* during the mid-1940s.

Murder with Music

It was ten o'clock at night. Sheriff John Martin, of Sandhill, Colorado, leaned back with a wide yawn on his ruddy, good-humored face, stretched his long arms, then turned off the radio beside his desk. He and Deputy Sheriff Lem Whitaker had lingered late in the Sheriff's office listening to the hour-long newscast over Denver's Mutual outlet.

The Sheriff tugged the wide brim of a soiled white Stetson down on his forehead, and said, "Ready to call it a night, Lem?"

Whitaker was a lean man with a body as tough and stringy as whipcord. His face was burned the color of old leather by the Colorado sun, and his legs were permanently bowed from many years in the saddle. He nodded and thumped his chair forward to get up. "Might as well get to bed," he agreed.

Sheriff Martin switched out the bright light over his scarred desk. Whitaker walked to the door, and the Sheriff followed him out, pulled the door shut, and they went together down the silent hallway of the otherwise deserted courthouse.

Whitaker pushed one of the big double outside doors open, and stopped abruptly, cocking his head to one side and gazing westward toward the towering peak of Lookout Mountain, against the base of which the town was nestled.

"Someone coming hell-bent down the old road," he muttered. "Twice as fast as it's safe to take those horseshoe curves."

The Sheriff listened with him a moment, and nodded. "Some crazy kids from the university," he surmised. "We'll have some broken necks up there one of these nights."

"There it comes down the last stretch," Whitaker pointed out. "Sixty miles an hour."

They started down the broad steps together, both officers listening to the roaring motor as it rushed toward the village at breakneck speed, both of them momentarily expecting a nasty accident.

"He's swinging up this way!" the Sheriff exclaimed as they reached the sidewalk. "Might be trouble. Let's wait a minute and see."

He stopped and got a sack of flaked tobacco and brown cigarette papers from the pocket of his tan corduroy shirt.

He was fashioning a cigarette when the car swung around a corner a block away and its headlights silhouetted the two men.

Brakes screamed and the big black coupe lurched to a stop in front of them. A door was flung open and a man jumped out excitedly. "That you, Sheriff? There's been an accident up on Lookout Mountain. A car went over the cliff and killed the driver."

The speaker was Nate Morris, a rugged young man who had a small ranch on Table Mountain and who lived in Sandhill during the winter months.

Martin asked, "You're sure he's dead?"

"Yes. I went down a drop of 200 feet to the car—at the foot of the third horseshoe curve. That place they call Inspiration Point. He's pinned under the car, dead."

"Get a wrecker and some men to help you," Martin directed his deputy, "and get the Coroner out here." Turning to Nate Morris, he asked the young man, "Do you want to drive me back up there and tell me more about it on the way?"

"Sally's with me. My wife." Morris indicated his coupe, and for the first time the Sheriff noticed a white-faced girl huddled in the front seat. "It's been a terrible shock to her and I'd like to take her home before I go back."

The Sheriff nodded briefly. "You saw it happen, eh?"

"Not exactly. We stopped there at the Point to park for a little while and watch the moon come up over Denver. We heard a radio playing very faintly as we sat there." Morris shivered and glanced at his wife.

"It was ghastly. We couldn't tell where the music was coming from. We were alone up there. Then I noticed a couple of those big guard rocks along the edge weren't in place. I got out and investigated with my flashlight and saw the tracks where a car had gone over. Then I realized the music was coming from an automobile in the bottom of the canyon. Sally stayed in the car while I went down to investigate. Then I came to town as fast as I could."

"We heard you," Martin told him dryly. "Lucky you're not at the bottom of a canyon, too. Go ahead and take your wife home and then come back."

Deputy Whitaker had already hurried off to get a wrecker and the Coroner. Sheriff Martin went around the corner to his parked car, got in and headed up the narrow twisting road that climbed sharply up the mountainside directly above Sandhill.

In its time, the Lookout Mountain road had been a marvel of engineering, with its steep grades and sharp curves, a portion of the main highway west from Denver over the Rockies. In later years it has been superseded by a wide, smooth highway following the gentle gradient of Mount Vernon Canyon a few miles south of Sandhill. Now the road was used only by local residents, sight-seeing tourists, or occasional night-roaming couples who found it a safe place for necking parties.

The Sheriff stopped his car 100 feet below the wide shelf on the edge of the cliff known locally as Inspiration Point. He turned the machine crosswise to block the highway, to prevent the wrecker or any other car from getting past to spoil the tracks at the scene of the accident. He got out a big focusing flashlight, stepped off the side of the road and circled down the mountain toward the canyon floor.

He felt a tingling in his spine when he heard the muted sound of music through the night silence. The moon had risen, casting an eerie light over the mountainside. The radio in the wrecked car was tuned to Station KFEL in Denver, and the orchestra was playing Don't Ever Leave Me.

His flashlight showed a light sedan turned up on its side in the bottom of the canyon ahead. The body of a man was pinned under the lower, right-hand side of the car. The upper part of his body protruded through the open window of the right door, with the steel top of the sedan crushing his chest. He had a nasty head wound and there was a pool of blood on the ground. He was a young man and his lips were crimsoned with a woman's lipstick.

The car radio continued to play softly while Martin flashed his light inside the wrecked car. There was a smear of blood on the instrument board where he could have received the head wound. The key was in the ignition and it was turned on. The headlight switch was also on, though all the lights were out.

Other cars were roaring up the road from Sandhill. They were halted by the Sheriff's parked car, and Whitaker's voice floated down to him. "Where are you, John?"

Martin flashed his light up the hillside. "Send the Coroner down here if he's with you. Don't let anybody go up to the Point until we look it over. I'm coming up now."

His flashlight clearly showed the course the automobile had taken as it plunged straight down, indicating that it had turned end over end in the course of its journey.

The Sheriff was puffing strenuously by the time he reached the top. Whitaker was there ahead of him, flashing his light around the unpaved parkway that had been smoothed outside the arc of pavement.

"This gravel doesn't show up tracks very well, but there's no sign of skidding or anything like that," he announced. "Looks like the car was driven straight over the edge."

Martin flashed his light on the heavy granite boulders, set about three feet apart in a curve on the very edge of the precipice to act as a guard wall. There was a gap where two of the boulders were missing.

"A light car couldn't possibly knock two of those boulders out of place," he protested. He went to the edge and knelt down with his light, carefully examined the two places where the dislodged rocks had been.

"They were pried up and pushed over the edge to make a gap," he surmised, pointing out marks in the hard ground such as might be made by a crowbar or similar tool.

"The outer edge was dug away first," Whitaker agreed, "so it didn't take much leverage to put them over." He straightened up and looked at the Sheriff grimly. "Looks like an intentional accident. Fellow pried the boulders out and then drove over."

Martin shrugged and switched off his light. "Looks that way. We'll have to find the tool he did it with. Might as well bring the wrecker up now and let a cable down. I'll go back down and see if the Coroner is through."

Coroner F. J. Fulgreen and Assistant County Attorney Albright were examining the wrecked car and the body when the Sheriff went back. The radio was still sending soft music out into the night, and the Coroner reached inside the car and switched it off with an exclamation of annoyance.

"It does sound sort of ghostly," Martin agreed, "but if it hadn't been for the radio playing we might not have known about the accident for days." He told them how Nate Morris had heard the radio and come down the slope to investigate, and then explained what he and his deputy had deduced from the physical evidence above.

"Suicide?" Albright asked doubtfully. He gestured toward the dead man. "That lipstick on his mouth looks mighty fresh to me."

"It is fresh," said Fulgreen quietly. "I wiped off a sample for possible laboratory analysis later. He kissed some woman a very short time before he died."

"Lots of neckers park up on the Point," Albright said.

"But where is she now? Where was she when the car went over? What do you get as the cause of death?"

Fulgreen disregarded the first two questions as rhetorical, and answered the third. "He's bruised badly around the head, and that blow on his forehead from the instrument board probably caused a concussion. Offhand, I'd say the life was crushed out of him by the weight of the car across his chest."

The wrecker had been brought up to the edge of the cliff above, and a steel cable was lowered to the battered sedan. A hook was attached to the rear axle, and the car was hoisted gently off the body.

The dead man was well-dressed and had the pale complexion and soft hands of an office worker. His billfold held $32 in cash, and papers that indicated he was William Petty of 127 South Race Street, Denver, Colorado, a bookkeeper. A driver's license and registration certificate in the leather key-container on the ignition substantiated this identification and showed the wrecked car belonged to him.

After it was hoisted up onto the roadway above, Martin had it examined carefully for fingerprints, and then directed a number of volunteers with flashlights to search all along the slope for a tool that might have been used to pry the boulders loose from the edge. This search was unsuccessful, though the rocks themselves were both found in the bottom of the canyon, and they showed traces of having been pried up and rolled over the cliff.

While this search was going on, Sheriff Martin drew Nate Morris aside from the others to question him more fully.

"I came back as soon as I felt I could leave my wife," the young rancher told him. "She was terribly upset."

"Murder is enough to upset any woman," the Sheriff said.

Morris looked surprised. "Murder? I figured the car had just gone out of control making the turn and plunged over."

"I don't think so." Martin didn't go into details, but said, "Tell me again exactly how it happened. Did you and your wife just drive up here to see the view?"

"It was a sudden impulse." Morris shrugged. "It was a pretty night and—well, we did some of our courting here on the Point two years ago."

The Sheriff nodded his understanding. "Did you meet any cars coming up?"

"I don't think—wait a minute! There was a car coming down just as we started up that first long slope. There was a woman driving and she crowded me pretty well over the edge."

"A woman? Alone?"

"Yes. As near as I could tell. She flashed by so fast I couldn't be positive."

"What kind of car?" Martin was taking notes.

"A sedan. Dark blue or black. I think it was a big car. Perhaps a Buick."

"Let's see. It must have been just about nine-thirty. We had been listening to 'I Love a Mystery,'" Morris recalled. "I turned it off when the program ended at nine-fifteen, and it was a few minutes later when we decided to drive up here."

"That the only car you met?"

"That was the only one. We drove on up and found the Point deserted. I guess we'd been parked there about ten minutes when we first heard that music drifting up and couldn't place it. Then, I've told you about seeing the guard rocks missing and going down to investigate."

"Did you touch anything down below?"

Morris shuddered. "Only the man's wrist. His body was still warm, but there wasn't any pulse."

The Sheriff snapped his notebook shut. "That helps a lot," he told the rancher. "Do you think you'd recognize the woman driver if you saw her again?"

"I'm afraid not. The moon wasn't even up, you know."

Whitaker came up just then to report that the searching party had been unable to find any trace of a tool that might have pried the boulders loose.

"I didn't expect you would find it," said Martin. "Whoever it was, carried the tool away with them. It's murder. Or a suicide pact that only one of them went through with. Come on with me."

With his deputy beside him as he drove down the steep grade, he told Whitaker about the fresh rouge on the man's lips and the woman driver whom Morris had met.

"I don't believe a woman could have pried those boulders loose," the deputy objected.

"That's why I mentioned a suicide pact," Martin agreed. "Either that or there was some other man in the vicinity who knocked William Petty unconscious and sent his car over the edge." He had reached the north and south straightaway at the bottom of the slope, and slowed to turn into a lighted filling station on the right.

The proprietor came out, and as soon as he recognized the Sheriff, he asked eagerly, "What's goin' on up to the Point? See a lot of cars up there."

"Car went over and killed a man. You been on duty long, Jeff?"

"Since six o'clock."

"Many cars go up or down the mountain tonight?"

Jeff shook his head. "That new highway has just about ruined my business. Several cars went up earlier, but none of 'em stopped for gas. I saw Nate Morris go by a-hellin' it right about ten o'clock."

"We know about him," Martin said. "Any others?"

"One. Only customer all evenin'. She bought five gallons on a C-stamp. That was about nine-thirty, I reckon."

"What kind of car, Jeff?"

"A big blue Buick. Had a Denver license, I recollect. She came down in a big hurry. Didn't wait for me to clean her windshield. An' you know I had a kinda funny hunch about her." Jeff laughed sheepishly. "You know how 'tis when you're alone an' not much to do. There was a sort of funny bundle on the back seat, an' I got the idea she didn't want me to clean the windshield on account of she didn't want me to look in.

"Well, sir, I made mention of it to her when I gave her the change. Just kiddin', you know. Said it looked like she had a body back there. She said her husband had drunk too much and passed out. Then she roared away in a big hurry."

The Sheriff thought about this information for a moment. Then he said, "Okay. Let me have her license number and I'll—"

Jeff broke in, "But I didn't notice the number. I can't remember all the—"

"You said she got gas on a C-stamp, Jeff."

The gas station proprietor nodded in a puzzled way and then suddenly grinned. "I see what you mean, Sheriff." He turned and hurried into the station.

Martin got out and followed him inside. He came back with a Denver license number, remarking grimly to Whitaker, "One good thing about those OPA rules. Person has to write his license number on the gas coupons. I'll stop by the courthouse and call this number in to the Courtesy Patrol in Denver. Save time by having them look it up while we're driving in. I got a pretty good description of her from Jeff," he added. "Young and thin and pretty. Wearing a little red hat and lots of lipstick."

Half an hour later the Sheriff and his deputy pulled up in front of Courtesy Patrol Headquarters in Denver. The sergeant in charge had checked the automobile registration number and had a name and address written on a slip of paper. Sheriff Martin took it. It read: "David L. Waring, 183 South Vine Street."

"This looks interesting," mused Martin as they went back to his car. "This address is just a block from where the dead man lived."

He drove out First Avenue to Vine and turned to the right. Number 183 was a small apartment building with a big garage at the rear, with private stalls for the cars of tenants. The Sheriff stopped in front and said to Whitaker, "Let's go back to the garage to look for that Buick before we go in."

They found a dark blue Buick sedan in one of the stalls. A woolen auto robe was crumpled up on the back seat. The truck was unlocked and there were a couple of tire tools inside, but neither of them showed any evidence of having been used to dig in the dirt recently. The motor of the Buick was warm, however, as though it had been standing in the garage not more than an hour.

They returned to the front of the apartment building and entered. Martin found a typed slip bearing the name "Mr. and Mrs. D. L. Waring" under the box marked 1-C, and the Sheriff led the way down a wide, richly carpeted hallway.

The door of No. 1-C was closed and there was no transom to indicate whether there was a light inside. Martin rang the bell and waited. After about thirty seconds he put his finger on the button and held it down.

The door finally opened. A black-browed young man scowled at the Sheriff and his deputy from beyond the threshold. He had broad shoulders and was in his shirtsleeves, wearing pants and shoes but no tie.

He nodded when Martin asked, "Mr. Waring?"

"Yes, what is it?"

"I'm Sheriff Martin from Sandhill. May we come in?" The Sheriff started forward.

Waring's scowl deepened and it seemed for a moment that he was going to block Martin's entrance. He stepped aside, however, with a surly, "I was going to bed. I don't know what you want here."

The living-room of the apartment was small, but nicely furnished. Martin looked around slowly and then asked, "Is your wife in?"

"She's in bed." Waring thrust his jaw out angrily. "See here. What do you want, anyway?"

"We'd like to see Mrs. Jessica Waring." Martin's drawling voice was deceptively mild.

"What about?"

"Murder."

The quietly spoken word seemed to reverberate through the room. The young man hesitated, then turned and strode across the room to jerk a door open. "Couple of cops out here want to see you, Jessica." He turned back, fuming. "I don't know what this is all about. What does my wife know about murder?"

"That's what we want to ask her," Martin told him. He got out the makings and rolled a brown-paper cigarette.

A tall, slender girl came out of the bedroom. She wore a polka-dot dressing gown. Her blond hair was worn in a long bob, and this combined with her unrouged face to give her a look of childish innocence. She looked curiously at the two officers and asked in a husky voice, "Did David say you're the police?"

"From Sandhill." Martin amplified watching her closely.

She blinked her eyelids and went across the room to a cigarette box. She lifted one out and lit it, went to a chair and sat down. "What on earth is this all about?"

"We want to know if you were in Sandhill this evening, Ma'am?"

"Of course she wasn't," Waring said violently. "She's been home all evening with a sick headache."

Martin sat down in a straight chair and said, "Let's let the lady answer the questions."

"That's right," Jessica Waring said. "I had to break a dinner engagement with my husband because I didn't feel like going out."

"But you were out?" Martin asked Waring.

"Yes. To dinner with some friends. I got home less than half an hour ago."

"Did you drive your Buick?"

"No. We're short on gas and I took a taxi," the man replied.

"Who did drive your Buick this evening?"

Jessica started slightly, but then sat back, veiling her eyes with long dark lashes.

"No one," Waring said harshly. "It's been in the garage."

"Is that right, Mrs. Waring?"

"I suppose so. I've been lying down since late afternoon."

Martin said, "The motor is still warm."

Waring glanced sharply at his wife. He thrust his hands deep into his pockets and strolled over to stand in front of her. "You have been lying down, I suppose?" His voice trembled slightly and was queerly harsh.

"Of course, dear." She fluttered her long lashes tremulously. "I told you I didn't feel like going out."

Martin said, "I'm sorry, but I have proof that your Buick stopped at a filling station just the other side of Sandhill for gas about nine-thirty tonight."

Waring swung about and demanded angrily, "What sort of proof?"

"A C-coupon was turned in for the gasoline. One that was endorsed with your registration number."

Mrs. Waring smiled lazily. "David is always giving his coupons away."

"The car we're looking for is a big blue Buick. And a woman answering your description was driving it. I'm afraid the filling station man will identify you, Mrs. Waring."

"All right. What of it?" She tossed her head and her voice sharpened. "Suppose I did get to feeling better and go for a little drive? I didn't want to tell you, David," she confessed, "because I knew you'd accuse me of having just pretended to be sick to get out of that dinner engagement."

Her husband snorted, went to the end of the divan and slumped down, glowering at the toes of his shoes.

"So you went up on Lookout Mountain just for a drive?" the Sheriff asked easily.

"Yes. I felt that I had to go out and get some air."

"Alone?"

"Of course I was alone. I often drive alone at night."

"Do you know the place they call Inspiration Point?"

The girl's hesitation was only momentary. "Do you mean that parking place where the college kids stop to neck?"

Martin nodded. "Did you stop there tonight?"

"Alone?" She laughed lightly. "I noticed a car parked there as I drove past. The couple who were in it didn't seem to need any company, so I kept on going."

"On your way up or down?"

"Driving up. That is, I'm not sure whether it was there when I drove back or not. I didn't notice."

"Who was the man in the back seat of your car when you stopped for gas?" the Sheriff shot at her suddenly.

She widened her eyes. "I told you I was alone." She glanced quickly at her husband, who had turned his head to stare at her. "It's the truth, David. I swear it is. There wasn't anyone with me."

"You told the man at the filling station it was your husband and that he had passed out from too much whiskey," Martin reminded her.

"Oh, that?" She laughed shakily. "It was just the robe bunched up on the back seat and I thought it would be a good joke to tell him that, when I saw him looking in suspiciously."

"He says it was a man."

"Jessica!" David Waring sprang to his feet, trembling violently. "Did you go out with that skunk again? After you promised me? Did you?"

Martin nodded to Whitaker. The deputy lunged forward and put his body between husband and wife. He gave Waring a little shove, and said, "The Sheriff'll ask the questions around here."

Jessica said, "No, David, I didn't. I swear I didn't. I haven't seen him since I promised you."

"What man?" Martin asked grimly.

She didn't look at him. She was staring past Whitaker at her husband, imploringly. Waring made a little defeated gesture with his hand, and muttered, "Skip it. Forget it."

"It's not that easy," Martin told him. "This is a murder investigation."

"Good heavens! You don't think my wife had anything to do with a murder, do you?"

"I don't know. That's for her to say. What man is he talking about, Mrs. Waring?"

"It's nothing, really. David got an absurdly jealous idea a couple of months ago. It was foolish on my part. Innocent, but foolish."

"What's the name of the man?" the Sheriff demanded of Waring.

"I don't even know his name," he muttered. "I found a note he'd written my wife. That's all I know about it. But I'm sure it's over. She wouldn't break her promise."

Martin said, "You'd better give us his name, Mrs. Waring, so we can check up."

She shook her head defiantly. "It was just an innocent flirtation, but my husband's so jealous I'm afraid of what he might do if he ever found out."

"And you insist that you were alone in the car tonight?"

"I do." She clamped her lips together tightly.

The Sheriff got up and went over to a low table near the door that held a red pocketbook, with a little red hat lying on top of it. He picked them up and asked, "This is the purse you had with you tonight?"

She nodded mutely.

He opened it and searched through it, finding and palming her tube of lip-rouge in his big hand. He laid the purse down, slid the lipstick in his pocket, told Whitaker, "We've got another stop to make in Denver," and stalked to the door.

Neither Mr. nor Mrs. Waring said anything as they went out.

Going down the hall, the deputy asked, "What do you make of it, John?"

"I don't know. If we can find anything to connect her with William Petty, I think we'll have something. It's a cinch she'll be up to something tonight. If her husband followed her out there and caught her with Petty—or if she drove out alone and caught Petty with another woman—anything might have happened. On the other hand, she may be telling the truth. All except being out there alone. I don't believe that for a minute."

"Neither does her husband," said Whitaker soberly. "I bet there's hell to pay in 1-C the rest of the night."

They went out to their car, and Martin drove around the block to 127 South Race. It was a big, old-fashioned dwelling that had been converted into housekeeping rooms. Though it was almost midnight, the porch light was on, and a silvery-haired old lady was knitting in the big living room when they walked in.

She looked up with a gentle smile, but shook her head sadly. "I haven't a single vacancy, gentlemen."

Martin said, "It's about one of your roomers, Mr. William Petty."

"Oh, yes. I was waiting up to let him in. I always like to know everyone's in and the door's locked before I go to bed. Has anything happened to Mr. Petty?"

"There's been an accident," the Sheriff told her. "Do you know where he went tonight—or with whom?"

"Why, I think he and Larry Johnson went out together. Larry's one of my roomers, too. But he came back an hour ago and he guessed Bill would be in soon. Mercy me! Is it serious?"

"He's been badly hurt, Ma'am. Could we see this Larry Johnson?"

"Yes. He's right upstairs. I'll show you his room." The landlady bustled out of her chair. "My, my. It's too bad about Mr. Petty. Such a nice young man. Always so jolly and full of fun."

She led the way up a wide staircase and knocked at a door at the top. A sleepy voice said, "Yes?"

Martin opened the door and switched on the light. A tousle-headed young man blinked at him in surprise from the bed.

"These gentlemen want to talk to you about Bill Petty, Mr. Johnson," the landlady announced from the doorway. "He's been hurt."

"That's too bad." Johnson sat up and pulled the blanket about his shoulders. He laughed, and said, "Don't tell me the husband came home unexpectedly."

"Why do you say that?" Martin asked sharply.

Johnson grimaced. "I really didn't mean anything. Only—well, Bill always had some woman on the string and I wondered—" He hesitated, then went on hastily, "I was just kidding. What did happen?"

"I understand you were out with him tonight."

"No. I went to a show by myself."

"Why, Mr. Johnson," the old lady reproved him from the doorway. "You know you and Mr. Petty went together. I heard you talking about what picture you'd go to at breakfast this morning."

"I know we did at breakfast this morning, Mrs. Crane. But Bill changed his mind this evening and went out alone."

"I don't think you had ought to fib about it," she said, shaking her head. "I saw you drive away with him in his car with my own eyes, right after supper."

"Sure, he drove me downtown. But he dropped me off at the Orpheum and I haven't seen him since."

"Can you prove it?" Martin asked.

The young man scowled at that. "I don't get it," he protested. "Why should I have to prove that?"

"Petty has been murdered!"

"Murdered?" Johnson's jaw dropped.

"I don't know anything about it," Johnson said soberly. "I'm sorry I kidded about Bill. He was a good guy. I can tell you all about the picture at the Orpheum. And I may have my ticket stub in my pocket. But I didn't see anybody I knew all evening."

"Did Petty tell you where he was going tonight?"

The young man hesitated for a moment, then shook his head. "No."

"Give you any idea what he planned?"

"I suppose I'd better tell you the whole thing," the youth said reluctantly. "We had planned to go to the show together tonight, but when I went into Bill's room after supper he told me it was all off. He showed me a note he'd gotten in the mail and said it was the kind of date he didn't want any company on."

"What did the note say?"

"It said—" Johnson screwed up his face in thought. "I think it's still lying on his dresser where I put it down." He slid out of bed. "I'll show you."

The officers stood back to let him go out into the hallway and into a room two doors down. He turned on the light, and sighed with relief as he pointed to the littered dresser top. "There it is. I thought I remembered him leaving it there."

The Sheriff and his deputy strode over to read the few words written in ink on a double sheet of heavy feminine notepaper.

Meet me tonight the same place. Must see you.
—Your Kitten.

The Sheriff put it in his pocket, careful not to ruin any fingerprints that might be on it. "You say Petty got this in the mail?"

"That's what he said."

"Did you see the envelope? Notice when or where it was mailed?"

"I didn't see the envelope."

"How about you, Mrs. Crane?" Martin asked the landlady. "Did you notice any mail that Petty received today?"

"I can't say as I noticed it particular. He got several letters."

"What did he tell you about this note?" Martin looked hard at Johnson.

"Nothing much. Except it was a pretty special date and he wouldn't need me along. I had an idea, well, that maybe it was a married woman."

"Why?"

"I don't know," Johnson shrugged defensively. "Except that he was always getting mixed up with married women."

"Can you give us any names?"

"No. He was always mighty closed-mouthed about his lady friends."

"Ever hear him mention one named Jessica, for instance?"

Johnson appeared to be thinking. "I don't think so. I don't remember."

He was unable to furnish any other relevant information concerning his friend's possible actions of the evening, nor did a thorough search of Petty's room reveal anything of consequence.

As the two officers drove back toward Sandhill a short time later, Sheriff Martin said optimistically, "We're coming along pretty well, at that. If this sample of Mrs. Waring's lipstick checks with what's on Petty's mouth, we'll get a sample of her handwriting and see if she wrote this note. That may clear it up."

"Suppose the lipstick and the handwriting don't check?"

"Then we'll have to start all over again," the Sheriff admitted. They were pulling into the environs of Sandhill, and he turned along a tree-lined street in the direction of the deputy's home. He slowed the car and seemed to be thinking deeply, then suddenly struck the steering wheel a blow with his fist. "I'm a fool, Lem!"

He pulled over to the curb in front of Whitaker's house and asked intently, "It was just ten o'clock when we left the office, wasn't it?"

"Not more'n a minute or so after. We listened to the end of that hour-long newscast over KFEL and went right out."

"And we heard Morris's car coming down the hill when we got to the front door," Martin went on, thinking aloud. "That couldn't have been more than five minutes past ten at the most."

"That's right."

"Even a young fellow like Nate Morris couldn't climb down that slope and back up again in five minutes," mused the Sheriff. "That sets the time exactly."

He put his car in gear again and swung in a U-turn to go back up the street. "I'm going to ask Mr. and Mrs. Morris just one question and then I'll know who murdered William Petty without waiting to get this lipstick analyzed or this handwriting checked."

"It's pretty late to rouse somebody out now," the deputy objected.

"Not too late to put the finger on a murderer. And Morris can do it for us. He lives out on Elm Street, doesn't he?"

Martin drove another block and swung to the right. As the houses along Elm Street became more scattered, Whitaker leaned out of his window to look ahead, and said, "It's the middle of the next block, I think. A white stucco house."

"They're still up." Martin indicated the lighted windows of the neat bungalow as he stopped in front.

The two men went up the path and the Sheriff pressed the electric button. They heard footsteps inside. Morris opened the door. He flung it wide open when he recognized the Sheriff and his deputy. "Come in. Glad you stopped by. Sally and I have been wondering what you've found out."

They entered a long, comfortable living-room with Indian rugs on the floor and deep, restful chairs arranged cozily. Sally Morris was seated in an overstuffed chair in front of a low coffee table. A silver percolator was bubbling on the table and a tall bottle of brandy stood beside it. She looked up, but there was no welcoming smile. "We are about to make ourselves a coffee royal, Sheriff. Will you join us?"

She was quite young, with freckles splashed across her nose.

Martin said, "The coffee smells mighty good. Wouldn't mind having a shot of royal first, I reckon, and then coffee on top of it."

"Get some glasses," the girl told her husband, and asked the deputy, "How about you?"

"I reckon I'll wait for the coffee, Mrs. Morris," he decided.

Morris brought two glasses from the sideboard. He stopped beside his wife and held them out while she poured the brandy. He handed one to the Sheriff, saying, "I'll drink one with you. How's the investigation been going?"

"Good." Martin gulped down the brandy and smacked his lips. "Just about got the whole thing tied up in a knot and all I need is to check one thing with you."

"Go ahead. If there's anything we can tell you, we'll be glad to help."

"It's the exact timing," the Sheriff explained. "That's the most important point right now. I want you both to think hard. You figure you reached the Point a little after nine-thirty?"

"It couldn't have been much later than that."

"And you sat there awhile and waited for the moon to come up and then heard soft music and couldn't figure where it was coming from. That right?"

"I imagine we were parked about ten minutes before I noticed the two guard rocks were gone. Then I realized the music must be coming from the radio of a car that had gone over and I told Sally to wait while I went down to investigate."

"That makes it about right," Martin agreed. "You were back in town by five minutes after ten. Give you three or four minutes to make the run—that'd give you ten or fifteen minutes to've got to the bottom and back up after hearing the music."

"That's about right," the rancher agreed. "It's a steep climb back up the cliff."

"Which sets it pretty definite as being between nine-thirty and ten o'clock when you heard the music?"

Nate Morris nodded. "That's a safe enough guess."

Sheriff Martin shook his head slowly. "It's a plumb bad guess, Nate. That car radio was tuned to Station KFEL. You forgot that KFEL has an hour-long news program without any music between nine and ten."

"But—we heard it, I tell you."

"You didn't hear any music and I'll tell you why, Nate. You were busy knocking Petty cold after finding him there kissing your wife—and then prying out those boulders and kicking his car in gear and guiding it over the edge from the runningboard. But couldn't take a chance on him still being alive, so you slid down the slope to check. Then you got scared we might find your footprints or something to indicate that you'd been there and you tried to think up some good story to explain how you'd been attracted to the wreck that couldn't be seen from above.

"The motor was dead and the lights were shorted out, and you thought of the radio. You turned it on, and by golly, it played. So you hiked back up to the top and listened for a moment, and that's when you heard the music. Right after the program changed at ten o'clock. I'm sorry, Nate. That's the only answer that fits the lie you told about hearing the music."

Morris was breathing hard. His wife leaned forward to put her face in her hands, elbows propped on her knees.

"It's absurd," Morris protested. "There must have been music. We heard it."

Martin said, "We'll need a sample of your wife's lipstick to compare with that on Petty's mouth. And you'd better write us a note, Mrs. Morris. Just write: Meet me tonight the same place. Must see you. And sign it: Your kitten."

Morris stepped forward with an angry exclamation, clenched fist upraised.

Sally leaped up with a cry of terror. "Don't, Nate! They know everything. It won't work. I told you it wouldn't work. Oh, God help us!" She buried her face in her hands and wept hysterically.

Morris said, "All right, Sheriff. I killed him. I went crazy when I drove up and saw Sally in his arms. I jumped out of my car and hit him. When I saw he was unconscious, saw how easy it would be to run his car over the edge and make it look like an accident. But I had to be sure he was dead. And after I'd gotten down to his car, I realized the police have ways of tracing footprints and things. And someone might have seen me driving up there.

"I read in a book once about a radio that kept on playing after a car was smashed up, and I reached in with my gloved hand and turned the knob. An announcer came on. I didn't think about what station it was. I just thought it would make a plausible explanation for me being down there."

Later that night in the Sheriff's office, Morris repeated his confession before both officers, Assistant County Attorney Albright and a court reporter. He willingly signed a typewritten transcript of his statement, which told in detail how he had suspected his wife of secretly meeting a certain Denver man whose name need not be mentioned here and how he had followed them to their fatal tryst that night.

An information charging him with first-degree murder was filed in District Court, and on April 19th, 1944, he was brought to trial before District Judge A. H. Belton, and his attorneys were prepared to fight the case on the grounds of the unwritten law that allows a man the right to protect his home.

In a surprise move, however, the prosecution agreed to accept a plea of guilty to second-degree murder, and Nate Morris was promptly sentenced to life imprisonment in the Colorado State Penitentiary.

DASHIELL HAMMETT

It is unfortunate DASHIELL HAMMETT blocked all efforts to collect his short literary works in one place. A good many of his stories, important ones that shed significant light on his development as a writer, have been inaccessible, out of print for more than sixty-five years, among them, "Who Killed Bob Teal?". It appeared in *True Detective* in November 1924, the magazine's second issue, and according to records at the Library of Congress, it has never before been collected. Determining which elements of this yarn are based on fact is a detective puzzle in itself. The story was attributed to "Dashiell Hammett of the Continental Detective Agency," an agency which existed only in Hammett's other fiction. Names have been changed to protect the innocent. And court records from this period in San Francisco no longer exist; no leads there. On the other hand, records at *True Detective*'s Manhattan headquarters make no mention of the fact that this story was fiction, something they normally acknowledged privately, if not always to the magazine's readership. Moreover, while this story shares much in common with Hammett's best fiction from this period, it has a pacing and style of its own. If indeed this story is true, it would appear to be the only true crime story he ever wrote. Or at least, it is the only one that has been rediscovered for today's reader. Judge for yourself.

Who Killed Bob Teal?

"Teal was killed last night."

The Old Man—the Continental Detective Agency's San Francisco manager—spoke without looking at me. His voice was as mild as his smile, and gave no indication of the turmoil that was seething in his mind.

If I kept quiet, waiting for the Old Man to go on, it wasn't because the news didn't mean anything to me. I had been fond of Bob Teal—we all had. He had come to the agency fresh from college two years before; and if ever a man had the makings of a crack detective in him, this slender, broad-shouldered lad had. Two years is little enough time in which to pick up the first principles of sleuthing, but Bob Teal, with his quick eye, cool nerve, balanced head, and whole-hearted interest in the work, was already well along the way to expertness. I had an almost fatherly interest in him, since I had given him most of his early training.

The Old Man didn't look at me as he went on. He was talking to the open window at his elbow.

"He was shot with a .32, twice, through the heart. He was shot behind a row of signboards on the vacant lot on the northwest corner of Hyde and Eddy streets, at about ten last night. His body was found by a patrolman a little after eleven. The gun was found about fifteen feet away. I have seen him and I have gone over the ground myself. The rain last night wiped out any leads the ground may have held, but from the condition of Teal's clothing and the position in which he was found, I would say that there was no struggle, and that he was shot where he was found, and not carried there afterward. He was lying behind the signboards, about thirty feet from the sidewalk, and his hands were empty. The gun was held close enough to him to singe the breast of his coat. Apparently no one either saw or heard the shooting. The rain and wind would have kept pedestrians off the street, and would have deadened the reports of a .32, which are not especially loud, anyway."

The Old Man's pencil began to tap the desk, its gentle clicking setting my nerves on edge. Presently it stopped, and the Old Man went on:

"Teal was shadowing a Herbert Whitacre—had been shadowing him for three days. Whitacre is one of the partners in the firm Ogburn & Whitacre, farm-development engineers. They have options on a large area of land in several of the new irrigation districts. Ogburn handles the sales end, while Whitacre looks after the rest of the business, including the bookkeeping.

"Last week Ogburn discovered that his partner had been making false entries. The books show certain payments made on the land, and Ogburn learned that these payments had not been made. He estimates that the amount of Whitacre's thefts may be anywhere from $150,000 to $250,000. He came in to see me three days ago and told me all this, and wanted to have Whitacre shadowed in an endeavor to learn what he has done with the stolen money. Their firm is still a partnership, and a partner cannot be prosecuted for stealing from the partnership, of course. Thus, Ogburn could not have his partner arrested, but he hoped to find the money, and then recover it through civil action. Also he was afraid that Whitacre might disappear.

"I sent Teal out to shadow Whitacre, who supposedly didn't know that his partner suspected him. Now I am sending you out to find Whitacre. I'm determined to find him and convict him if I have to let all regular business go and put every man I have on this job for a year. You can get Teal's reports from the clerks. Keep in touch with me."

All that, from the Old Man, was more than an ordinary man's oath written in blood.

In the clerical office I got the two reports Bob had turned in. There was none for the last day, of course, as he would not have written that until after he had quit work for the night. The first of these two reports had already been copied and a copy sent to Ogburn; a typist was working on the other now.

In his reports Bob had described Whitacre as a man of about thirty-seven, with brown hair and eyes, a nervous manner, a smooth-shaven, medium-complexioned face, and rather small feet. He was about five feet eight inches tall, weighed about a hundred and fifty pounds, and dressed fashionably, though quietly. He lived with his wife in an apartment on Gough Street. They had no children. Ogburn had given Bob a description of Mrs. Whitacre: a short, plump, blond woman of something less than thirty.

Those who remember this affair will know that the city, the detective agency, and the people involved all had names different from the ones I have given them. But they will know also that I have kept the facts true. Names of some sort are essential to clearness, and when the use of the real names might cause embarrassment, or pain even, pseudonyms are the most satisfactory alternative.

In shadowing Whitacre, Bob had learned nothing that seemed to be of any value in finding the stolen money. Whitacre had gone about his usual business, apparently, and Bob had seen him do nothing downright suspicious. But Whitacre had seemed nervous, had often stopped to look around, obviously suspecting that he was being shadowed without being sure of it. On several occasions Bob had had to drop him to avoid being recognized. On one of these occasions, while waiting in the vicinity of Whitacre's residence for him to return, Bob had seen Mrs. Whitacre—or a woman who fit the description Ogburn had given—leave in a taxicab. Bob had not tried to follow her, but he made a memorandum of the taxi's license number.

These two reports read and practically memorized, I left the agency and went down to Ogburn & Whitacre's suite in the Packard Building. A stenographer ushered me into a tastefully furnished office, where Ogburn sat at a desk signing mail. He offered me a chair. I introduced myself to him: a medium-sized man of perhaps thirty-five, with sleek brown hair and the cleft chin that is associated in my mind with orators, lawyers, and salesmen.

"Oh, yes!" he said, pushing aside the mail, his mobile, intelligent face lighting up. "Has Mr. Teal found anything?"

"Mr. Teal was shot and killed last night."

He looked at me blankly for a moment out of wide brown eyes, and then repeated: "Killed?"

"Yes," I replied, and told him what little I knew about it.

"You don't think—" he began when I had finished, and then stopped. "You don't think Herb would have done that?"

"What do you think?"

"I don't think Herb would commit murder! He's been jumpy the last few days, and I was beginning to think he suspected I had discovered his thefts, but I don't believe he would have gone that far, even if he knew Mr. Teal was following him. I honestly don't!"

"Suppose," I suggested, "that sometime yesterday Teal found where he had put the stolen money, and then Whitacre learned that Teal knew it. Don't you think that under those circumstances Whitacre might have killed him?"

"Perhaps," he said slowly, "but I'd hate to think so. In a moment of panic Herb might—but I really don't think he would."

"When did you see him last?"

"Yesterday. We were here in the office together most of the day. He left for home a few minutes before six. But I talked to him over the phone later. He called me up at home at a little after seven, and said he was coming down to see me, wanted to tell me something. I thought he was going to confess his dishonesty, and that maybe we would be able to straighten out this miserable affair. His wife called up at about ten. She wanted him to bring something from downtown when he went home, but of course he was not there. I stayed in all evening waiting for him, but he didn't—"

He stuttered, stopped talking, and his face drained white.

"My God, I'm wiped out!" he said faintly, as if the thought of his own position had just come to him. "Herb gone, money gone, three years' work gone for nothing! And I'm legally responsible for every cent he stole. God!"

He looked at me with eyes that pleaded for a contradiction, but I couldn't do anything except assure him that everything possible would be done to find both Whitacre and the money. I left him trying frantically to get his attorney on the telephone.

From Ogburn's office I went up to Whitacre's apartment. As I turned the corner below into Gough Street I saw a big, hulking man going up the apartment house steps, and recognized him as George Dean. Hurrying to join him, I regretted that he had been assigned to the job instead of some other member of the Police Detective Homicide Detail. Dean isn't a bad sort, but he isn't so satisfactory to work with as some of the others; that is, you can never be sure that he isn't holding out some important detail so that George Dean would shine as the clever sleuth in the end. Working with a man of that sort, you're bound to fall into the habit—which doesn't make for teamwork.

I arrived in the vestibule as Dean pressed Whitacre's bell-button.

"Hello," I said. "You in on this?"

"Uh-huh. What d'you know?"

"Nothing. I just got it."

The front door clicked open, and we went together up to the Whitacres' apartment on the third floor. A plump, blond woman in a light blue house-dress opened the apartment door. She was rather pretty in a thick-featured, stolid way.

"Mrs. Whitacre?" Dean inquired.

"Yes."

"Is Mr. Whitacre in?"

"No. He went to Los Angeles this morning," she said, and her face was truthful.

"Know where we can get in touch with him there?"

"Perhaps at the Ambassador, but I think he'll be back by to-morrow or the next day."

Dean showed her his badge.

"We want to ask you a few questions," he told her, and with no appearance of astonishment she opened the door wide for us to enter. She led us into a blue and cream living-room where we found a chair apiece. She sat facing us on a big blue settle.

"Where was your husband last night?" Dean asked.

"Home. Why?" Her round blue eyes were faintly curious.

"Home all night?"

"Yes, it was a rotten rainy night. Why?" She looked from Dean to me.

Dean's glance met mine, and I nodded an answer to the question that I read there.

"Mrs. Whitacre," he said bluntly, "I have a warrant for your husband's arrest."

"A warrant? For what?"

"Murder."

"Murder?" It was a stifled scream.

"Exactly, an' last night."

"But—but I told you he was—"

"And Ogburn told me," I interrupted, leaning forward, "that you called up his apartment last night, asking if your husband was there."

She looked at me blankly for a dozen seconds; and then she laughed, the clear laugh of one who has been the victim of some slight joke.

"You win," she said, and there was neither shame nor humiliation in either face or voice. "Now listen"—the amusement had left her—"I don't know what Herb has done, or how I stand, and I oughtn't to talk until I see a lawyer. But I like to dodge all the trouble I can. If you folks will tell me what's what, on your word of honor, I'll maybe tell you what I know, if anything. What I mean is, if talking will make things any easier for me, if you can show me it will, maybe I'll talk—provided I know anything."

That seemed fair enough, if a little surprising. Apparently this plump woman who could lie with every semblance of candor, and laugh when she was tripped up, wasn't interested in anything much beyond her own comfort.

"You tell it," Dean said to me.

I shot it out all in a lump.

"Your husband had been cooking the books for some time, and got into his partner for something like $200,000 before Ogburn got wise to it. Then he had your husband shadowed, trying to find the money. Last night your husband took the man who was shadowing him over on a lot and shot him."

Her face puckered thoughtfully. Mechanically she reached for a package of popular brand cigarettes that lay on a table behind the settle, and proffered them to Dean and me. We shook our heads. She put a cigarette

in her mouth, scratched a match on the sole of her slipper, lit the
cigarette, and stared at the burning end. Finally she shrugged, her face
cleared, and she looked up at us.

"I'm going to talk," she said. "Never got any of the money, and I'd be a
chump to make a goat of myself for Herb. He was all right, but if he's run
out and left me flat, there's no use of me making a lot of trouble for myself
over it. Here goes: I'm not Mrs. Whitacre, except on the register. My
name is Mae Landis. Maybe there is a real Mrs. Whitacre, and maybe not.
I don't know. Herb and I have been living together here for over a year.

"About a month ago he began to get jumpy, nervous, even worse than
usual. He said he had business worries. Then a couple of days ago I
discovered that his pistol was gone from the drawer where it had been
kept ever since we came here, and that he was carrying it. I asked him:
'What's the idea?' He said he thought he was being followed, and asked
me if I'd seen anybody hanging around the neighborhood as if watching
our place. I told him no; I thought he was nutty.

"Night before last he told me that he was in trouble, and might have to
go away, and that he couldn't take me with him, but would give me
enough money to take care of me for a while. He seemed excited, packed
his bags so they'd be ready if he needed them in a hurry, and burned up
all his photos and a lot of letters and papers. His bags are still in the
bedroom, if you want to go through them. When he didn't come home last
night I had a hunch that he had beat it without his bags and without
saying a word to me, much less giving me any money—leaving me with
only twenty dollars to my name and not even much that I could hock, and
with the rent due in four days."

"When did you see him last?"

"About eight o'clock last night. He told me he was going down to Mr.
Ogburn's apartment to talk some business over with him, but he didn't go
there. I know that. I ran out of cigarettes—I like Elixir Russians, and I
can't get them uptown here—so I called up Mr. Ogburn's to ask Herb to
bring some home with him when he came, and Mr. Ogburn said he hadn't
been there."

"How long have you known Whitacre?" I asked.

"Couple of years, I guess. I think I met him first at one of the Beach
resorts."

"Has he got any people?"

"Not that I know of. I don't know a whole lot about him. Oh, yes! I do know that he served three years in prison in Oregon for forgery. He told me that one night when he was lushed up. He served them under the name of Barber, or Barbee, or something like that. He said he was walking the straight and narrow now."

Dean produced a small automatic pistol, fairly new-looking in spite of the mud that clung to it, and handed it to the woman.

"Ever see that?"

She nodded her blond head. "Yep! That's Herb's or its twin."

Dean pocketed the gun again, and we stood up.

"Where do I stand now?" she asked. "You're not going to lock me up as a witness or anything, are you?"

"Not just now," Dean assured her. "Stick around where we can find you if we want you, and you won't be bothered. Got any idea which direction Whitacre'd be likely to go in?"

"No."

"We'd like to give the place the once-over. Mind?"

"Go ahead," she invited. "Take it apart if you want to. I'm coming all the way with you people."

We very nearly did take the place apart, but we found not a thing of value. Whitacre, when he had burned the things that might have given him away, had made a clean job of it.

"Did he ever have any pictures taken by a professional photographer?" I asked just before we left.

"Not that I know of."

"Will you let us know if you hear anything or remember anything else that might help?"

"Sure," she said heartily; "sure."

Dean and I rode down in the elevator in silence, and walked out into Gough Street.

"What do you think of all that?" I asked when we were outside.

"She's a lil, huh?" He grinned. "I wonder how much she knows. She identified the gun an' gave us that dope about the forgery sentence up north, but we'd of found out them things anyway. If she was wise she'd tell us everything she knew we'd find out, an' that would make her other stuff go over stronger. Think she's dumb or wise?"

"We won't guess," I said. "We'll slap a shadow on her and cover her mail. I have the number of a taxi she used a couple days ago. We'll look that up too."

At a corner drug store I telephoned the Old Man, asking him to detail a couple of the boys to keep Mae Landis and her apartment under surveillance night and day; also to have the Post Office Department let us know if she got any mail that might have been addressed by Whitacre. I told the Old Man I would see Ogburn and get some specimens of the fugitive's writing for comparison with the woman's mail.

Then Dean and I set about tracing the taxi in which Bob Teal had seen the woman ride away. Half an hour in the taxi company's office gave us the information that she had been driven to a number on Greenwich Street. We went to the Greenwich Street address.

It was a ramshackle building, divided into apartments or flats of a dismal and dingy sort. We found the landlady in the basement: a gaunt woman in soiled gray, with a hard, thin-lipped mouth and pale, suspicious eyes. She was rocking vigorously in a creaking chair and sewing on a pair of overalls, while three dirty kids tussled with a mongrel puppy up and down the room.

Dean showed his badge, and told her that we wanted to speak to her in privacy. She got up to chase the kids and their dog out, and then stood with hands on hips facing us.

"Well, what do you want?" she demanded sourly.

"Want to get a line on your tenants," Dean said. "Tell us about them."

"Tell you about them?" She had a voice that would have been harsh enough even if she hadn't been in such a peevish mood. "What do you think I got to say about 'em? What do you think I am? I'm a woman that minds her own business! Nobody can't say that I don't run a respectable—"

This was getting us nowhere.

"Who lives in number one?" I asked.

"The Auds—two old folks and their grandchildren. If you know anything against them, it's more'n them that has lived with 'em for ten years does!"

"Who lives in number two?"

"Mrs. Codman and her boys, Frank and Fred. They been here three years, and—"

I carried her from apartment to apartment, until finally we reached a second-floor one that didn't bring quite so harsh an indictment of my stupidity for suspecting its occupants of whatever it was that I suspected them of.

"The Quirks live there." She merely glowered now, whereas she had had a snippy manner before. "And they're decent people, if you ask me!"

"How long have they been here?"

"Six months or more."

"What does he do for a living?"

"I don't now." Sullenly: "Travels maybe."

"How many in the family?"

"Just him and her, and they're nice quiet people, too."

"What does he look like?"

"Like an ordinary man, I ain't a detective. I don't go 'round snoopin' into folks' faces to see what they look like, and prying into their business. I ain't—"

"How old a man is he?"

"Maybe between thirty-five and forty, if he ain't younger or older."

"Large or small?"

"He ain't as short as you and he ain't as tall as this feller with you," glaring scornfully from my short stoutness to Dean's big hulk, "and he ain't as fat as neither of you."

"Mustache?"

"No."

"Light hair?"

"No." Triumphantly: "Dark."

"Dark eyes, too?"

"I guess so."

Dean, standing off to one side, looked over the woman's shoulder at me. His lips framed the name "Whitacre."

"Now how about Mrs. Quirk—what does she look like?" I went on.

"She's got light hair, is short and chunky, and maybe under thirty."

Dean and I nodded our satisfaction at each other; that sounded like Mae Landis, right enough.

"Are they home much?" I continued.

"I don't know," the gaunt woman snarled sullenly, and I knew she did know, so I waited, looking at her, and presently she added grudgingly: "I think they're away a lot, but I ain't sure."

"I know," I ventured, "they are home very seldom, and then only in the daytime—and you know it."

She didn't deny it, so I asked: "Are they in now?"

"I don't think so, but they might be."

"Let's take a look at the joint," I suggested to Dean.

He nodded and told the woman: "Take us up to their apartment an' unlock the door for us."

"I won't!" she said with sharp emphasis. "You got no right goin' into folks' homes unless you got a search-warrant. You got one?"

"We got nothin'." Dean grinned at her. "But we can get plenty if you want to put us to the trouble. You run this house; you can go into any of the flats any time you want, an' you can take us in. Take us up, an' we'll lay off you: but if you're going to put us to a lot of trouble, then you'll take your chances of bein' tied up with the Quirks, an' maybe sharin' a cell with 'em. Think that over."

She thought it over, and then, grumbling and growling with each step, took us up to the Quirks' apartment. She made sure they weren't at home, then admitted us.

The apartment consisted of three rooms, a bath, and a kitchen, furnished in the shabby fashion that the ramshackle exterior of the building had prepared us for. In these rooms we found a few articles of masculine and feminine clothing, toilet accessories, and so on. But the place had none of the marks of a permanent abode: there were no pictures, no cushions, none of the dozens of odds and ends of personal belongings that are usually found in homes. The kitchen had the appearance of long disuse; the interiors of the coffee, tea, spice, and flour containers were clean.

Two things we found that meant something: A handful of Elixir Russian cigarettes on a table; and a new box of .32 cartridges—ten of which were missing—in a dresser drawer.

All through our searching the landlady hovered over us, her pale eyes sharp and curious; but now we chased her out, telling her that, law or no law, we were taking charge of the apartment.

"This was or is a hide-out for Whitacre and his woman all right," Dean said when we were alone. "The only question is whether he intended to lay low here or whether it was just a place where he made preparations for his get-away. I reckon the best thing is to have the Captain put a man in here night and day until we turn up Brother Whitacre."

"That's safest," I agreed, and he went to the telephone in the front room to arrange it.

After Dean was through phoning, I called up the Old Man to see if anything new had developed.

"Nothing new," he told me. "How are you coming along?"

"Nicely. Maybe I'll have news for you this evening."

"Did you get those specimens of Whitacre's writing from Ogburn? Or shall I have someone else take care of it?"

"I'll get them this evening," I promised.

I wasted ten minutes trying to reach Ogburn at his office before I looked at my watch and saw that it was after six o'clock. I found his residence listed in the telephone directory, and called him there.

"Have you anything in Whitacre's writing at home?" I asked. "I want to get a couple of samples—would like to get them this evening, though if necessary I can wait until tomorrow."

"I think I have some of his letters here. If you come over now I'll give them to you."

"Be with you in fifteen minutes," I told him.

"I'm going down to Ogburn's," I told Dean, "to get some of Whitacre's scribbling while you're waiting for your man to come from Headquarters to take charge of this place. I'll meet you at the States as soon as you can get away. We'll eat there, and make our plans for the night."

"Uh-huh," he grunted, making himself comfortable in one chair, with his feet on another, as I let myself out.

Ogburn was dressing when I reached his apartment, and had his collar and tie in his hand when he came to the door to let me in.

"I found quite a few of Herb's letters," he said as we walked back to his bedroom.

I looked through the fifteen or more letters that lay on a table, selecting the ones I wanted, while Ogburn went on with his dressing.

"How are you progressing?" he asked presently.

"So-so. Heard anything that might help?"

"No, but just a few minutes ago I happened to remember that Herb used to go over to the Mills Building quite frequently. I've seen him going in and out often, but never thought anything of it. I don't know whether it is of any importance or—"

I jumped out of my chair.

"That does it!" I cried. "Can I use your phone?"

"Certainly. It's in the hallway, near the door." He looked at me in surprise. "It's a slot phone; have you a nickel in change?"

"Yes." I was going through the bedroom door.

"The switch is near the door," he called after me, "if you want a light. Do you think—"

But I didn't stop to listen to his questions. I was making for the telephone, searching my pockets for a nickel. And, fumbling hurriedly with the nickel, I muffed it—not entirely by accident, for I had a hunch that I wanted to work out. The nickel rolled away down the carpeted hallway. I switched on the light, recovered the nickel, and called the "Quirks'" number. I'm glad I played that hunch.

Dean was still there.

"That joint's dead," I sang. "Take the landlady down to Headquarters, and grab the Landis woman, too. I'll meet you there—at Headquarters."

"You mean it?" he rumbled.

"Almost," I said, and hung up the receiver.

I switched off the hall light and, whistling a little tune to myself, walked back to the room where I had left Ogburn. The door was not quite closed. I walked straight up to it, kicked it open with one foot, and jumped back, hugging the wall.

Two shots—so close together that they were almost one—crashed.

Flat against the wall, I pounded my feet against the floor and wainscot, and let out a medley of shrieks and groans that would have done credit to a carnival wild-man.

A moment later Ogburn appeared in the doorway, a revolver in his hand, his face wolfish. He was determined to kill me. It was my life or his, so—

I slammed my gun down on the sleek, brown top of his head.

When he opened his eyes, two policemen were lifting him into the back of a patrol-wagon.

I found Dean in the detectives' assembly-room in the Hall of Justice. "The landlady identified Mae Landis as Mrs. Quirk," he said. "Now what?"

"Where is she now?"

"One of the policewomen is holding both of them in the Captain's office."

"Ogburn is over in the Pawnshop Detail office," I told him. "Let's take the landlady in for a look at him."

Ogburn sat leaning forward, holding his head in his hands and staring sullenly at the feet of the uniformed man who guarded him, when we took the gaunt landlady in to see him.

"Ever see him before?" I asked her.

"Yes"—reluctantly—"that's Mr. Quirk."

Ogburn didn't look up, and he paid not the least attention to any of us.

After we had told the landlady that she could go home, Dean led me back to a far corner of the assembly-room, where we could talk without disturbance.

"Now spill it!" he burst out. "How come all the startling developments, as the newspaper boys call 'em?"

"Well, first-off, I knew that the question *Who Killed Bob Teal?* could have only one answer. Bob wasn't a boob! He might possibly have let a man he was trailing lure him behind a row of billboards on a dark night, but he would have gone prepared for trouble. He wouldn't have died with empty hands, from a gun that was close enough to scorch his coat. The murderer had to be somebody Bob trusted, so it couldn't be Whitacre. Now Bob was a conscientious sort of lad, and he wouldn't have stopped shadowing Whitacre to go over and talk with some friend. There was only one man who could have persuaded him to drop Whitacre for a while, and that one man was the one he was working for—Ogburn.

"If I hadn't known Bob, I might have thought he had hidden behind the billboards to watch Whitacre; but Bob wasn't an amateur. He knew better than to pull any of that spectacular gumshoe stuff. So there was nothing to it but Ogburn!

"With all that to go on, the rest was ducksoup. All the stuff Mae Landis gave us—identifying the gun as Whitacre's, and giving Ogburn an alibi by saying she had talked to him on the phone at ten o'clock—only convinced me that she and Ogburn were working together. When the landlady described 'Quirk' for us, I was fairly certain of it. Her description would fit either Whitacre or Ogburn, but there was no sense to Whitacre's having the apartment on Greenwich Street, which if Ogburn and the Landis woman were thick, they'd need a meeting-place of some sort. The rest of the box of cartridges there helped some too.

"Then tonight I put on a little act in Ogburn's apartment, chasing a nickel along the floor and finding traces of dried mud that had escaped the cleaning-up he no doubt gave the carpet and clothes after he came home from walking through the lot in the rain. We'll let the experts decide whether it could be mud from the lot on which Bob was killed, and jury can decide whether it is.

"There are a few more odds and ends—like the gun. The Landis woman said Whitacre had had it for more than a year, but in spite of being muddy it looks fairly new to me. We'll send the serial number to the factory, and find when it was turned out.

"For motive, just now all I'm sure of is the woman, which should be enough. But I think that when Ogburn & Whitacre's books are audited, and their finances sifted, we'll find something there. What I'm banking on strong is that Whitacre will come in, now that he is cleared of the murder charge."

And that is exactly what happened.

Next day Herbert Whitacre walked into Police Headquarters at Sacramento and surrendered.

Neither Ogburn nor Mae Landis ever told what they knew, but with Whitacre's testimony, supported by what we were able to pick up here and there, we went into court when the time came and convinced the jury that the facts were these:

Ogburn and Whitacre had opened their farm-development business as a plain swindle. They had options on a lot of land, and they planned to sell as many shares in their enterprise as possible before the time came to exercise their options. Then they intended packing up their bags and disappearing. Whitacre hadn't much nerve, and he had a clear remembrance of the three years he had served in prison for forgery; so to bolster his courage, Ogburn had told his partner that he had a friend in the Post Office Department in Washington, D.C., who would tip him off the instant official suspicion was aroused.

The two partners made a neat little pile out of their venture, Ogburn taking charge of the money until the time came for the split-up. Meanwhile, Ogburn and Mae Landis—Whitacre's supposed wife—had become intimate, and had rented the apartment on Greenwich Street, meeting there afternoons when Whitacre was busy at the office, and when Ogburn was supposed to be out hunting fresh victims. In this apartment Ogburn and the woman had hatched their little scheme, whereby they were to get rid of Whitacre, keep all the loot, and clear Ogburn of criminal complicity in the affairs of Ogburn & Whitacre.

Ogburn had come into the Continental Office and told his little tale of his partner's dishonesty, engaging Bob Teal to shadow him. Then he had told Whitacre that he had received a tip from his friend in Washington that an investigation was about to be made. The two partners planned to leave town on their separate ways the following week. The next night Mae

Landis told Whitacre she had seen a man loitering in the neighborhood, apparently watching the building in which they lived. Whitacre—thinking Bob a Post Office Inspector—had gone completely to pieces, and it had taken the combined efforts of the woman and his partner—apparently working separately—to keep him from bolting immediately. They persuaded him to stick it out another few days.

On the night of the murder, Ogburn, pretending skepticism of Whitacre's story about being followed, had met Whitacre for the purpose of learning if he really was being shadowed. They had walked the streets in the rain for an hour. Then Ogburn, convinced, had announced his intention of going back and talking to the supposed Post Office Inspector, to see if he could be bribed. Whitacre had refused to accompany his partner, but had agreed to wait for him in a dark doorway.

Ogburn had taken Bob Teal over behind the billboards on some pretext, and had murdered him. Then he had hurried back to his partner, crying: "My God! He grabbed me and I shot him. We'll have to leave!"

Whitacre, in blind panic, had left San Francisco without stopping for his bags or even notifying Mae Landis. Ogburn was supposed to leave by another route. They were to meet in Oklahoma City ten days later, where Ogburn—after getting the loot out of the Los Angeles banks, where he had deposited it under various names—was to give Whitacre his share, and then they were to part for good.

In Sacramento next day Whitacre had read the newspapers, and had understood what had been done to him. He had done all the bookkeeping; all the false entries in Ogburn & Whitacre's books were in his writing. Mae Landis had revealed his former criminal record, and had fastened the ownership of the gun—really Ogburn's—upon him. He was framed completely! He hadn't a chance of clearing himself.

He had known that his story would sound like a far-fetched and flimsy lie; he had a criminal record. For him to have surrendered and told the truth would have been merely to get himself laughed at.

As it turned out, Ogburn went to the gallows, Mae Landis is now serving a fifteen-year sentence, and Whitacre, in return for his testimony and restitution of the loot, was not prosecuted for his share in the land swindle.

NUNNALLY JOHNSON

. . . And then there are those who only occasionally made crime their business like Dashiell Hammett's old drinking buddy, NUNNALLY JOHNSON. Johnson is remembered today for writing, producing, and directing powerful westerns such as *The Gunfighter* (starring Gregory Peck), gripping tales of suspense like *The Dark Mirror* (starring Olivia de Havilland), social commentaries like *The Man in the Grey Flannel Suit* (Gregory Peck, Jennifer Jones, Lee J. Cobb, Frederic March), and lighthearted comedies like *Mr. Peabody and the Mermaid* (starring William Powell and Ann Blyth) and *How to Marry a Millionaire* (starring Marilyn Monroe and Betty Grable). In the mid-1920s, before Hollywood beckoned, Johnson was a fledgling newspaperman for the *Brooklyn Daily Journal* and a short story writer for *The Saturday Evening Post* and H. L. Mencken and George Jean Nathan's *The Smart Set*. That's when this never-before-collected, true crime story appeared. Written in the as-told-to format (the teller is one Maxwell Livingston), it purports to offer "the inside facts about jewel thefts in exclusive society." It has a quirky and amusing style all its own.

A Scream in the Dark

Nan shuddered. "I'm nervous," she explained, drawing her scarf tighter under her chin. I nodded sympathetically. The situation was disturbing.

"I feel as if something were going to happen again," she went on, then paused before adding: "And yet, I'm glad I came. It really is thrilling, don't you think, Max?"

My nod this time was not so sympathetic. I suspected that whatever thrill was on the way, would probably be a bit more extravagant than my taste liked.

"Just think"—eagerly—"there's a thief in our crowd, a real Raffles, working right at his trade! Twice now he's got away with stuff, valuable stuff, from under our very noses."

"You've been reading the papers too much," I objected. "It's nonsense to think that any of the people who came to the Brandons' a month ago, or those who came to the Merritts', would be capable of that. It was a chance, pure chance both times, that a robbery took place. A professional yegg did it, or two professional yeggs. Remember, there've been more than two house parties this year on Long Island."

"Perhaps"—unconvinced; "but I have a feeling you're wrong. That sheriff, Ruel, says—"

"Ruel is a fathead," I broke in, "a caricature of a sleuth. Who, pray, could it have been? Your own brother? Ted Harrison? Polly Gleason? Mrs. Fothergill? Harry Fothergill?"

"None of those, silly. But there has always been one or two others, people we didn't know very well."

"Who then?" I insisted. "Count them off. First there was Tim Crosby." I stopped to see what effect this name would have on her.

She leaped at the bait.

"You are silly!" she said, flaring up. "You've known Tim as long as you've known me."

"But," I reminded her, "Tim has been away—been away very very mysteriously. Even you hadn't seen him for two years until he walked into the Brandons'. What has he been doing? How is he making his living? He certainly doesn't toil, and yet he doesn't borrow. The Crosby fortune has evaporated. Where, please tell me, does the money come from?"

There was anger in her eyes as she returned snappily: "You should be ashamed of yourself, Max, claiming to be a friend of Tim's, and talking of him like that! I won't listen to it. Unless you stop I'll go in."

"Please understand," I insisted, "this is purely an academic discussion. I no more think Tim would steal from the Brandons or the Merritts than you do. I was simply going over the situation. And as for my having betrayed a friendship, you've, in exactly the same manner, betrayed all of your friendships here, by suspecting a thief among them."

"Oh, I didn't mean— Go ahead then." She cooled off. "This is all impersonal, of course."

"Of course," I agreed. "Next, then, we may mention two men, both complete strangers to all of us, and both introduced and sponsored by Tim."

Again she rose. "Why Tim all the time?" She demanded. "You are directly intimating something, Max, and it is not impersonal, either. You know very well that the first man—I forget his name—was an old army friend of Tim's; and the second man—"

"The second," I assisted her, "was an old college friend. Did you ever see anybody look less like a college man—old or young? Or act less like a college man?"

"It's outrageous!"

"Well"—I was willing to pass over the matter, for it really was chance that had led me to mention Tim again—"there was this Englishman, Darcy, who claims to be a journalist and novelist and what-not. And he"—the idea occurred to me suddenly—"has been present at the Brandons', at the Merritts', and is coming here to-night. Otherwise, he's been nowhere else so far as we know."

Nan was stumped. "I don't know," she said after a pause, very slowly. "Polly Gleason vouches for him. Polly surely wouldn't bring a crook in. And besides—"

"Yes, I know—and besides, he hasn't any of the earmarks of a crook, of the kind of crook you've read about," I finished the sentence for her. "He's charming, isn't he?"

"I think so."

The list, so far as I could remember, went no further. And it was Nan who broke the silence.

"Why," she demanded, "do you think Tim keeps bringing strangers in?"

"They are old army and college friends," I reminded her slyly. "Why? Does it worry you?"

Her only answer was to jump down from the balustrade where we had been sitting, and start toward the door.

"Let's go in," she said. "I think somebody's just arrived."

I took one more puff on my cigarette and, throwing it away, followed her in. Nan was almost at the reception-room door. She had stopped and was listening. Beyond the door the usual introductions for a newcomer, a stranger, were going on. A voice, Tim Crosby's:

"And I was sure you wouldn't mind, so I brought him along. Mrs. Gleason, Mr. Durling, another of my old army pals."

An odd light came into Nan's eyes, a queer, troubled light, as she turned to me.

"Another stranger is here!"

Then, laughing, as though at her own suspicion, she parted the curtains which separated us from the reception room. The next minute she was acknowledging an introduction to Mr. Durling.

As I say, I was nervous too. So much had been said in the newspapers about the two robberies, and so lurid and persuasive—to me—had been the intimations of a Raffles, that I half believed it to be true. Only, who among these people, among this coterie of ours, could it be?

I had catalogued the names as much for myself as for Nan. All of the others were friends for whose honesty I would have bonded my life. But of Tim Crosby I knew nothing beyond the fact that he was a companionable lad who had been God knows where for the two years since his father's death. He had inherited nothing, so people said, and yet—and this is the kind of thing that always puzzles me—he lived well, upheld his end financially in whatever the crowd did, and never worked. Men who can live without work invariably hold a fascination for me.

As for his apparently endless number of old college and army friends, I was willing to suspect any and all of them, particularly the latest, Mr. Durling. They all, the three, were of a stripe—gaudily dressed, inclined to be overly familiar on short acquaintance, and altogether too willing to be taken for granted.

I acknowledge, though, that in mentioning Leo Darcy as I had, I had done him an injustice. I had no reason on earth for suspecting him any ill intentions at all. He was Polly's own guest, and without doubt he had brought the best of references, even assuming that she had not known him abroad. Well bred, well read, well mannered, he had quite won the liking of all of us—except me.

But I don't count in such a respect. It was only that in him I seemed to see a little too much eagerness to be affable, to be accepted; indeed, just such another quality as I had found in Tim Crosby's friends, with more polish. But then, I'm a bit diffident socially, and so no fit judge of such things.

The subject of the thefts came up, of course, at dinner. It was Leo Darcy who started it.

"I know," he said in his pert little way, "that we've all been thinking at one time or another this evening about these little unpleasantnesses. It's quite a revelation to me, I assure you. Never before did I fancy that some evening I might be sitting in er—er—in terror, you might say, lest a robber spring in the window."

"Stuff!" Polly declared. "There's little here in this house to tempt a robber."

It was Durling who denied this. "Look at those pearls around your neck. Look at Mrs. Fothergill's wrist watch, worth every bit of five hundred dollars. Look at—"

By chance my eyes strayed to Tim Crosby. He was glaring at his old army pal. But Durling failed to notice.

"Yes," Nan chimed in, "and look at Polly's rings."

We looked, all of us, for some reason, though we knew them, had seen them a hundred times. Three platinum and diamond affairs that glistened wickedly as Polly held them up. She was proud of them, reveled in having them on her fingers. But fascinating as they were, they stirred some sense of danger in all of us, I believe.

Anyway, nobody spoke for a while. Again I glanced at Tim Crosby. His face was white as he busied himself with his food, and he kept his eyes on his plate. Durling, who sat at Polly's left, stared blandly at the stones, and Darcy smiled affably across the table at Nan, as though they shared a secret between them.

"When we dance," he presently said to her, "I'd like to have the first with you. May I?"

It was this ease, this ability to say things I couldn't in a way that I couldn't that set me a little against Darcy. I should have waited to ask that question until afterward, when so many attentions were not alert to be centered on anything that came to hand.

Nan nodded.

"I danced with Lady Diana once," he went on. "She is tall, you know, and I am not so tall. It must have been torture to her, and certainly I was most fearful that she would say: 'I can't go on with this; you are not tall enough for me.' But she is as tolerant as she is beautiful, and so we finished it."

A maid came in and stopped beside Polly.

"Excuse me," she nodded to Darcy, "but shall I serve coffee now?"

Polly nodded, and the maid withdrew. The girl returned in another minute, and presently, in spite of the suppressed tension, we all felt pleasantly stimulated.

Darcy took up his story where he left off, a rambling but lightly narrated account of another week-end, in England, when there came a second interruption. Tim Crosby had risen from the table.

"Excuse me," he said hurriedly, "but I think it's started to rain and my car's in the drive."

He went around the table toward the door. Polly called to him: "Go through the pantry, Tim. It's quicker."

"I was going to," he replied. He pushed the swinging door and disappeared. We heard him stumble.

Polly laughed. "Golf sticks," she explained.

The words were scarcely out of her mouth when, astonishingly, the lights went out. For a second we sat struck silent, startled, our nerves suddenly taut. I, for one, hadn't realized the tension. Then Polly giggled.

"He fell against the switch button," she said. "Will somebody—"

I pushed my chair back hastily. Another chair scraped on the floor. I put out my hands to grope my way.

"It's on the left side—"

The voice broke, raised into an ear-splitting scream, a scream of fright, of panic. A chair turned over. There were sudden noises, as somebody sprang up, and I heard Nan crying: "Polly! Polly! What is it, Polly?" I dashed through the dark for where I took the door to be, bumping against the table. Then I found it, flung it open, and collided with—Tim Crosby.

"What the devil!"

"Turn on those lights."

"What lights?"

I knocked him aside, slid my hand down the left wall, and found the button. I returned in time to hear Polly sob:

"My rings! My rings! Somebody snatched them!"

I looked around, dumbfounded. Nan was holding Polly in her arms, begging her to tell what had happened. Tim Crosby stood at my shoulder, apparently trying to make out the scene. Harry Fothergill and Fletcher Gleason stared at each other, dazed. Durling seemed to be trying to catch Tim's eye, and Darcy stood by Polly's chair.

"What do you mean?" he demanded. "Somebody snatched your rings off then?"

Polly bobbed her head against Nan's shoulder and held out her hand. The third finger was red and scratched—and bare.

"Good God!"

Fletcher Gleason shook himself, as if to see that he was wholly awake. "But there was nobody else—" He stopped.

"No," Durling continued for him, "nobody but us."

The silence that followed this must have lasted a year. Tim Crosby broke it.

"I don't know," he began. "That is, I didn't know—oh, I didn't know I'd turned off the lights."

The lights! Almost with one accord we faced him, and his face blanched. Somebody struck a match—Durling. He lighted his cigar slowly, deliberately. It must have been what came to our eyes, automatically, against our wills, that prompted him to shoot an answer at our unuttered thoughts.

"Suppose you search me, then!"

At that Gleason waved his hand. "This is nonsense!" he said. "Don't fly off the handle, Tim. Nobody has been accused." He paused. "It isn't the rings," he said, "but—is one of us a thief?"

"Well," spoke up Durling, "I suppose I'm the only stranger here. This may not be exactly the proper thing to do, but I'm willing that I should be searched from head to foot before I leave this room."

Again Gleason raised his hand, but this time he was unanimously voted down. Darcy assumed the spokesmanship for all of us. "Mr. Durling's suggestion is perfectly proper, it seems to me," he said. "I too am comparatively a stranger. But I think these other gentlemen will all join me in a belief that we all ought to be searched, and thoroughly, from top to bottom. We should find out here and now er—er—whatever is to be found out." He glanced around and we all nodded.

"This is terrible!" Gleason objected, obviously distressed. "And yet—"

"And yet," I interrupted, "one of us here is undoubtedly responsible."

Polly was sitting up straight again. Her eyes were red, and she was rubbing her finger. Nan and Mrs. Fothergill rose. "Perhaps," Nan said, "Polly could help us."

Polly shook her head. "I know nothing," she declared, "except that just as I started to speak, two hands grabbed mine, and before I could clinch my fist they had slipped the rings off. Strong hands."

"If I may offer a suggestion," I said, "suppose Tim—Tim was out of the room at the time—search every man here. I assume that—"

"Why the devil should I have to say it? Durling, though, helped me out."

"Of course," he finished the sentence, "the ladies are eliminated."

"Then," said Nan, rising briskly, "we might as well get out and let you get to it. Please, please, be quick."

They rose, led by Polly, and started to leave the room. Nan last. As she passed me she pulled me aside. "Max! Max!" she whispered. "Do something—anything!"

I shook my head. "Go outside," I said. "I'll let you know in a minute." She hurried after the others.

There were nine of us left when the door closed behind her. Gleason, Fothergill, Ted Harrison, Cully Mason, Nan's brother, Durling, Darcy, Tim Crosby, and myself. Gleason was impatient.

"Go to it, Tim," he said.

Tim glanced around uncertainly. I stepped forward. "Begin with me," I suggested. With a half-apology he began the ordeal—and I'll vouch for its thoroughness. My pockets, the lining of my coat and vest, the hollows of my bat tie, my waistband—he went through everything.

Next came Fothergill. And then Gleason. And then Darcy. The little Englishman chattered away, offering possible and impossible hiding places for inspection. Then Harrison, Cully, and finally Durling. Tim hastened, was stepping back from the man he'd brought to the house, when Darcy spoke.

"Just a minute, Mr. Crosby!" he said sharply. "Mr. Durling has not been searched as thoroughly as he might be. We're all, you know, to be treated with equal disrespect." This last was with a cold, humorless smile.

Durling growled something. "Don't slight me, Tim," he said then. "Look good."

Without comment Tim extended his search—his futile search. Completed, he made his report—the report that we already realized.

"They're not here."

Automatically I glanced about the room. It was comparatively bare, not a possible place where the rings could have been placed in the fraction of a second that followed the theft. The windows were down. The floor was hardwood—and glistened with a clear expanse.

Gleason sat down. "Will somebody call the girls?" he asked. I went into the next room. The occupants sprang to their feet. "Gleason will make the report," I said, and they filed past me.

We took our chairs. Darcy was speaking.

"It makes the situation beastly awkward," he said as I sat down. "One of us has got away with it, as you say here. One of us so far is an uncaught thief. We all suspect one another. I don't dare suggest that the police be called—"

"Not all," Gleason interrupted. "This is a private robbery." He smiled grimly.

"Personally," Darcy resumed, "I should object to being held. But I would understand your point of view. The point is, shall we all remain here? Wouldn't we be trying your nerves to remain any longer—what with so many other trinkets about, as Mr. Durling has pointed out"—he smiled the same cold, humorless smile at Tim's friend—"and the lights likely to go out again at any moment"—and this time the smile was for Tim.

"I told you," Tim sprang up, "that it was accidental. If you wish to question—"

"I meant nothing, Mr. Crosby," the Englishman explained placidly. "You are too impetuous."

Choking another angry word, Tim sat down again, his face as white as a sheet, for we could not help it; but the circumstances—the lights, Durling, Darcy's notice that the search had not been regular at first—compelled in our faces, no doubt, something akin to skepticism. And when I turned to Nan, she was in tears.

"Then," Darcy went on, "if there are no objections, and if Mr. and Mrs. Gleason will understand that we mean only to relieve them of an undesirable situation, I move that we make our adieus."

"There is an objection."

"From whom?" Darcy turned in surprise to face Tim Crosby.

"From me."

"Tim," spoke Durling, "Mr. Darcy's right. Let's go."

"I won't."

"You will."

Durling's voice held a command. His words were short, snapped out, and we looked at him in surprise. Tim met his gaze for a minute and then, after a pause, submitted.

"All right," he said.

Durling and I rose uncertainly. Gleason followed us. Darcy smiled around.

"I'm sure," he said, picking up his demitasse, "that we all regret to the very bottom of our hearts what has taken place here. It is the most unfortunate thing I've ever known."

He put the cup to his lips, and at that second Tim Crosby jumped to his feet.

"Grab him!" he cried.

Durling flung himself directly across the table, crashing the cups and glasses and dishes recklessly, while his hands shot out and seized Darcy's.

It was pandemonium. Tim was around the table in a flash. Nan screamed. I shouted something—I don't know what. All I could tell was that Durling was being dragged across the table, sweeping everything to the floor, that Tim was shouting unintelligibly, and that Darcy was fighting furiously, desperately, to break Durling's hold. And then Tim struck the Englishman.

His fist caught Darcy on the point of the jaw, a blow that might easily have broken it, and the fight ended there. Darcy dropped to the floor, unconscious. In a flash Tim was astride the prostrate form, had turned it face up, and was running a finger around inside Darcy's mouth. A smile came to his face. He withdrew the finger, held it up. There were Polly's three rings!

A half-hour later Darcy, sullen and silent, was sitting awkwardly in a stuffed chair, his hands bound behind him.

"Now," Nan spoke, "tell us."

Tim sat down. "Well," he began, "I want first to give you Mr. Durling's correct identity. He is from Scotland Yard, in this country on important business. And Mr. Darcy—he is wanted certainly for one theft and homicide case in London, and suspected of several others. He has a few aliases that I can't remember. I recognized him, I thought, when we met at the Brandons', from the pictures published in the London papers while I was over there last summer. After what happened I was pretty certain of it.

"I cabled to Scotland Yard. It happens that I am interested in such matters. I'll confess it—I am a detective. What my professional connections are doesn't matter. But before Durling came, there was the Merritts' party, so I brought along another detective—my old 'college chum.'"

"And the first man—at the Brandons'—who was he?"

"What he said he was—what I said he was—really and truly an old army pal. But the detective flunked me. We got nowhere, could do nothing. The Merritts' coup—planned—turned out a failure. Then Durling came.

"Briefly, Durling recognized Darcy at once. We had planned to get him outside after dinner, make the arrest with as little fuss as possible and let the party go on. Then came that clumsy accident when I turned off the lights, which really was an accident. Evidently Darcy was waiting to take advantage of the first opportunity that came up. And then we couldn't arrest him until we found out what had become of the rings.

"The search failing, we were up a tree until at last, when Durling had a hunch that something might turn up as Darcy prepared to go. Darcy started to drink his demitasse—and it was cold as ice! It flashed on me what he had done—he had dropped the rings in his black coffee. And to put me in a more humane light, I hit him on the jaw to prevent his swallowing Polly's rings. Does that answer all the questions?"

We nodded, speechless.

"And now," Tim said, "I have a question—for Nan." He turned to her. "You thought I had taken them, didn't you?"

She turned red. "Yes," she replied truthfully, "only—only, I didn't care if you had."

DAY KEENE

With only so many plots to go around, the difference between a top-notch crime writer and a pedestrian crime writer is often subtle. What distinguishes DAY KEENE's sauciest novels is his sense of humor—ruthlessly dark and foreboding—his sentences—crisp and abstemious—and his eccentric and often harrowing story lines. Keene published more than 50 novels from the late 1940s through the mid-1960s. Since all of them currently await reissue in this country, may I suggest three to any publishers who may be reading? There's *Dead Dolls Don't Talk* (Crest, 1959) with its outrageous cover blurb, "He figured her for just another one-night stand... until he found her still there in the morning—murdered." There's *Too Hot to Hold* (1959 Gold Medal). This time the cover copy cried out, "She was a female Judas leading men to torture... and death." But Keene's foremost treasure is *Sleep with the Devil* (Lion Books, 1954), featuring Les Ferron. An enforcer for a loan shark who moonlights as a model for a true crime magazine, Ferron tries to make a new start in life, in upstate New York and $150,000 the richer. But when he meets comely and virginal Amy Stanton, he discovers country life isn't what he bargained for. One suspects much of Keene's knowledge about true crime magazines came from writing for pulps like Lionel White's *Underworld Detective*. *Underworld* published this grim tale about a killer criminology student, under Keene's William Richards pen name in 1951.

Strangled

It was a glum day in the Federal Housing Administration offices in Fresno, California.

For though the sun shone outside and flowers bloomed and the glad sounds of spring were all about, on this Monday, April 2nd of 1951, something was amiss.

What was amiss was that Benny was not at work and there'd been no explanation of her absence. Benny was Hazel Benson Werner, 30-year-old former WAC, whose ebullient personality and irrepressible vitality had kept the office morale on an upward arc for three years.

Married to a GI student at Fresno State College, a handsome girl, tall and lush bodied, with an unfailing smile and a gay retort for all sallies, Benny was the bellwether of the office. As Benny went, so went the work, and since Benny always went the sunny route, good will and ambition prevailed in her orbit.

First Emily Bonne, who worked at the desk next to Benny and was one of her closest friends, telephoned her apartment and got no answer. Then Irene Elliott tried and finally Evelyn Hersey, and still no reply to the call. It wasn't like Benny to go away without letting her office and her friends know of her plans.

Someone thought of calling the college. Someone called and learned that Edgar A. Werner, Benny's 31-year-old husband, had not attended his classes during the day. This offered a possible solution: the two had decided on a sudden holiday and had driven somewhere for just a brief rest. The girl friends, however, were not satisfied. It simply wasn't like Benny to leave her office in the lurch.

Work done for the day, Emily, Irene and Evelyn went to Benny's apartment on College Avenue. They found a note tacked to the door. It said, "Darlings, whoever you are, I've gone to visit Lee and Lorna. Won't be at the office, so don't bother them there."

The girls knew Lorna and Lee to be friends Benny had met through the WAC's. Benny had not mentioned visiting them, or expecting to see them, but the note was calm and normal enough and the girls were satisfied... for the moment.

Even the fact that the signature had been typewritten, as was the remainder of the note, didn't upset them.

It also was quite likely that Benny and Ted, her husband, had gone to visit Lorna and Lee together. It wasn't unlikely that they should drive to Auburn, near Sacramento, for the visit and certainly they wouldn't be expected to make the two hundred mile trip and return in a day.

In the office the following day, Benny's friends explained her absence and all was well... that is, temporarily. A few minutes after eleven o'clock,

C. S. Wooton, Mrs. Werner's direct chief, appeared at Emily Boone's desk to show her a telegram. It had come from Los Angeles and it said:

"Dear Chief. Sorry to let you down on job. Must settle problems for Ted. Plan to be back next Monday."

The telegram was signed "Hazel Werner."

"But that can't be," Miss Boone protested. "The note on her door said she was going to Auburn and that's 600 miles from Los Angeles."

"Well, the telegram's from Los Angeles," Wooten said. "Maybe she didn't want to tell you everything."

"But," interposed Irene Elliott, "I just remembered something. Benny doesn't have a typewriter in her apartment. That note was written somewhere else."

"That's right, she doesn't," Miss Boone said. "It is strange, isn't it?"

The two girls looked at each other. It was Emily Boone who said slowly, "I've got a terrible premonition. This whole thing just isn't like Benny. She simply wouldn't tell some people one thing and someone else another. I'm going over to her apartment as soon as I get off here."

The day wore slowly on. Promptly at five o'clock, the Misses Boone, Elliott and Hersey hurried from the office and drove to Benny's College Avenue apartment. They tried the door and got no answer. They tried the windows, found them locked, with the shades tightly drawn . . . also unlike Benny.

They drove to the telephone office and put a call in to Auburn for Lorna. When she answered, they asked about Benny. Lorna seemed surprised. She hadn't heard from Benny for more than two weeks. No of course she hadn't been to Auburn, she knew nothing about the note saying Benny would visit her.

The three ordinarily circumspect girls with no more than the normal young woman's interest in mysteries and crime suddenly became Pinkertons in petticoats. They sped off to the Western Union office, persuaded the manager there to contact Los Angeles and learn, if he could, whether the wire sent to Wooton on that morning had been filed by a man or woman.

The reply came back in an hour. The wire had been sent by a man, but the clerk remembered little of his appearance. Could the original message be sent, air mail, special delivery, to the Fresno office of the Western Union? No reason why it couldn't be, said the manager, and the girls asked that it be done.

Fast as air mail might be, it would not arrive in Fresno until the following morning, so the three left the telegraph office and returned to the building in which Benny had her apartment.

En route, they began to ponder the state of Benny's affairs. The notation in the telegram about settling problems for her husband seemed ambiguous. The girls knew that the pair, once so happy and seemingly ideally mated, had not been seeing eye-to-eye in all things recently. In fact, Ted had taken a room of his own, near the college, so that he could have quiet for his studies. He was making a desperate effort to finish his schooling and land his degree within the year and, since Benny often had friends in, he had sought solitude.

They were together much of the time, nonetheless. He took most of his meals with her and their weekends they spent together. But what affairs Ted could have, especially in Los Angeles, that would require help from Benny, puzzled the three friends. They pondered it apprehensively as they drove back to the apartment house and rang the bell at the landlady's flat.

The landlady responded. The girls asked her if she'd had any word from Mrs. Werner. The landlady hadn't, had not seen Benny leave the flat. Miss Boone then suggested that she open the door to Benny's flat. The landlady demurred, but when the girls told her they had reason to believe Benny might be ill in her quarters, she finally opened the door.

Emily Boone was the first to step inside. She found a scene of violent confusion. Rugs had been kicked out of place, a chair was overturned, a drape had been pulled down from one of the windows. The bedclothes were disheveled and a pillow lay on the floor.

Beyond the bed, huddled in a pool of blood, her head a mass of gashes and contusions, lay the body of Benny Werner. Loose now about her neck, but showing signs of having been closely knotted there was a brown shoe lace and near her, the handle broken away from the bloodsmeared head was a carpenter's type of claw hammer.

A few minutes after the landlady had called Fresno headquarters, Lieutenant S. G. Vind and Chief of Detectives Dan Lung arrived.

They found the room covered with the unmistakable dark brown spots left by drying blood. The dead girl's skull had been fractured in at least four places. Yet her staring eyes and the purplish gray pallor of her face indicated, to the trained officers, that the blows, obviously from the broken hammer, had not been the real cause of death. Instead, they concluded, she had been strangled to death, presumably by the shoe lace.

Immediately Lung inquired about Benny's marital status. He learned that, although she had been temporarily estranged from her strapping, six foot, two hundred pound student husband, they had been reconciled only recently and appeared to be on the best of terms. At Fresno State College, he discovered that Werner had made plans to be away from school for at least two, possibly three weeks, hence his absence had aroused little interest.

Learning that he still lived, part of the time, at the quarters he had taken when he and Benny had separated, they went there. There was no sign of him. Two of his bags were missing and some of his clothing. So, too, was his small automobile, purchased on a GI loan plan. His landlady said that he had told her he expected to be away for two weeks, explaining that he had been ill and needed a rest from his studies.

They found a series of fingerprints, including Benny Werner's and those of two other persons, obviously, from the broad impressions, male. All three series seemed to be of approximately equal age, as if three persons had been in the apartment within the last forty-eight hours, two of them male.

The officers took the fingerprints to headquarters for study and classification. A few hours later a check with the records of GI students at Fresno state college revealed that one of the two male series belonged to Ted Werner. The other, however, remained unexplained.

The identification of Werner's fingerprints occasioned no unusual interest. There was no reason why Werner should not have been in the house. In fact, it was appropriate that he should have been. Not only had he told his school of planning a vacation, but his wife had indicated that she expected to be away. What more likely than that he had gone to her apartment to pick her up in his car as they started their vacation?

By this line of reasoning, suspicion led naturally to the owner of the third set of fingerprints. Who was he and what had he been doing in the apartment? Prints had been found on an ash tray, on a chair arm, on a tumbler out of which he apparently sipped beer, the doors leading to the bathroom, the bedroom and the kitchen, in addition to the prints on the entrance door. He had gotten around, but there was an even more significant showing of his fingerprints.

They were on the broken handle of the claw hammer with which the victim had been beaten.

Couldn't it mean that an intruder had entered the Werner home, strangled and bludgeoned Benny Werner and been interrupted at this grisly task by the arrival of Werner?

Couldn't it have meant that the thug and Werner had struggled for the hammer—hence the discovery of fingerprints of both on the broken handle—broken the weapon in their struggle and resorted to some other tactics, such as a gun drawn by the intruder to intimidate and even kidnap Werner? Not only was it possible, it was highly probable. It would have been difficult for the intruder to beat Werner into unconsciousness, or even kill him, and then drag his body from the house, dump it into a car and escape without attracting some notice.

On the other hand, two men walking out of an apartment, even though they walked close together, would not be too noticeable. The bandit might very easily have forced Werner into his car, ordered him to drive and made his escape, leaving the murdered Benny Werner lying in her life blood.

What motive could the thug have had for kidnapping Werner? He'd already committed one murder; certainly he could not suffer more, if caught, for the commission of a second.

But what reason could he possibly have for kidnapping Werner, who had no money? Could they have wanted his car, and his ability to drive it? Could it have been that the killer did not drive and that, in this emergency, he saw a chance to make a well covered get-away by forcing Werner to drive him beyond the city, possibly northward toward San Francisco and Oakland, where he could dispose of Ted at his leisure?

Certainly this sounded the most logical of all the possibilities, but what of the note left on the door? Did the bandit write it before arriving... there was no typewriter in the apartment... and if so, how did he know Lee and Lorna? Or had Benny had Werner write it on his typewriter. Bring it to the apartment, tack it to the door and leave it before he entered the house? If this were so, there was every reason why it should have been left, as it was, by the bandit. It would provide an extra time killer for him, giving him further opportunity to put distance between himself and the scene of his heinous deed.

But how about the telegram from Los Angeles? That had been sent by someone who knew the Werners. And it had been sent by the killer to further obfuscate the Werner friends and keep them away from the charnel house as long as possible. It indicated, unquestionably, that the slayer had picked the Los Angeles area for a hideaway instead of the San Francisco Bay district. Furthermore, it also showed that the slayer, if he had sent it and had been the one who left the strange fingerprints, had known a very great deal about the Werners, consequently must have been a reasonably close friend.

Detective Sergeant L.M. Morris of the Fresno police and Assistant District Attorney Richard Shepard now took over the case. One of their first moves was to forward the unidentified fingerprints to the FBI in Washington.

Before nightfall of the following day, Shepard and Morris had their identification of the mysterious fingerprints. They corresponded to those of a sailor named Roland Berger stationed at the Port of Los Angeles in Wilmington. Immediately Shepard asked for a check on Berger, and received the information that he was on his ship. He had, however, the report said, spent the preceding week-end visiting relatives in Fresno.

Shepard and Morris started at once for Los Angeles. Before leaving, they asked Western Union to hold the copy of the Wooton telegram— already requested by the girls, but not yet received—in the southern city. They could check it there against a specimen of the writing of both Benny and Ted Werner taken from the dead girl.

Arriving in Los Angeles, the two went first to the Western Union office from which the telegram had been dispatched. The manager nervously handed it to them. It had been written on a sheet of plain, white paper . . . and with a typewriter.

"Keep it," Morris advised as Shepard disappointedly moved to throw it away. "Maybe we can check it against a typewriter somewhere."

They went to Berger's ship. His commanding officer summoned the sailor. He came into the presence of Shepard and Morris, almost eagerly, it seemed. He was a pleasant faced, blond youth, somewhere in his early twenties, but his young face was drawn and lined and there was a certain shocked terror in his blue eyes. Introduced to his visitors, he spoke before either could fire any questions.

"What happened to her?" he said. "What happened to my aunt?"

"Your aunt?" It would have been impossible to determine whether Shepard or Morris spoke first, so spontaneous was their reaction. Finally Shepard said, incredulously, "What do you mean, your aunt?"

"My Aunt Hazel...Mrs. Werner," the youth said. "The papers say she's dead."

"She's your aunt?" Shepard repeated dazedly.

"She's my aunt...yes, she was my aunt," Berger said, doggedly, "and I want to know who killed her."

"Seaman Berger visited with his aunt last week-end," the commanding officer said. "He came to me as soon as he read of her death in the papers and told me the story."

Shepard and Morris obviously were stunned. They looked at each other, then at Berger. Finally Morris withdrew the broken hammer from a package he had carried to the interview.

"Did you ever see this before?" he demanded. Berger studied the bloody fragments, then nodded slowly.

"She had a hammer like that in her apartment," he said. "I used it just before I came away to fix some shelves."

He stopped and looked anxiously at his commanding officer for reassurance.

Morris said, quickly: "Go on. You haven't told us the whole story about this hammer."

Berger stood silent for a long time. There was terror in his eyes, a terror heightened to near panic by his indecision. His commanding officer said:

"I'd advise you to tell everything you know, Berger," he said. "I have every confidence in your innocence, and I'm sure these men want only the truth, that they don't want to persecute anybody."

Berger gulped. Then he turned to Shepard and Morris. "I spent the week-end with my aunt...that is, Mrs. Werner," he began. "I stayed with Ted, her husband, over Saturday night and we went back to her apartment on Sunday. They got into a quarrel and once I took the hammer from Ted and hid it, or thought I did. The quarrel passed once, but they started fighting again later.

"I went out for a while and when I came back, Ted was threatening her and had hit her once or twice when she refused to allow him to move back into the apartment.

"It got so bad that my entire week-end was being loused up, so I decided to pull out for good. I went back to Ted's place, got my luggage and came back here. As soon as the papers reached camp telling about my aunt's body being found, I came to my commanding officer to ask for another leave to go to Fresno . . . that was only a couple of hours ago."

Once more the C.O. bore out Berger's story. There was nothing for Shepard and Morris to do but accept his story, especially when the commanding officer guaranteed that he would be available at all times if wanted. They returned to Los Angeles and located the clerk who'd taken the Wooton message on Monday morning. She recalled, dimly, the man who had sent it.

"He was a big guy," she said, "and sorta good looking in a long-hair kind of way. He wore big horn rim glasses. He acted pretty nervous and looked like he hadn't had much sleep. I'd say he was an inch or two over six feet and weighed two hundred pounds or more."

Back in Fresno the officers returned to Werner's apartment. They seized his typewriter and turned it over to the police laboratory for the purpose of comparing its type with the telegram. When the results appeared identical, the officers were ready for a thorough casing of the Werner rooms.

With three uniformed officers, Shepard and Morris returned to Werner's rooms. It was apparent that he had taken some clothing with him in a suit roll and a hand grip. But there was considerable clothing left in the apartment, along with two items which aroused more than passing interest: a shirt and a pair of slacks, obviously belonging to Werner, dug from the bottom of the clothes hamper in a closet, both bearing unmistakable blood spots.

Came now another report from the police laboratory. The note found on Benny's door ostensibly had been written on Werner's typewriter. The conclusion was that he had prepared it before going to his wife's apartment for the last time, an obvious indication of premeditation. When Werner's fingerprints were taken from the door upon which the note had been tacked, the authorities were then entirely certain that they had now identified their quarry.

Shepard now asked for a murder indictment against Werner. When it had been granted, he sent out an all-points bulletin, with a description of Werner and the car he was driving, asking for his arrest. Then, with Morris, he began checking Werner's movements and his past.

All trace of the hunted man ended in Los Angeles. That he had gone directly there, was admitted. There were vague clues placing him at the Mexican border, at Tijuana, but no reason to believe that he had remained in Mexico. Shepard now checked his background at Fresno State College.

The records showed that he had spent a year at Oklahoma A. and M. at Stillwater, Oklahoma. From there he had gone into the service. He had been born near Kinderhook, up the Hudson River from New York City, a small town chiefly distinguished as the birthplace of President Martin Van Buren.

When a search of Stillwater and surrounding country failed to reveal any trace of the fugitive, the FBI was brought into the case by means of a fugitive warrant. The federal agency at once instituted a search of New York City, at the same time setting up a check on Kinderhook, where Werner still had relatives. The mails to and from Kinderhook were placed under particular observation. So, too, were the telephone lines and the telegraph wires.

Meantime, Morris developed a new angle. At Fresno State, Werner ostensibly had prepared himself for a life of dubious emergencies by specializing in Criminology and the Psychology of Crime. In his examination of Werner's school records, Morris came upon a thesis in which the fugitive had written that the homing pigeon instinct in first-time criminals, while almost unconquerable, was not completely uncircumventible. It was natural for a man in trouble, he wrote, to want to be in friendly, or at least, familiar environs, but he could achieve this, not by such hazardous maneuvering as returning to his regional beginnings, but to a similar environment reasonably near (or as near as would be prudent) to his home.

When Morris communicated this information to the FBI, Federal Agent Edward Scheidt in New York set up a check of the Hudson River littoral, but carefully avoided Kinderhook. Newburg, Peekskill, Poughkeepsie, Hudson, Kingston, et al, fell under his scrutiny.

Then, one day, his peregrinations took him to Garrison, the little town that clings to the east bluff of the broad river just across from West Point. Here was a town somewhat smaller than Kinderhook, but in much the same pattern and atmosphere. Here was a hideout where communications were readily accessible, but in which strangers attracted little notice,

since it was the United States Military Academy on the other side of the
stream.

With one agent working beside him, Scheidt began to comb the little
river community. At the end of 36 hours the two had checked every male
resident of the town between the ages of 28 and 35, and were ready to
strike.

Together, they waited at a restaurant a few yards off the main street.
Dinner time came and the usual flow of men in working clothes arrived for
their evening meal. One or two women ate alone, a family appeared, more
men in working clothes, and finally a tall, burly man, his myopic eyes
blinking, edged up to the lunch counter and Scheidt gave the signal.

With his partner, he waited for the man to finish his dinner. As he quit
the counter, the two preceded him to the door and waited just outside on
the sidewalk. The big man stepped through the door and Scheidt and his
aide fell in on either side.

"Take it easy, Werner," Scheidt said evenly. "We're FBI. We want you
for the murder of your wife."

For the moment it seemed that Werner would sink to the sidewalk in
complete collapse. Scheidt and his partner supported him by the arms.

"Let's walk on over to your lodgings," Scheidt said. "Act like nothing
unusual was happening and we'll all do better."

Werner obeyed. The three reached the fugitive's cheap rooming house.
Werner volunteered the information that he had been living in similar
places since leaving California. Asked why, he replied that he felt it was
better to escape detection.

"I heard that Benny was dead," he said, "and since I'd fought with her,
I knew they'd be after me and that I'd never be able to prove I didn't do
it. That's why I hid out."

"But you did do it, Ted," Scheidt said. "They've got all the proof they'll
ever need out there in California."

"No," Werner said, quietly, "I didn't do it. I loved her too much to
harm her."

"But you slugged her a couple of times," Scheidt said. "I wouldn't call
that love."

"Maybe not, but I didn't kill her," Werner insisted.

"Who did, then?"

"I don't know. There was a fella visiting her . . . her cousin, she said.
Why don't you ask him?"

"They did," Scheidt said. "He knew plenty."

Werner steadfastly refused to admit the slaying. He also refused to return to California without due process of law. Back in New York, working with Fresno authorities, they took up the task of obtaining extradition papers.

The Fresno authorities were in no mood to temporize. Even as Werner fought extradition, Shepard and Morris were building their case against him, convinced that no conceivable alibi available to Werner could save him.

ELEAZAR LIPSKY

ELEAZAR LIPSKY was the assistant district attorney of New York County, and for a time his star shone brightly, in the literary world and in Hollywood. His first novel, *The Kiss of Death* (later published as *The Hoodlum*) attracted the attention of all the major Hollywood studios. Director Henry Hathaway brought it to the screen. A smash hit starring Victor Mature as a noble stool pigeon who smashes the racket led by crazed gunman Richard Widmark, it is generally thought to be a masterpiece of late-1940s realism. On the heels of its success, Lipsky quickly published two uneven novels, *Murder One* and *The People Against O'Hara*. After that, he turned to true crime. This story about a perfectly normal, harmless man who faced death for a crime he didn't commit appeared in the premier issue of *Detective: The Magazine of True Crime Stories*. Founded in 1951, publisher Lawrence Spivak declared his magazine would be "characterized by accuracy, restraint and an intelligent literate approach," one that would "leave the gory photographs, the lurid illustrations and the sensational exaggerations to others." Readers accustomed to getting their murder straight up and bloody responded indifferently to this classy publication. It folded less than two years later.

Shield of the Innocent

There is a popular idea, spread by the movies and the radio, that district attorneys and detectives spend the best years of their lives pinning murders on innocent suspects who happen to fall into their hands. Well, maybe.

But in my own practical experience, I have seen it work more often the other way. Police sometimes are wrong. All men can be wrong. But if we were to insist on perfection, we could have no police force and no workable system of justice.

Some years ago, the Homicide Bureau of the Office of the District Attorney of New York County "caught" a case. It was a hot Saturday morning in late June. The young assistant district attorney on duty received a call from Detective Joseph Hennessy of the Homicide Squad who put the matter to him. The conversation ran along in this order:

"What have you got, Joe?"

"A cutting in the Seventh. They've got a prisoner there."

"What's it about?"

"It seems that this guy cut a man's throat early this morning. The man's at the hospital and it looks as though he's going. They don't give him much time."

"What's there for me?"

"Well, this prisoner is making a statement—"

"Do you mean a confession?"

"No— He claims they've got him wrong. But there's no doubt about it. They've got a pack of witnesses. They all saw him do the cutting."

"What was it for?"

"Just one of those things."

The prosecutor said, "I'll call the stenographer. Can you pick me up?"

"In twenty minutes. I've got the squad car."

A short time later the homicide detective and the young prosecutor were at a precinct station in the lower East Side where Detective Morris Schreiber of the Seventh Squad Detectives was "carrying the case."

Despite the green shades pulled down against the blazing sun, the squad room on the second floor was hot. Detectives were working in shirtsleeves, and a sweating group of eyewitnesses sat about in sleepy boredom. Schreiber took the prosecutor and the homocide detective aside and pointed to the prisoner—a trembling white-faced boy of nineteen whose torn shirt was smeared with blood. His face was bruised and cut. Schreiber summed up:

"These witnesses saw the whole thing. They tell us this cutting took place at two A.M. outside of a saloon and this boy, Kennedy"—he pointed to the trembling youth—"did the job. Three of these witnesses"—he pointed to a woman and two men, all Negroes—"saw Kennedy walk down the street with two other men. The woman says she kept her eye on

Kennedy. Now the old man who was stabbed was sleeping on the stoop of the house where he lives which is about fifty feet from the saloon. It was hot and that's why he was sleeping outdoors. Kennedy and his friends went past the old man and walked west to the corner. Then Kennedy turned back. He walked up to the old man and cut his throat, just like that. The woman screamed and a whole mob started after Kennedy. They caught him and gave him one hell of a beating. An officer came along and saved his life."

"What started it all?" the prosecutor asked.

Schreiber shrugged. "It was about nothing. The old man was asleep. No words passed between them. Kennedy just came up and cut his throat."

The prosecutor considered this information and asked, "Where's the arresting officer?"

Schreiber stuck his head into the corridor and called, "Fitz!" A stocky officer in a trim blue uniform entered the room. The prosecutor asked:

"Do you have any information on this, officer?"

The other shook his head. "I was on patrol in the car. I saw a mob chasing somebody in a white shirt. When I caught up, they were fit to kill him. I had to take out my gun before they would let up."

"He's pretty bruised up," the prosecutor observed.

"Don't look at me," the officer said. "That's the way I found him."

"It doesn't look good when a man comes in with injuries," the prosecutor said earnestly. "It takes the edge off a confession."

"You won't get a confession," the officer predicted. "He's been yelling not guilty since I dragged him in."

"We'll see." The prosecutor dismissed the officer and turned back to Schreiber. "What does Kennedy say?"

"He doesn't say anything," Schreiber answered. "He claims he was walking along the opposite side of the street with two friends. He was on the south side walking west. He says they were standing at the corner when suddenly they saw a mob running at them and he beat it because he was afraid. He didn't know what they were after. He just ran. So did his friends, Butch and Louie."

"Butch and Louie? Who are they?"

Schreiber grimaced expressively. "He doesn't know their last names or where they live. He doesn't know how to reach them. He says they were just out walking and talking when this happened. Butch and Louie sound phony."

The case so far was typical of many assaults on the streets of New York. A man without motive, goaded by an impulse known only to himself, savagely attacked a harmless bystander. When caught he offered a weak alibi. The problem seemed to require only the examination of the eye witnesses to verify identification.

Hennessy, who was a philosopher, wondered out loud, "Now why would Kennedy do a thing like that?"

"Drunk, doped, or just plain nuts." Schreiber was not concerned with the impulse behind the crime—police are not required to show motive.

"It's funny," the prosecutor said doubtfully. "Let's talk to the witnesses."

Schreiber motioned to a woman who had been dozing behind a typewriter desk. She came forward and the detective said, "This is Mary Jones. Mary, this is the district attorney. He's your friend. You can tell him the truth."

"I'm telling the truth," she said simply.

The prosecutor offered the witness a cigarette and motioned her to the inner office. When they were seated, he asked quietly:

"Did you see what happened this morning?"

"I saw it with my own eyes," she said emphatically. "He cut old Caspar's throat. I saw it."

The prosecutor lit her cigarette. "You want to help us catch the man who did this thing to old Caspar, don't you?"

"Mister, you got him." She puffed the cigarette.

"Is there any chance you might be mistaken?"

"Not a chance."

The prosecutor thought Mary Jones sensible enough. She worked as a buttonhole maker in the garment district. She had a daughter at home and had been waiting near the tavern for her husband who was due from his job as an elevator operator. These were some of the things she told him before he asked her what had happened. She said:

"I was standing on the corner under the lamp post. I wasn't talking to anyone. I was just waiting for my husband. We were going to have a beer together and go home. There were two men standing around. I know them as Fred and Terry. After a while three men, I mean Kennedy and his two friends, passed in front of me. They walked along the street on the same side as me away from the East River. Then they crossed to the downtown side of the street. I saw them pass old Caspar the first time. There were no words between them. Nothing happened to draw my attention. I had nothing to do so I watched them. When they got to the corner, they stood around talking. Then Kennedy came back alone. He walked up to old Caspar and made a pass at his throat. I didn't know what he was doing. Then he walked away slowly. Old Caspar got up and put his hand to his neck. I was wondering what it was all about. Then Caspar looked at his hand and started to walk toward where I was standing. I saw blood coming down his shirt and I saw this cut along his neck. I pointed to Kennedy and I screamed, 'He cut old Caspar's throat. The one in the white shirt. Get him!' Then Fred and Terry started after him. I kept screaming and pretty soon, maybe five seconds or so, a whole crowd came running. They caught this Kennedy. I pointed him out right away to the cops and then to the detectives."

The prosecutor resumed. "Between the time you saw old Caspar's throat cut by someone and the time you screamed, did you take your eyes off the man who did the cutting even for an instant?"

"I did not," she said firmly.

"You keep using Kennedy's name," the prosecutor said. "Did you even know him before this? Do you have anything against him?"

"I learned his name here in the station house. I never saw the man before." She left the room.

Fred and Terry, young powerful men employed in the subways, agreed with Mary Jones's statement. They had been standing near her engrossed in conversation, but they recalled three men passing a few minutes before the woman screamed. When they looked up, they saw the street was empty except for the dazed victim and "the man in the white shirt" whom they identified as Kennedy.

"When I saw him," Fred said, "he was only a short distance from old Caspar. No one else was on the street. Couldn't be anybody else did it but this man. I lit out after him. He turned two or three corners, but I ran wide and I never lost sight of him. I collared him and then the rest came and started to beat him up."

"You didn't see him do the cutting?"

"No, but it just had to be him. Nobody else was in sight."

The prosecutor asked each in turn:

"When you turned around, was this the man in the white shirt near Caspar or near the far corner?"

They were sure he was near Caspar.

"How many drinks did you have in you?"

"We weren't drunk," Fred said sturdily. "I had maybe two shots but I knew what I was doing. I couldn't be wrong. Not this wrong."

And there it stood. Three eyewitnesses, an immediate hue and cry, the chase, and capture. It was a simple case.

Yet Schreiber seemed unhappy. "You better talk to the boy."

Hennessy, of Homicide, a red-haired intellectual with the manner of an instructor in philosophy at a military academy, put the questions.

"I don't know what this is about," Kennedy protested. "I was just walking around after supper with these fellows, Butch and Louie. We had a beer apiece at about ten o'clock on Canal Street. We walked along the river front for a while and then turned into this street. I was never on the side where the old man got knifed. We walked on the opposite side to the corner and were standing there when we heard a mob yelling and running at us. We all ran away together. I didn't run because I stabbed anybody. I ran because I was afraid. This is a mixed neighborhood. I saw they weren't white. I thought it might be a riot. I don't know where Butch and Louie live. I don't know their last names. They're fellows I met around the neighborhood."

"This is a serious business," Hennessy said. "You'd better know where to get Butch and Louie."

The prosecutor asked, "Do you claim the police beat you?"

"No, they saved my life. But they act like I did it. I had nothing to do with this at all. Why should I hurt him? I don't even know who he is."

"Did you see anybody else on the street at the time who could have cut him?" Hennessy demanded.

Kennedy was trembling. "No, I didn't."

"Somebody did it and they all say it was you." Hennessy waited a moment. "You could make it easier for yourself by telling the truth."

"I've told you the truth." Kennedy conceded a minor record of delinquency, neither good nor bad. He had a spotty employment record. He lived with his family. "What reason would I have? Answer me that," he asked.

"Whoever did it had no reason," Hennessy said, "and it might as well be you."

Kennedy was taken outside and the investigators sat around in the inner room, drinking soda pop, and standing in the breeze of the fan. "What do you all think?" the prosecutor asked.

Schreiber finished his bottle. "Let's try the old man. He ought to be coming around now."

Kennedy was taken to the hospital where old Caspar lay in the emergency ward with a wad of bloody cotton at his throat. The prosecutor put questions but the old man could not talk because of the blood welling up in his mouth. Schreiber and Hennessy brought in Kennedy and the prosecutor asked, "Is this the man who cut you?"

For a moment the old man could not move. Then with an effort he raised himself and pointed at Kennedy and nodded. He sank back weakly and closed his eyes.

"Now what does that mean?" Schreiber asked heavily.

"It means we charge this Kennedy with assault," the prosecutor said. "If the old man dies, we'll arraign him again for homicide."

"I didn't do it," Kennedy protested.

The officials stood on the hot street in front of the hospital and summed up. Three eyewitnesses questioned separately had given a story which made the prisoner's guilt appear unmistakable. The victim had pointed him out. His "alibi" of Butch and Louie appeared to be fictitious.

"Still, I don't like it," Schreiber grumbled. "This is a vicious crime. I don't for the life of me see how this kid could do it. He's a weakling."

The prosecutor also had his doubts. "I don't like it for another reason. If he was the kind who could commit this assault, why doesn't he invent a story? He's too passive."

"Well, you're right," said philosopher Hennessy, "but what can you do against three eyewitnesses?"

"We can get a plate of borscht—that's what we can do," Schreiber said, and they adjourned to a dairy restaurant on nearby Delancey Street.

That afternoon the old man died, and automatically the charge against Kennedy became homicide.

There seemed no chance of mistaken identity. The harmless life of the victim ruled out a planned killing. It was a neighborhood affair, a cutting done on impulse. Little further police work was indicated. Ordinarily, with that kind of evidence, a prisoner immediately would be indicted, tried, and convicted for murder. Kennedy had neither the brains, the resourcefulness, nor the money to fight his way out of the trap.

However, neither the police nor the prosecutor were satisfied. They continued to worry and work. Schreiber continued to dig around the neighborhood. On Monday, Margaret Kennedy, the prisoner's sister, applied at the district attorney's office for a pass to see her brother in City Prison.

The prosecutor made it a rule to interview members of the family and he invited her to his office. The young woman was good-looking with an intelligent air, but with a definitely hostile manner. She worked in a millinery shop on Second Avenue as a sales assistant. "My brother's innocent," she said bitterly.

"How do you know?" the prosecutor asked. "We always hear that."

"I know," she said flatly.

The prosecutor looked at her curiously. It was natural for a sister to protest her brother's innocence. But something in her manner pointed to definite knowledge of some sort. Her chin was up and her mouth was clamped tight. He asked mildly, "Is there anything you want to tell me?"

"Is there any reason I should?"

He was not annoyed at her hostility. She was right to view him with suspicion. From her viewpoint he meant her brother no good. "Do you think I'd take advantage of any information you might give me?"

Her shrug was answer enough.

"Do the police know your brother?"

"Not especially."

"Did I ever meet your brother before Saturday?"

"No," she admitted.

"Then what makes you think he means anything to me?" he demanded.

"I've got nothing to tell you," she said firmly.

"I think you do," he said sharply. "You've got something on your mind. Why not spill it?"

"How do I know how you'll use it?"

He laughed. "Your brother means nothing to me. There's no election turning on this case. Nobody's going to get to be governor by convicting your brother. The whole idea is just tiresome. Now, let me tell you—we have overwhelming proof that your brother killed this old man. We believe that proof. But our minds aren't closed. We'll take anything now. If the evidence goes to his innocence, we'll follow it there. If it goes to his guilt, well, that's where we are already."

She stuck to her guns. It took an hour's hammering and cajoling to break her down. "All right!" the prosecutor shouted. "Somebody told you he was innocent. Who was that man?"

"I can't tell you."

"Where did you hear the news?"

"I was in a bar."

"What bar?"

"Farley's Bar," she muttered, "on Henry Street."

"When?"

"Early Saturday morning a man came in and said, 'They got your brother, but he didn't do it.'"

"What does that add? He didn't say any more than you've been saying."

"He saw the whole thing," she burst out, and then bit her tongue.

"An eyewitness?"

She nodded.

"What's that man's name?"

"I won't tell you."

"Why not?"

"I promised I wouldn't get him in trouble."

The prosecutor was incredulous. "Your brother is facing the chair. We've got an airtight case against him. You're his sister. You claim you have evidence to prove his innocence. Now you tell me that you'll let a promise to this man stand in the way of saving your brother."

She said stubbornly, "I can't tell you. I gave the man a promise."

Finally after several hours of tedious harangues and pleas and arguments, the girl promised to ask her witness to come in voluntarily the next day. As she left, she said, "I hope I'm doing the right thing."

Schreiber called in to say, "I got something for you."

"What is it?"

"There might be something in Kennedy's story at that. I finally got the owner of the bar and his bartender. There was a fight there just before this cutting. Two civilians and a sailor. I've got a feeling one of the civilians could be our man."

Within the hour, Schreiber produced a white-haired old man who owned the bar, and his stocky bartender. A few threats directed against the liquor license loosened their tongues completely. They agreed that one of the civilians, a tall powerful man, had been drinking heavily. Finally, in an ugly mood, he had quarreled with the bartender. "Mr. District Attorney," the Negro bartender said quietly, "the things he said about me and mine I wouldn't take off any man. Besides, he was making a nuisance of himself. So I asked the boss for the okay and I threw him out. He wasn't gone five minutes when I saw my sandwich knife was gone. Then a little after that, maybe five, ten minutes, I hear this woman scream, and everybody ran out. I closed up the place and went home. I didn't want to be around if there was trouble. Of course if I'd have known old Caspar was going to die, I'd have stuck around. But I thought they got the man."

"Who was the tall man you threw out?"

The bartender shook his head. "I never got his name. I remember seeing him in the neighborhood."

The prosecutor showed both a photograph of John Kennedy. "Was it this man?"

They studied it carefully. "No."

The prosecutor had the witnesses outside and asked Schreiber, "What does this prove?"

"How many men are roaming around that hour in the morning looking for trouble with sandwich knives?" Schreiber protested. "What do you want—moving pictures?"

"There's a chance you're right," the prosecutor admitted. "But we've got to do better. What about Butch and Louie?"

"I passed the word along to have them come in, if they exist," Schreiber said.

Statements were taken and the witnesses were released. The following morning, Margaret Kennedy's missing witness proved he was not a myth by showing up. He was a man of thirty, short, with a pimpled face, wavy hair of which he was proud, a low grade of intelligence, and frazzled nerves. He sat pulling at his knuckles.

"What's your name?"

"Jerry Capone!"

"Capone?" the prosecutor studied the witness. "You're kidding."

"I wish I was," Jerry said sadly. "I get a lot of ribbing."

"All right, what happened—Capone?"

"It wasn't Johnny Kennedy." Jerry licked his lips. "I don't know anything else. I just came because they asked me."

The prosecutor arose. "Are you trying to insult the district attorney's intelligence, Jerry? I don't mind a man's lying to me. I get to expect that. But I won't tolerate anyone's insulting the intelligence of the district attorney."

Jerry shrank back. It was as though "insulting the district attorney's intelligence" was a graver crime than murder. He started talking.

"Well, I saw the whole thing. I was across the street with some friends. We were sitting on boxes drinking rum colas. I went into the bar and I saw a sailor and two civilians. One of the civilians, a big man in a white shirt, started a fight with the bartender. I picked up my drinks and left. I wasn't interested in any fights that night. About fifteen minutes later, I saw these two men and the sailor walk out and go west. They stood at the corner a while looking back. One of them, the big one, turned back. I thought he was going back to the bar to finish the fight. But he stopped at this old man and made a pass at him. I didn't know what he was doing at that time. Then he went back to his friends and I lost sight of him. Then Kennedy and two boys walked right past me, as close as you are to me, and said, 'Hello.' I said 'Hello' back. Then I didn't watch. A few seconds later I heard screams and I saw the mob running after Kennedy. I hung around until they caught him. Then I beat it. You never know where those things end. I found Kennedy's sister and told her about the trouble."

The prosecutor took careful notes and asked, "Was anyone with Kennedy?"

"I told you, two other boys. I never saw them before."

"Did you hear what they were talking about?"

"Sure. Women."

After a moment, the prosecutor asked, "All right now, who was the big man?"

"I don't know," Jerry said nervously.

"Sure you know. Out with it."

"I wouldn't like to say," Jerry pleaded. "I'm scared."

Schreiber took over. In other circumstances, his manner might have been regarded as unduly harsh. Jerry cowered and finally wept, "They call him Herman. I'm scared he'll find out I told on him."

The prosecutor asked the detective, "Does that give you an idea?"

"It sure does," Schreiber said grimly. "I think that could be a tough one from the neighborhood." He prodded Jerry. "You mean Herman Schweppes?"

Jerry nodded.

The prosecutor asked, "Do you have any idea, Jerry, why Herman did this job?"

"He couldn't get at the barkeep," Jerry said simply, "so he got at the first man he could."

Schreiber added, "You don't need to be a lawyer to see that."

Jerry was placed in the antechamber and the prosecutor said, "We'll need something more than Jerry. Three eyewitnesses, all friends of the dead man, tell us a different story. Jerry is a friend of Kennedy's. It could be a frame."

Schreiber picked up his straw hat. "Let me dig into it."

It took a bit of doing. Herman Schweppes was located and a surveillance kept on his associates. Within two days, Schreiber identified his companions of the night. They were questioned vigorously until the story was developed.

The sailor did the trick. He was loyal to his friend—up to a point. But when the interrogation reached a peak of intensity he decided to get out of the middle. He gave Schweppes away.

Jerry Capone was right. Herman Schweppes had reason for his impulse. He had left the bar with rage in his heart because of his humiliation at the hands of the bartender. Schweppes was a parolee with a vicious criminal record. Any man in his path was in danger. Perhaps a white man might not have been attacked. But the defenseless sleeping old Caspar reminded him of the wounds from which he was smarting.

So, there it was—a flash of violence in the streets, a ready victim of suspicion and a routine investigation.

Kennedy would have been lost except for the uneasy feeling, shared by police and prosecutor, that he did not look and act like a killer. Until Jerry came in, there was no reason to doubt the eyewitnesses. They in turn were suspicious that the police were trying to save Kennedy, a white man, from punishment for killing a Negro. Because they would not credit the police with good faith, they refused to concede the possibility of error. The harder they were pressed, the more obstinately they insisted that they could not be wrong.

And yet the simple explanation was that in a short time interval between the criminal act and the alarum, Herman Schweppes had turned the corner and John Kennedy had stepped into his place.

If Kennedy had had a bad criminal record, there would have been another story. What else do the police have in the average case except eyewitnesses upon whom they must rely?

John Kennedy was lucky that Jerry Capone saw the killing and told the story to his sister, Margaret. He was lucky that the prosecutor took the trouble to get the truth from his reluctant sister. He was lucky, in fact, that Jerry Capone reached the prosecutor before he reached a defense lawyer—the story believed in the prosecutor's office would have been torn apart under cross-examination in Court.

Clues, evidence, ratiocination, brilliant sleuthing, the embellishments of fiction—these have their place. But for the ordinary case, experience and sound instincts and a deep sense of responsibility are the strongest shield of the innocent.

STUART PALMER

Of all the literary forms, comedy has the shortest shelf life. STUART PALMER'S, on the other hand, has outlived its creator, and thanks to International Polygonics Ltd., some of his finest books from the 1930s through 1950s, landmarks in the comic crime tradition, are back in print. Included in this new series is his first critical and commercial triumph, *The Penguin Pool Murder* (1931). It chronicles the life and times of "that meddlesome old battle axe," Miss Hildegarde Withers, a spinster schoolteacher with a taste for fancy headgear. Later in his career, Palmer introduced a second character, Howie Rook, "an old newspaperman turned out to the pasture." Rook, like Palmer, occasionally wrote true crime. Rivaling his most outrageous fiction, the story before you now takes you on a doomed voyage with Captain Walter Wanderwell, "a world traveler, adventurer and soldier of misfortune," and his crew of madcap, but wholly incompetent, Argonauts. It goes to prove even real murder can be fun—when it's in the right hands.

Once Aboard the Lugger

Curtain rises on a lonely, deserted dock on the Long Beach waterfront, where the rakish black schooner *Carma* has just been moored that afternoon. The date is December 6, 1932; the hour 9:30 of a dank and dripping evening. One feeble 20-watt bulb dangles overhead and there is a faint glow from a few lighted portholes of the gently-rocking old vessel, a former rum-runner with still a bit of stagger to her.

That is the setting of Act One. Enter the chorus, consisting of eight very pretty girls and seven handsome men, most of them in their early twenties. They are all living aboard the schooner, supposedly engaged in preparing for an adventure cruise to Tahiti and Samoa and the glamorous

South Seas. It is nice casting. One girl is a bewitching authoress and poet from Atlanta, one a bob-haired student from Boston and Wellesley . . . there's a cute, plump secretary from Manhattan, another poet, a painter, a dishwasher, a sailor or two (but not very salty) and an actress who had played Juliet in summer stock. And there is even a handsome young man with a heavy Oxford accent who claimed to be the son of a British peer—and was!

We might have a fanfare of martial music while the principals enter. In the top starring role is Captain Walter Wanderwell, leader of the expedition. He is a tall, handsome, stiffly-military chap who always wears boots and a self-designed uniform—a distinct Nordic type with cold blue eyes and a jutting chin, very much resembling Hairbreadth Harry. If you can't remember *that* hero of the comics, then consider the Captain a combination of Fearless Fosdick and Superman with a dash of Clyde Beatty. He is a world-traveler, adventurer, and soldier of misfortune.

There is also, as heroine and leading woman, his wife Aloha Wanderwell. She is six feet and 140 pounds of blonde, curly-haired pulchritude, with a figure which has to make concessions to no stack of wheat-cakes, in spite of the fact that she almost always dressed in another of those home-designed, stiffly military uniforms. Aloha was—and for that matter is—a woman in whom I and the other newsmen assigned to the story took an obviously deep interest, and for whom we have a most healthy respect.

For further audience sympathy we have also the Wanderwells' two children—Valerie, aged seven, and Nile who is pushing six, both members of the strange "crew." Little Val was the nominal owner of the vessel, since her father was not an American citizen and thus could not own a ship under United States registry. She was no doubt the youngest shipowner in history.

And—to round out the cast—there is a slight, wavy-haired, good-looking young man in a gray cravanette raincoat. You can choose his role yourself—juvenile lead, very heavy villain . . . or comedy relief. He later stood trial for his life on the charge of having shot Captain Wanderwell through the back of the neck. Certain highlights of that memorable trial, presented here for the first time from my own records and with the amiable assistance of Judge Robert W. Kenny, who presided, are worth bringing up in this account.

Captain Wanderwell and his fifteen merry, madcap adventurers were all living aboard the *Carma* (the new name of the old rum-runner being

Wanderwell's own misspelling of Karma, the Buddhist word for Fate), although the rickety vessel had not been conditioned nor fully provisioned, and her sailing date for Tahiti and points south was, to say the least, highly indefinite. But they had no place else to live, since each had contributed all the loose cash he or she had toward the trip's expenses. Wanderwell himself had somehow raised the considerable amount of $22,000 with which to buy the ship, although his last venture—in the wilds of South America—had been spectacularly unsuccessful. He had purchased the old rum-runner at a government auction of seized ships, and had managed to have her towed to her present berth.

So, with all their money—in most cases their life savings—invested in the common kitty, the would-be Argonauts lived on canned beans and waited for the great day. Captain Wanderwell was a natural-born leader, imbuing them with confidence, a brave and dashing figure—while he lasted.

Only recently, within the last year, he had led a similar group of starry-eyed explorers north from Buenos Aires through some of the most impassable jungles of South America, travelling by means of two specially-built, high-slung Ford trucks and stopping now and then to shoot movie film footage starring crocodiles, head-hunters, and of course the beautiful Aloha. She had shown herself in the film, of which more later, to be a crack shot with rifle or pistol, a real Amazon on the Amazon.

That particular expedition, as I have said, had wound up somewhat short of its announced goal of Beverly Hills, California, due to the fact that no motor cars had yet been built which could travel through those parts of South America where roads didn't exist. Wanderwell and Aloha and their seventeen aides had finally worked their way to the Ecuador coast; they had taken passage on various tramp steamers and by the time they reached the Canal Zone had lost several people by the wayside and had also had a sort of mild mutiny among their staff. The trip had been a considerable disappointment and disillusionment to the members of the crew—the girls who had been promised roles in the picture found themselves fighting mosquitoes and snakes and doing chores around the camp or carrying lights and cameras for the photography which centered on Aloha and of course on Wanderwell himself.

The group broke up completely at Colon, and there a number of lawsuits against the Wanderwells were immediately instituted by members of the party. But the Captain and his fair bride managed to sail for Los Angeles before the suits came to trial. So now—after a few months of much-needed rest—Wanderwell was ready to take off again. His new volunteer crew had been recruited through advertisements in newspapers and magazines and literary weeklies by offering any footloose adventurer the opportunity of having his or her investment (which might range from $400 to $2,000 apiece) repaid tenfold from the profits of the new voyage—profits from the sale of the adventure movies they expected to make, from picture postcards, from curios and strange shells to be collected—and also possibly from the discovery of millions in buried treasure in case they happened to put in at the fabled Cocos Island or any other historic pirate hangout.

It may seem to contemporary skeptics that the investors were making a rather poor gamble. But it must be remembered that in that sad year 1932 the nation was gripped tight in depression, with no jobs anywhere for anybody; strong, able men with college degrees were selling apples on street corners and it was a time when many young, imaginative persons yearned for any kind of escape from the hopeless doldrums of ordinary existence. Somewhere else—anywhere else!—was the cry.

The fifteen who had signed on as the volunteer, amateur crew of the *Carma* did not know that the ship had already been condemned as unseaworthy, that an experienced marine engineer and carpenter had both quit in disgust after a couple of days aboard, and that the aged vessel had taken two days to make a run of a few nautical miles from San Pedro to Long Beach, during which both of her auxiliaries had broken down completely and the moldering queen of the seas finally was ignominiously towed to her new berth.

Here the Argonauts awaited her, ready to take off for anywhere. So, fifteen youths and maidens plus the Wanderwell family of four crowded aboard the cranky old *Carma* which boasted only three cabins furnished with six double bunks and a few sofas. On the night when the fantastic comedy-tragedy really got under way, not all were aboard. The majority of the crew were out enjoying the dubious pleasures afforded by the Long Beach waterfront at the time—movies and speakeasies—and the fair Aloha had gone up to Los Angeles to visit her sister. The Captain was alone in his cabin aft; the remaining members of the crew were crowded in a cabin, amusing themselves after their wont, presumably listening to an accordion on which one of the boys had some facility and probably trying to harmonize the popular songs of the day—"Moonlight Bay" and "I'd Love to Call You My Sweetheart" and "I Can't Give You Anything But Love, Baby...". Or else they were taking turns reading aloud—Jurgen, perhaps, or the poetry of Edna St. Vincent Millay. There was certainly a jug of dago red nearby, or a few bottles of home brew.

But it was testified later that at least two of the crew saw a face suddenly appear at one open porthole, and heard a husky "Germanic" voice ask for Wanderwell. The visitor was directed to the other cabin—some said he was even guided there by one of the boys, but there is considerable conflict in the testimony about this point. Some of the gay young people in the cabin claimed not to have heard or seen anybody. Yet a while later—either a few minutes or an hour or so, you can take your pick—there was the sound of a shot.

The little group of intrepid adventurers investigated, and found Captain Walter Wanderwell kneeling against a sofa in his cabin in utter darkness. He was dying, having been shot through the back of the neck, the bullet ranging downward and through his heart. Rushing out on the deck, they saw no sign of anybody—the fog had settled over them... where it was to remain.

After some delay, the situation was reported by telephone to the Long Beach police, who proceeded to take charge after their fashion—a fashion which we sincerely hope has changed with the years. It is understandable now why the local authorities found themselves somewhat out of their depth in dealing with a murder case of this type but even so, the investigation could well go down in history as a horrible example.

The boys from Long Beach headquarters had a fresh corpse on their hands, and immediately ruled out suicide since there was no gun around and since it was unlikely even to them that a man could shoot himself in the back at a range of four feet or more. Then the officers remembered about the paraffin test (since officially discarded by crime investigators as useless and confusing) and spent most of the rest of the night giving it to everyone aboard, with negative results everywhere. All got a clean bill of health, including Aloha Wanderwell herself who had been brought back from her sister's apartment on Santa Monica Boulevard in Hollywood (about twenty minutes away by auto, or half an hour by street car or bus).

By next morning the Los Angeles police were in on the case after their fashion—aided and abetted by Carlton Williams, brilliant police reporter for the Los Angeles *Times*. It was immediately clear to all parties

concerned that some old enemy of the Captain had done him in.
According to police records, there was only one old enemy—a former
member of his group, who had been jettisoned midway on the auto-boat
jaunt upward through South America, and who later had the temerity to
come to Los Angeles and ask for his money back, finally even appealing
to the juvenile authorities and to the bunco squad at headquarters. This
man's description was printed in the *Times*—Carl Williams's paper—and
picked up by the other Los Angeles dailies, though for some reason his
name was carefully withheld. And he was put on the police "Wanted"
docket.

Meanwhile, down at Long Beach, there was much consternation and
many alarums and excursions. The fifteen adventurers were coached,
primed, questioned all night, and shown photographs of the wanted man.
Some of them were placed under technical arrest for twenty-four hours.
Even the two Wanderwell children were drawn into it. Rudely awakened
from their bunk where they had been sleeping at the time of the killing,
they were questioned to the point where they would (and did) swear to
almost anything.

At the same time a parallel investigation was being made through
regular Los Angeles police channels, during which it was discovered
without too much difficulty that Captain Wanderwell had been in the
custody of the Secret Service during the late war and had been interned
for a while at the federal penitentiary at Atlanta as a German espionage
agent. His real name was Valerian Johannes Riecynski, a Polish national;
his military background and his captaincy were purely fictional. But he
had been a world-traveler and, in fact, had skipped out of half a dozen
ports without bothering to clear with the customs or the immigration
authorities.

The glamorous Wanderwell couple had also appeared on police records
in Los Angeles in March 1925, charged with wearing United States Army
uniforms without authorization. Actually, both Walter and Aloha (giving
them the benefit of their assumed names) were only wearing their
home-designed uniforms plus Army officers' Sam Browne belts as part of
the act. It was, however, an offense for which both paid the not
inconsiderable fine of $200. It was also revealed at that time, 1925, that
Aloha—who claimed that Wanderwell had picked her up in a French
convent (place unnamed) and swept her off her heels at the age of
seventeen, was traveling around with him as his sister. She was immedi-

ately, under the circumstances, made a ward of the Los Angeles juvenile court, but charges were naturally dropped when the dashing couple eloped to Riverside and were legally married. It is not a matter of record as to whether or not their two children were attendants.

It was a somewhat complicated case—for the investigating authorities of Long Beach and Los Angeles as well as for my associate Bill Moore, then police reporter of the Los Angeles *Herald-Express*, and for me as the visiting kibitzer who was supposed to supply "atmosphere"—as if the affair didn't have enough and to spare of that commodity.

We were definitely hampered by the fact that by this time Carlton Williams, star reporter of the opposing paper, was working hand-in-glove with Detective-Lieutenant Filkas who was in charge of the Los Angeles aspects of the case. Witnesses were being brought up to the *Times* office, questioned and interviewed and photographed by the *Times* staff. We were handicapped. However, we did have a composite photograph made up, showing round-faced, Spanish-Irish, Bill Moore peering through the porthole of the *Carma* where the mysterious murderer was supposed to have been, and at least one of the witnesses obliged with a positive identification of it as being that of the mysterious Peeping Tom!

It was a time when few, if any, holds were barred. But the news leaked out that the entire investigation centered on one man, that man who had been a member of the earlier Wanderwell expedition. He and the Captain were supposed to have had a scene in the Wanderwells' Wilshire Boulevard apartment, during which the ex-Argonaut had demanded his money back. And—even though the disillusioned voyager had but one friend with him while Wanderwell was flanked with two aides—the Captain had shattered a window and yelled for help.

Aloha had then dropped in, and smoothed things out. Wanderwell had promised to pay the money later, thus stalling off his angry antagonist—whom he outweighed by 60 pounds and towered over by five inches. All in all, Captain Wanderwell seems not to have shown up too well on that occasion. Of course, it hadn't been rehearsed and he wasn't as usual the director. However, he didn't make good his promise. So, the man who had challenged him, flanked by several others of the indignant South American contingent, finally went to the police bunco-squad, where they got no help at all.

The story that this man told the officer on the bunco-squad was that he and his pretty young wife had joined the previous Wanderwell expedition in Buenos Aires; that they had contributed all their available funds and then had been stranded in Panama. He and his wife had been left strapped, then they had been forced to separate since she could get a subsistence job as an entertainer and B-girl in a Colon bar and he obviously could not. So, he alone had worked his way north to Los Angeles to try to retrieve all or part of the original investment from the self-styled "Captain."

Early reports of the fracas in the Wilshire Boulevard apartment differed considerably. Aloha Wanderwell, who hadn't been present for much of the time, said that her husband had been threatened, and that his coat and tie were disheveled. All others present said that there had been no threats but only a demand for an accounting of funds, and that twice the instigator of the interview had suggested that they call the police and have a showdown—something for which Wanderwell had no taste.

At any rate, the day after the murder the investigation speedily narrowed itself down to this one target, this mysterious man who had been a member of the previous group—although police records showed that he was anxious to work if at all through proper legal channels. Photographs of the missing man were produced and suddenly several people conveniently remembered that they had seen someone of that general description lurking around the Pacific and Orient docks—where the *Carma* was moored—at 6 P.M. the night of the murder. Others (or the same ones) testified that he had been noticed in the same vicinity at 11:30 P.M. that night, asking directions as to how to return to Los Angeles. Certainly such evidence, given to the grand jury and later to the court—if true—displays a surprising lack of enterprise on the part of the murderer, both before and after the crime. In five and a half hours the murderer of Captain Wanderwell should have been able to arrive, do the job, and disappear— without asking his way of anyone. And if he had been able to find his way to the dock where the *Carma* was moored, he certainly should have been able to find his way away from it . . . after the crime. None of this evidence made much sense, even to the police—though it was repeated at the trial.

But on Thursday December 8, acting on information received, as the old saying goes (which was actually Reporter Williams's dope on the previous fracas between Wanderwell and the accused), Detective-Lieutenant Filkas of the Los Angeles police, backed up by the intrepid Carl Williams, swooped down on a house at 2045 Blake Street, near Riverside Drive and the Los Angeles River. The dismal little cottage was dark, empty, almost unfurnished, without heat or light save that of a candle.

As the detective and the newspaper reporter descended upon the place, a man emerged from the house with his hands in the air. So enters our major suspect, one William James (Curley) Guy. He had been in residence there, fortified by some oranges and delicatessen food, all the late newspapers and the aforesaid candle.

Curley Guy, as we came to know him, was the adventurer who had dared to approach Wanderwell and ask for his money back. He was a native of Wales, an authentic flyer, navigator and ship's officer: a slightly built man with clear-cut features, wavy hair, and a ready, apologetic smile. He said he had rented the abandoned house the morning after the murder, had stocked it with a few comestibles, and had then sat still and waited for the inevitable. When questioned by police and reporters at the *Times* offices—where he was taken instead of to the police station—he explained that he had gone into hiding because he knew he would be the primary suspect of the much-publicized murder, and didn't want to involve his friends, the DeLarms, with whom he had been living.

Besides, Curley Guy was in no position to face investigation. In his attempt to establish American citizenship (to which he had no legal right whatsoever) he had been cutting numerous corners. A humble seaman-navigator aboard the palatial Vincent Astor yacht, he had jumped ship some months before when the vessel was docked near Los Angeles. Then, he had registered and voted at the recent elections—in order to make himself eligible for a pilot's or a navigator's license—then only granted to American citizens.

A grayish raincoat was found among his meager effects and the police then marked the case Closed. There were various identification parades, held both at the *Times* offices and at police headquarters, some without Guy being present. But several important witnesses identified his raincoat— which they had seen through a twelve-inch porthole on the Carma on a dark and foggy night, if at all. Guy was given the nitrate-paraffin test and passed it, but the police explained that too much time had elapsed and that in the meantime he might have washed his hands, or even at the time of the murder he might have worn gloves—though never did anybody in officialdom suggest that the same ruse might have been used by any other potential suspect.

The case, which had up until this time been largely centered in a newspaper office, finally came to preliminary hearing (Guy was booked December 13) and the comedy of errors got into full swing. Before a magistrate, the lovely Aloha Wanderwell, who had been very dry-eyed all this time, gave her testimony. She also smiled encouragingly at the prisoner all the while, which mightily confused the press who were properly trying to build her up as the bereaved widow. Also smiling and nodding to him was pretty Marian Smith, the girl from Atlanta who thought that she had seen somebody like him through the porthole on the fatal night, but wasn't too sure...

What really flabbergasted the working press was the fact that after the hearing was over, the beauteous Aloha walked across the room and made a point of warmly shaking hands with the prisoner and whispering a few words to him. It was certainly evident at the time that there were no hard feelings anywhere. It made no sense to the boys on the *Times*—nor to us on the *Herald-Express*, the opposition paper, who naturally resented being caught off base. With the arrest of Curley Guy reporter Williams and his friend Lieutenant Filkas had scooped everybody in town. But the thing was just beginning...

The trial of William James (Curley) Guy opened February 3, 1933 in Long Beach, with Judge Robert W. Kenny (more recently Attorney General of the State of California and now a prominent attorney specializing in labor law and relations) presiding. At the request of the city editor of the *Herald-Express*, I was assigned to cover the highlights of the trial. This may have been because of, or in spite of, the fact that my early stories on the case had accented my belief that Curley Guy was innocent—at least of the crime for which he had been indicted. I had even gone so far as to begin one story with the famous Gallic cliché, *"Cherchez la Femme!"*

Weeks ahead of the trial our opposition paper, the *Times*, intimated that Curley Guy was guilty all over its front pages. The *Herald-Express* inclined toward the opposite viewpoint—not only because of my own hunch but because Bill Moore, their regular police-reporter, agreed that the case against Guy was as full of holes as a Swiss cheese. The thing became a battle between two great rival newspapers, with no holds barred.

Meanwhile, the ceremonies attendant on the burial of Captain Walter Wanderwell—né Valerian Johannes Riecynski—had taken place with considerable fanfare; ceremonies from which the working press were excluded but which must have been something for the book. The body had been cheaply cremated in Long Beach, then taken back aboard the old schooner and in the midst of a rainstorm and a howling gale had been transported out to sea, with the full crew aboard. Since the *Carma* could not yet move under her own power of either sails or auxiliaries, she was lashed to a fishing vessel, aptly named the *Sunshine 2nd*, and ignominiously hauled out past the breakwater. The remains were wrapped in a flag— whether that of the United States, of his native Poland or something like his uniforms designed especially for the occasion is not recorded—and consigned to the deep. Then when it came time to play Taps it was found that no bugle was aboard! But by that time most of the disillusioned mourners were too seasick to care. On the way home the fifteen Argonauts got together and unanimously agreed to call off the projected tour to story-book islands of the South Seas.

Besides, most of them had been subpoenaed for the trial of Curley Guy and they wouldn't have missed that for anything.

Judge Kenny, looking like an Alaskan billikin or an Oriental Buddha, dominated the proceedings. The Judge ruled with cautious fairness— though some of the newspapermen who lunched with him gathered that in his private opinion he felt rather sure that the trial was a dry run; there would be no victory for the State.

Representing the defense was Eugene McGann, a fine old Irish warhorse in the tradition of Fallon and Jerry Geisler, who operated from the beginning as if he knew that he had the world by the tail with a downhill drag. From whence came his fee—which must have been considerable—nobody knows. It is part of the record that Guy was down to his last ten dollars when arrested. Nor did our defendant pad his coffers by signing up with any one of the numerous newspapers and press services who would have gladly paid him plenty for his "life story" (to be ghost-written of course by some hack sob-sister) as has happened in so many other murder cases. Curley Guy played it close to his chest, but I said in print then and I still maintain that he played it like a man in a poker game who had two aces showing and one in the hole.

Buron Fitts, a prominent legal light at the time, was then District Attorney of Los Angeles, and his jurisdiction covered the scene of the crime. But at the last minute he decided to send in this third team, a couple of bright young men fresh out of law school. Bill Brayton and Clarence Hunt carried the case for the People, doing their level best with what they had—which wasn't too much. There was a faint uncertainty about their courtroom manner—they went through their roles and read their lines in a manner which reminded me of the old story of Eugene Field as dramatic critic who said of Mr. Creston Clarke as King Lear that he "played the King as if he momentarily expected someone to play the Ace."

The two were bright and able young men and they had a true bill presented by a picked grand jury. But I always felt that they realized that the facts of the Wanderwell killing were still obscured and deep beneath the surface. They did their best, but they had to sit in on a tough poker game with nothing better than two pairs.

And Curley Guy had an ace in the hole, as I wrote at the time and still maintain.

On the opening day of the trial at Long Beach, thanks to the fact that while I was a pro tem *Herald-Express* reporter I was allowed an interview with the prisoner in his cell, and later was permitted to walk with him and his aged, tobacco-chewing deputy sheriff several blocks through the busy streets of Long Beach to the courtroom. Guy was under no restraint; the old man wore a rusty .38 but certainly would never have used it in a crowd and probably hadn't fired it in ten years or more anyway. It occurred to me at the time that Guy could easily have made a break for it anywhere along the way—the deputy in charge could have been pushed over with a nudge, and I for one would not have lifted a finger to stop the man, since I had already come to my own conclusions about who had actually shot Wanderwell—and who should be standing in the dock!

As we walked slowly along the streets, I tried to make the most of the time—tried to probe a little into the mind of the man accused of murder. As a mystery author, who had been brought for the first time into contact with the real thing, I thought that innocent or guilty, Curley Guy's reactions would be story material. But he had little to say. He disposed of Wanderwell in a few well-chosen if unprintable phrases. The man had been only a twenty-one-carat phony, who had made his living out of taking bows for adventures he had never had—and of taking money from little people who were seduced by his talk. The bullet through the back of his neck had been too good for him, but Curley laughed at the suggestion that he himself had put it there.

My impression of Guy at the time was that he was a right little, tight little Welshman, who knew planes and the navigation of ships, who would—for all his slight stature and boyish profile—have been a bad man to push around. But I also felt that he would, under any pressure, be the sort of person who would only hit above the belt. I realized that he despised Captain Walter Wanderwell—but I could not believe that he would have shot Wanderwell or anyone else in the back, under any circumstances whatever.

I tried to turn the conversation toward the topic of the lovely lost Vera, the wife from whom he had separated in the Canal Zone some months ago, and whose loss was supposed—according to the findings of the grand jury, the *Times*, and the prosecution—to have inspired his murder of Wanderwell. Guy shrugged that off. They were stranded in the Canal Zone. Vera had a chance to become an entertainer in a cafe, a B-girl, maybe worse. So, she chose to remain there and eat regularly, while he worked his way north.

"Water over the bridge—or do Americans say 'dam'?" queried Guy. More important to him at the moment was the question of whether or not, after the trial was over, he would be deported. He was determined to secure American citizenship, somehow or other.

I tried to explain to him that his situation was precarious, since he had been born in Wales and later had become a citizen of Australia. The only way he could legally enter the U.S.A. was on a quota, and this particular police record certainly would not help him with any of the immigration authorities.

About the trial and the Wanderwell murder itself, he would say very little. But I did discover the fact—which no detective had yet bothered to elicit—that Guy did not know that on the day of the murder the yacht *Carma* had been moved to new moorings at the P. and O. docks.

Which response could, of course, have been faked. Perhaps, as the prosecution argued on the first day of that memorable trial, Curley Guy had hated Captain Wanderwell so violently as a result of the failure of the South American expedition and the ensuing humiliation of himself and his wife, that he had first tried to get his money back and then had resorted to murder.

It made sense on paper, it made sense to the grand jury, and it sounded very likely as presented to the jury by Mr. Brayton and Mr. Hunt. Things looked not too good for Curley Guy during the first days of the trial, but he remained confident and unruffled.

Prominent in the courtroom during the trial was Aloha Wanderwell— and her sister, Margaret B. Hall—each done up in picturesque uniforms consisting of open silk shirts with loose Russian sleeves, dark, tight vests, breeches and shiny boots. The sister had never been on any of the expeditions, but she certainly went along with a gag. They were a striking couple. Aloha had her fair hair done up in tight ringlets under a tam-o-shanter cap and added considerably to the tone of the affair. Her innocent, little-girlish face, topping an Amazonic six-foot form, made a policeman next to me whisper that she looked like a .22 on a .45 frame. Everyone waited hopefully for the day when she would be called to testify, but the trial dragged on and on with interminable medical evidence that "proved" that Wanderwell had been shot at close range—that he had been shot from a distance outside the porthole—that the bullet had ranged here, there and everywhere . . . !

The course of the trial was then brightened by the announcement of Curley Guy to a lady reporter from still another Los Angeles newspaper that if freed he would gladly volunteer for a trip into the stratosphere with the famous Professor Auguste Picard, who was then out in Hollywood raising money for another of his balloon ascensions. There was no immediate comment from the Professor. It was the only statement Guy had to make to the press after my interview with him en route from the jail.

Still the trial dragged on, with days spent on the testimony of Guy's friend Eddie DeLarm (owner of a plane which had been making mysterious trips to Mexico), of Eddie's wife and of his two teen-age daughters— all of whom swore that Guy was in his room in their Glendale house at the time of the crime. Considerable time was spent on the boy-friends of the cute little DeLarm girls, who had or had not been sitting around in the living room playing jazz records on the fatal evening, and had or hadn't seen Guy about the house. The jury had a field day, making trips to look at the schooner *Carma* (where one juror shocked the court and panicked the newspapermen by making Rabelaisian suggestions concerning the way in which fifteen crew members and four Wanderwells must have utilized the limited sleeping arrangements of the ship) and to the original slip where the *Carma* had been tied, and even to the shack where Curley Guy had gone into hiding the morning after the murder.

DeLarm, not the most co-operative of witnesses, testified that most of his original statements to the police had been obtained under duress. He cited a night when he and his wife had had their home invaded by Lieutenant Filkas and reporter Williams—without warrant—during which time they had taken it for granted that Williams was an officer and not just a *Times* reporter on a field day. The DeLarms had been bounced around a bit and felt reasonably annoyed. Some of the witnesses who had testified to seeing Curley Guy's face in the porthole just before the murder—after having been prompted by glimpses of his photograph or looks at his raincoat—hedged on their testimony. It was also brought out that DeLarm's car, the only vehicle to which Guy had ready access, had stood in DeLarm's driveway all the time during the evening of the murder.

Although the case for the prosecution began to go all to pieces, it had a momentary life when a trimotored plane registered in the name of DeLarm was nabbed at Corona Airport, near San Diego, and found to hold 500 gallons of alcohol illegally imported from below the border. DeLarm insisted that he had sold the plane to somebody else a few days ago, but he was undoubtedly making a living running a shoe-string air transport and Curley Guy—a pilot and navigator—worked for him and lived with him. Perhaps we here have an indication of the one basic secret which Guy was really anxious to hide. The serious student of the case could certainly keep that fact in mind. All this happened in the days of prohibition, when an enterprising man with an airplane could make $4,- or $5,000 by importing a load of schnapps from south of the border. There were also numerous Chinese who waited in Mexican cities, ready to pay almost anything for an entree into the U.S.A. All this is not to speak of the traffic in drugs which went on and still goes on between Tijuana and points north. At any rate, DeLarm and his friend and associate, Curley Guy, had been making twice-weekly flights across the border for some months. The record does not show that they delivered any cargoes of Mexican serapes or huarachos.

Like most newspapermen assigned to the trial, I got awfully bored with it finally, and went around the corner to a nearby Long Beach burlesque theater which offered as its main attraction a double bill consisting of the personal appearance of the luscious Aloha Wanderwell together with the first showing of the film her late husband had made in South America, *The River of Death*. The show, at the time of my attendance, was a sell-out, with standing room only. I must admit that Aloha was a considerable disappointment, since she only appeared briefly and in a tight military uniform not designed to do justice to her junoesque charms. Aloha recited in flat midwestern accents a short introduction to the film, then gave its narration. The picture itself was definitely in the home-movie category, not too professionally directed or photographed. There were interminable scenes of the fair Aloha hemmed in by cannibalistic

head-hunters and head-shrinkers who mugged happily for the camera;
there were scenes of her knocking off predatory crocodiles and jungle cats
with her trusty rifle and pistol. But the picture dragged. Before the second
reel had run off some of the cash customers in the back rows were
shouting "Take it off, take it off. . ." in the old burlesque tradition, and
making wolf-whistles at the lady on stage.

Aloha, obviously somewhat at loss—a Trilby without her Svengali—
didn't take the hint from the audience. When the "show" ended, a
number of newsmen who had been in the audience went around outside
and down the alley, and waylaid Aloha as she left the stage door, trying
vainly for an interview. have vainly for an interview. One reporter
remembered that she claimed to have been a French orphan of mysterious
and noble lineage who had been discovered by the late Captain Wanderwell
in a convent somewhere in southern France and, in my hearing, spoke to
her in her native language, whereupon Aloha said "Huh?" We all
concluded that her particular convent must have been one in which for
some reason only English was spoken.

Two blocks away from the burlesque theater the trial still dragged on
and on, becoming less and less newsworthy. And then, in the middle of a
dull afternoon, with almost no reporters at hand, the prosecution suddenly
called Aloha Wanderwell to the stand. She was, of course, the most
interesting, exciting, glamorous figure in the entire case—she was front-
page stuff. But everybody thought she would be held in reserve for
another day or so, and her appearance in the witness chair at that time
was a surprise.

Her testimony, delivered in a faint, cautious voice, was nothing
unexpected. She told of the scene in the Wilshire Boulevard apartment
house when Curley Guy and his friend and employer DeLarm had come
visiting Wanderwell, who had been flanked by two associates but still had
felt it necessary to smash a window and holler for help.

From her own separate apartment next door she had heard the appeal
and come running, whereupon she smoothed things over between the five
men and got Guy and DeLarm to leave after her harried husband had
promised to square the financial thing at a restaurant that night—a place
where he and Aloha were making a personal appearance. It is not
recorded that he ever kept the date.

The witness was perhaps a little disappointing to the two bright young assistant district attorneys, for her testimony—while it matched what she had said at the preliminary hearing and before the grand jury—was not too strong against the prisoner at the bar. But all the same, that was a tense half hour in the courtroom—an hour which I am sorry to have missed. But all was not yet lost.

His Honor, Judge Kenny, had been a newspaper reporter before he took up the study of law and rose to his present eminence. Realizing that Aloha's testimony was the high spot of the trial, a most newsworthy moment indeed, and also realizing that her appearance at this hour would give a big break to the morning newspapers and leave the afternoon sheets out in the cold, he reverted to type. Once a newspaperman, always a newspaperman. His Honor quietly and firmly exercised his judicial prerogative and recessed the session for ten minutes on the grounds that he had to make a long distance telephone call.

This fact has never previously been made public, but with Bob Kenny's permission I can now let out the secret that his call was to the office of the *Herald-Express* (the Los Angeles newspaper on which he had once years ago been a cub-reporter) and that he gave the city editor of his old paper enough of the story on Aloha's testimony so that instead of being scooped, we had an exclusive front-page story. I doubt if there had ever been in recorded history another major murder case in which the presiding judge has sneaked back into his chambers and phoned in a red-hot story to a friendly newspaper.

Not, of course, to intimate that Judge Kenny wasn't impeccably fair in his handling of the Wanderwell murder trial. Most of his rulings, as the transcript shows, were in favor of the People. Messrs Brayton and Hunt had a certain amount of evidence, mainly circumstantial, on their side. They had a lot of law. But they were still, in the opinion of most of the newspapermen covering the trial, trying to convict a nice young man of murder when he was actually only guilty of jumping ship, illegal entry into the U.S.A., possible smuggling activities via DeLarm's plane and of having tried in a childish fashion to hide out when he learned that an avowed enemy of his had been killed.

The case finally went to the jury, after a good bit of heart-rending oratory from Counsellor McGann and a dry, factual summing-up from the prosecution, at 4 o'clock in the afternoon. Before 6 the twelve good men and true were back—with the expected verdict of Not Guilty. It is, as Judge Kenny points out, one of the few cases in history where a jury has

failed to stay out long enough to get an extra dinner at the expense of the
public. It was a verdict which surprised nobody who had followed the
course of the trial, and one which I think was concurred with by His
Honor and by the press and public.

Which brings us inevitably to the gaps in the story; faces us with the
certain question of who actually did put a .38 bullet through Captain
Walter Wanderwell's back? Your guess may be as good as mine. I am not
able to answer that question, any more than can the police even at this
late date—though I have reason to think that some of the boys down at
Homicide have come to the same conclusion as have I. Of course the
investigating officers muffed the thing completely; they set their sights on
one suspect and never bothered to look anywhere else.

There were some interesting questions which I raised at the time, and
still raise.

Was it likely that Curley Guy, a two-fisted forthright aviator and
navigator, even with a grievance against Captain Wanderwell, would have
shot the man in the back over a matter of a few hundred dollars? To me,
from a psychological standpoint, it seems out of character. Guy had
already faced Wanderwell and had scared the much bigger and heavier
heroic adventurer into spasms—and into smashing a window and calling
for help.

Then too, what were the reassuring words that the fair Aloha whispered
to Curley Guy at the time of the preliminary hearing, and why did she and
certain other members of the group smile and nod at him in such a
fraternal manner that afternoon?

Then too, Wanderwell was found to have been killed by a bullet from a
.38 pistol. No evidence was ever brought forward to show that Curley Guy
ever owned or possessed such a weapon, or any other gun. He was a
young man who, in my considered opinion, would have resorted to his
fists in any argument. But the evidence does show that Wanderwell did
have—in addition to a surprisingly heavy stock of rifles and carbines
aboard the vessel—a .38 pistol. It disappeared about the time of the
murder. Where did it go?

And why was he found dying in the dark? The murderer, knowing that
people were in the next cabin, waited on the scene for an extra second to
turn out the light. Why?

At the time the jury and the press made an inspection of the *Carma*, we
discovered that in the cabin where Wanderwell died, concealed by a rag,

there was a hatch leading down into the hold and the bilges, easily raised from above or below. From the hold there were half a dozen other hatches opening into the cabins, the mess-hall, and out on deck. It is within the bounds of possibility that someone who hated Wanderwell and who knew the ins and outs of the schooner could have crept through the hold, raised the hatch, and shot the man, then escaped the way he came.

One cannot sensibly accept the theory that Wanderwell was killed by a visitor who showed his face at the porthole to at least four people. Wanderwell was a nervous, jittery character in spite of his imposing presence—he would never have turned his back on Curley Guy or any other of his numerous enemies. Yet he had obviously turned his back and had been leaning over backwards at the moment he was shot—the bullet entered his neck and ranged down to the heart. Was he, perhaps—at the request of someone he knew and trusted—engaged in reaching up toward his collection of scrap-books on a high shelf in his cabin when the shot was fired?

Various other interesting theories have been put forward by writers interested in the case. It has been seriously suggested that Wanderwell, realizing that he had sunk $22,000 in a useless hulk of a vessel and that he was at the end of his rope, had taken his own life with his .38 pistol but changing the suicide into the semblance of murder by previously tying the gun to a weight and dangling the weight out of the porthole, so that when in death he released his grip the gun would disappear forever into the muddy bottom of the harbor. This ingenious theory still does not explain why he should have shot himself in the back at such an angle, but one cannot say it was absolutely impossible. There are records in the medico-legal textbooks of men who have shot themselves three times through the head, who have stabbed and then shot themselves—and from seemingly impossible angles.

It has also been seriously suggested that one of the Wanderwell children, inspired by seeing movies of Bill Hart or Jack Holt or some other tough two-gun shooting hero of the time, had come upon their father's loaded pistol and had pulled the trigger at the wrong time and place, causing an accidental death which was hastily hushed up by the crew members. Such things have happened, but in the light of the extensive grilling given the Wanderwell children it seems unlikely that they could have kept their lips sealed.

In my own opinion the true solution would have come, if at all, from a close study of the situation on board the schooner *Carma*. With no less than eight exceptionally attractive young women aboard, with Captain Wanderwell a handsome, dashing figure right out of a movie serial or a radio soap-opera, there could have been conflicts and frictions, romances and jealousies and broken hearts and revenges unguessed at by the thumb-fingered authorities. The Wanderwells were not close at the time—Aloha had months before made her own apartment next door to her husband's in the place on Wilshire. And she had had no compunctions about leaving him on the ship, with all the pretty crew members, while she went up to Los Angeles to stay with her sister. Was it not within the realm of possibility that Wanderwell had tired of the pretty blond wife he had married (under the shadow of the State's shotgun) and was carrying on with one or more of his charming feminine Argonauts? Could not that have led to disastrous results?

It is of course within the bounds of possibility that Curley Guy, or some other outraged and vengeful former voyager, did come down to the P. and O. docks that night, did appear at the *Carma*'s porthole, and ask for Wanderwell. If so, that person may not have come armed, and may not have fired the shot. It seems, from this perspective, unlikely that a would-be killer would show himself so openly to the group in the social hall, even through a porthole—or that he would be seen some hours after the murder wandering around the waterfront area, asking his way back to Los Angeles.

These questions will never be answered now. The Los Angeles police force—and particularly its homicide squad—have in recent years been completely torn down and rebuilt, with even a Marine general brought in at one time to make some order out of the chaos. Many of the old-timers still remain in uniform, however, and at least two of them have admitted to me, off the record, that they have finally come to the conclusion that Wanderwell wasn't killed by Curley at all, but by—

Guy himself, when released, put up a stout fight to resist being transported back to Australia—the boy wanted most desperately a chance to become an American citizen. The odds were against him, though he even paid a call on Judge Kenny, then living in a big beach-house at Malibu, and asked the jurist's help. Kenny was friendly but dubious, and finally lent the young man a pair of trunks and took him out for a swim in the ocean. At the same time, as a guest of Judge Kenny's next door neighbors, the district attorney of Los Angeles, Mr. Buron Fitts, was also swimming. Kenny held his breath, but Mr. District Attorney didn't recognize the defendant his assistants had just failed to send to the gallows, and Curley Guy didn't recognize the D.A., so everybody splashed around and had a wonderful time.

While changing back into his clothes, Curley Guy made a last appeal to the Judge. Couldn't something be done to square off his American citizenship? After all, he had voted Democrat at the last election...

The comments of Judge Kenny at this admission that a citizen of the Commonwealth of Australia had voted in an American presidential election are not recorded. But the young man kept in touch with the judge through letters and postcards, even after he was deported. He popped up a few years later, as a fighter pilot for Haile Selassie in Abyssinia, against the far superior odds of Mussolini's air legions. He reported in again at the beginning of World War Two—he had a job ferrying Hudson bombers from the U.S.A. to Britain. On his fifth trip he got into trouble off Newfoundland, and had only time to radio back "Ditching, tanks all empty, cheerio" before he went down into the cold bitter waves of the North Atlantic—not a bad end for a true soldier of fortune, who actually did many of the things and had many of the adventures to which the late Captain Wanderwell pretended.

But most of the questions are still unanswered. Carlton Williams, now a graying veteran newspaperman and still on the staff of the *Times*, remembers the Wanderwell case perfectly. He has just now stated to me that in his opinion there was never any doubt about the murder at all; Curley Guy pulled the trigger and that was that, and besides, Wanderwell probably had it coming to him. Mr. Williams had said to me that nobody who had been with him and Lieutenant Filkas at the time of the arrest of Guy in the house on Blake Street could have had any possible doubt about his guilt, there were certain statements and admissions made then which indicated the truth. It may be so—even on the track of a front-page story, reporter Williams would not tamper with the truth as he saw it.

But it is also important to remember that a man may be an enemy of society in a small way and not in a big way. A man may have something to hide—when confronted with the police and the press—and yet not be guilty of the major crime of which he is accused. Curley Guy had been cutting corners all over the lot since he jumped ship—there were half a dozen possible charges against him. He knew that he had had a fracas with Wanderwell, that he was in the country illegally, and that he had been piloting DeLarm's plane on certain flights over the American-Mexican border . . . bearing cargo not to be officially scrutinized. He had a lot to cover up, if not a murder.

Anyway, Curley Guy is dead. When his plane crashed into the sea, the story of the murder on board the schooner *Carma* was effectively ended. Long before that, however, the fifteen Argonauts had left for home—most of them hitchhiking. But they had had their hour, their little crowded hour. One of them, Lord Edward Montagu, the noblest born of the little group, returned to England by invitation of the American immigration authorities, and he was heard of only a few years later when he was reportedly hauled into magistrate's court on the charge of trying to peddle American hot-dogs outside the gates of his father's palatial, 400-acre estate. Later, so I have heard, he came into the title and now is presumably sitting in the House of Lords and voting Conservative.

For some time after the trial the fair Aloha haunted the Hollywood casting offices, offering her talents and late husband's film *(River of Death)*; both commodities had a very limited appeal. After a few weeks she disappeared—perhaps she retired to that incredible French convent where only English is spoken. But it is certain that the newspapermen, the judge, lawyers, police and court attendants who came into contact with Aloha will long remember her tall icy loveliness.

As for the schooner *Carma*, a few weeks after the end of the Wanderwell trial she was officially condemned as hopelessly unseaworthy and was towed out to sea and sunk. Her secrets are now and for all time secure in Davy Jones's locker.

PATRICK QUENTIN

PATRICK QUENTIN was a pseudonym for the writing team of two Harvard-educated Englishmen, Hugh Wheeler and Richard Webb. And their "Puzzle" mysteries featuring dapper, ex-alcoholic theater producer Peter Deluth is one of the most evocative series of the late 1930s to early 1940s. It was by no means hard-boiled, and it wasn't just a collection of isolated novels; Deluth's character truly developed over the course of six novels—by turns tragically and comically. Quentin seemed to delight in bringing to life the dark side of otherwise lighthearted characters. This is especially true in the first of the Deluth novels, *Puzzle for Fools* (1936), set in a small but exclusive sanitarium for the drunk and the deranged. Darker still are the Quentin novels Hugh Wheeler published after the death of his collaborator, beginning in the early 1950s. Judging from reprints, Quentin's later writings attracted a smaller readership. If you can find them, two are quite good: *The Man with Two Wives* (Dell, 1955) and *The Black Widow*, which Nunnally Johnson adapted for the screen in 1954. Reprinted here for the first time in more than forty years is "The Last of Mrs. Maybrick." A masterfully written story which appeared while the partnership was still going strong, Quentin leaves little doubt with whom his sympathies lie.

The Last of Mrs. Maybrick

On October 23, 1941, in a small, woodland shack between Gaylordsville and South Kent, Connecticut, a little old woman died. It was the lonely, inconspicuous death of an obscure eighty-year-old recluse, and her body might have lain undiscovered had it not been for a kindly neighbor whose habit it was to supply her with the milk that she needed to feed her innumerable cats.

The neighbor, peering through the fly-spotted window pane, saw the crumpled little body lying dead amidst the filth and disarray with which, in life, she had chosen to surround herself. A cat or two, perhaps, nosing at one of the many grimy, milkless saucers, might have felt that life had changed for the worse. There was nothing or no one else to mourn the passing of this forlorn and eccentric character whom Gaylordsville and South Kent had known as Mrs. Florence Chandler.

"Mrs. Chandler," after a residence of twenty years, had become a familiar if somewhat shy figure in those parts, especially on the campus of the South Kent School where she was often seen, a dowdy, meagre little figure with a face wrinkled as a walnut, carrying over her spare shoulder a gunny sack stuffed with newspapers salvaged from academic ash cans. These newspapers comprised almost her only form of reading matter. Once she had written a book herself, but that was long ago and South Kent School knew nothing of her as a woman of letters. Now, too poor to buy books, she was too proud to borrow them. As intellectual nourishment for her, therefore, there was nothing but old copies of *The New York Times* and an occasional *Bridgeport Sunday Post*.

"Mrs. Chandler's" gunny sack served another less literary purpose. On outgoing journeys it would often be filled with indeterminate scraps of food which were dumped at strategic points, usually on the school campus, for the delectation of the neighborhood cats. "Mrs. Chandler" had definite views on the care of cats. It was her belief that the summer folk went junketing off with the first fall of autumn leaves, leaving their cats to starve. Hence the amateur filling stations for orphaned pets.

This humanitarian impulse of "Mrs. Chandler's" was, on the whole, detrimental to the high seriousness of the South Kent students and a headache to certain members of the staff.

Headache! The word is pregnant. For when the kind neighbor discovered the pathetic body of "Mrs. Chandler" in the desolate New England shack, he had no idea that he was looking at all that remained of one of the world's greatest headaches. That tiny, dishevelled creature had, in her day, caused more headaches possibly than any woman since Helen of Troy. She had been a headache to several American Presidents; to Secretaries of State; to their wives; to many famous journalists; and to a vast army of organized American women. She had been more than a headache to one celebrated English judge, in that she is reputed to have pushed him off the teetering brink of his sanity. Indeed, she had been a fifteen-year migraine to no less august a personage than the Queen-Empress Victoria.

And the name of that headache was Mrs. Florence Maybrick.

Mrs. Maybrick. To those in their carefree twenties, the name may ring a distant bell. To those in their thirties, it may conjure up dim memories of a murderess, an adulteress—or something interesting. To those over forty-five, Mrs. Maybrick will be remembered for what she actually was—an international incident.

She was born Florence Chandler in Mobile, Alabama, in 1862, and came from what is usually referred to as "good American stock," boasting among her forbears, direct and collateral, a Secretary of the Treasury, a Chief Justice, a bishop and two Episcopal rectors, co-authors of a work entitled: "Why We Believe the Bible." As an appendix to this illustrious list of ancestors, her mother had married, a second time, the Baron Adolph von Roques, a distinguished German officer of the Eighth Cuirassier Regiment. Little Florence was educated, partly in America, partly abroad, by a succession of the most impeccable "masters and governesses." Nothing had been overlooked that might insure for her a cultivated and ladylike future.

As it happened, however, these fair beginnings did not help her much, for, from an early period, Florence Chandler was dogged by bad luck. At the age of eighteen, when the other Mobile maidens of her generation were fluttering toward good clean American romance, it is reliably reported that Florence, during a rough Atlantic crossing, stumbled on the sundeck of the liner carrying her to Europe. She stumbled and fell—literally and catastrophically—into the arms of a Cad, an English cad, at that. And, after all, the English invented the word.

The Cad was James Maybrick; he was old enough to be her father; and he married her. Probably it was the least caddish thing he ever did. But it was an ill day for Florence.

The April-October romantics lived for a while in Norfolk, Virginia. But Florence's dark angel soon put a stop to that and, through difficulties concerning James Maybrick's business, shuttled them off to a suburb of Liverpool, England, a city where almost anything unpleasant is liable to happen.

The unpleasantness soon set in. James, reverting to caddishness, started going merrily to hell with the belles and race horses of Liverpool. And Florence, a young mother though still quite "unawakened," started herself to toy with the idea of the Primrose Path or, as the Victorians called it, "going her own way." It is even reported that she went her own way into a London hotel bedroom with an anonymous gentleman, but at this far date it would be rancorous to cast stones—particularly when one remembers James.

For James was going from bad to worse and from worse to worst. Eventually he reached a peak of Victorian depravity from which there was no going back and little going forward. He took to drugs. Not exclusively, however, to the conventional cocaine or the hackneyed hashish. James was too exotic for that. He favored the heavy metals. And his pet pick-me-up was arsenic. With increasing frequency he began to patronize the Liverpool chemist shop of a Mr. James Heaton where he would replenish his stock of *liquor arsenicalis*—an arsenic solution which he imbibed sometimes as often as five times a day. He found it just the thing for that morning-after queasiness.

Oddly enough, while Mr. Maybrick was guzzling arsenic to repair the ravages of his dissipations, Florence had decided that arsenic was just what she needed as a skin lotion to repair the facial ravages caused by her unhappy married life. To obtain this unusual cosmetic, she is reputed to have soaked arsenic out of flypapers (the old-fashioned sort), a rather messy procedure at which she was unfortunately observed by one of the maids, a certain Alice Yapp, who eventually became as loquacious on the subject as her name might indicate. Why Mrs. Maybrick needed to endure the sufferings of soaking flypapers *pour être belle* (to make herself beautiful) is a mystery since, at a later date, enough professionally prepared arsenic was found in the house to poison a whole Panzer Division.

The Maybricks were distinctly an arsenic-conscious family.

In May, 1889, James, a gay dog to the end, went to the Wirrall Races, got wet and returned home next morning feeling very sick to the stomach. For religious reasons and for the sake of the two young children, the Maybricks had manfully tried to gloss over the shortcomings of their marriage and were still living in technical harmony. James was put to bed, visited by a doctor and, in due course, provided with a day nurse and a night nurse, Nurse Gore and Nurse Callery. Florence, however, guided by a stern sense of duty, was not willing to leave her ailing husband to the care of strangers. She herself was a frequent visitor to the sick room. According to the nurses, she was too frequent a visitor. While

James went on feeling sicker and sicker to the stomach, she would try to tempt him with little delicacies of her own contriving, much to the disgust of the dietetic Nurse Callery. Also she developed a nervous habit of shuffling bottles and medicaments around on the patient's bedtable. Her sick room manner was later described as "both suspicious and surreptitious." And she does seem to have behaved in a rather silly fashion. One of the silliest things she seemed to have done was to bring together a bottle of Valentine's Meat Juice and a punch of some white powder, believed by many to have been arsenic.

It is hardly startling that, in spite of the ministration of Nurse Gore and Nurse Callery, in spite of his wife's tender solitude, James Maybrick did not improve. On May 11, 1889, he finally passed away.

Since he had shown symptoms suggesting irritant poisoning, officious busybodies insisted upon an autopsy, and arsenic was found—not surprisingly, perhaps—in his body. Actually, the amount discovered was merely one tenth of a grain, a dose not sufficient to kill a normal respectable citizen, let alone James. But people feeling the way they do about arsenic in stomachs, Mrs. Maybrick was arrested and charged with the murder of her husband. Immediately all the silly things she had done around the bedside came to light. Alice Yapp remembered the flypapers. And, before long, the anonymous gentleman and the London hotel bedrooms were dusted off too.

To make matters worse—a sorry fact due perhaps less to bad luck than bad management—Mrs. Maybrick began to discover that nobody liked her. Her husband's two brothers had never been able to abide her. Now they acted in a most highhanded and spiteful manner, whisking off her children and branding her even before she was accused. Also, Alice Yapp, her fellow servant, Mrs. Briggs, Nurse Gore and Nurse Callery showed the most unfriendly symptoms. They had nothing to say in Mrs. Maybrick's favor and seemed to take savage delight in bringing out evidence to her discredit.

Later, when she was brought to trial, the English public didn't like her either. There was something about her.

Perhaps her American blood had a little to do with it. In the Golden Jubilee years of Victoria, American women were frowned upon in England. Perhaps they dressed better, looked smarter and managed to be more amusing than their stolider English sisters. Even the most impeccable Victorian male was not above rolling an appreciative eye at them, so long

as they stayed out of trouble. But once they were in the soup, the men
were as ready as the women to trace the scarlet A blazing forth beneath
the chic American camisoles.

As if this weren't bad luck enough, Mrs. Maybrick had bad luck with
her jury and terrible luck with one aspect of her defense.

The jury, consisting mostly of simple-natured men, were not the type
accustomed to think for themselves on nice points of law. Their profes-
sions, perhaps, speak for them. There were three plumbers (three of
them!), two farmers, one miller, one wood-turner, one provision dealer,
one grocer, one iron-monger, one house-painter, and one baker.

In preparing her defense against this literal-minded group of her peers,
Mrs. Maybrick was advised not to bring forward any evidence as to the
true character, the immortality, the dissipation, the general caddishness
of her husband. Sentimentalists have held this as a virtue in Florence
Maybrick that she adhered so rigidly to the principles of *de mortuis nil nisi
bonum* (say nothing bad about the dead). Actually, it was the smart, but
not smart enough, idea of her solicitors that the less James was discredited,
the less apparent motive there would seem for his wife's having wanted to
murder him.

In consequence of this blunder in psychology, Mrs. Maybrick faced
trial as an American hussy who had mistreated and deceived a perfectly
good English husband, a man, as far as the jury knew, without a blemish
on his character. To add to her troubles, her star witness, Mr. James
Heaton, the chemist from whom Mr. Maybrick had so constantly purchased his swig of *liquor arsenicalis*, was so sick when he came to court
that his vital evidence was all but inaudible. Even the brilliant rhetoric of
her attorney, Charles Russell, later Lord Chief Justice Russell, could not
soar above these obstacles.

And, as a final disaster, Mrs. Maybrick was not merely facing trial, she
was facing Mr. Justice Stephen on the bench. In the light of his future
career, which ended one year later in the madhouse, Mr. Justice Stephen
was a little more than even the most callous of murderesses deserved.
This one illustrious personage was already losing grip on his sanity before
the trial started; all he needed to complete the process was Florence
Maybrick. From the beginning he liked her no better than anyone else
had. As the trial limped along with no one exactly knowing who did what,
his dislike for her swelled within him until it reached almost psychopathic
proportions. This manifested itself finally, in his summing up, as a

two-day harangue of impassioned malignity and misogyny. In one of the most biased speeches ever to come from the English bench, he referred to poor Mrs. Maybrick as "that horrible woman" and branded her as the epitome of all that was vile. Startling even the prosecution, he vindictively maneuvered the Valentine's Meat Juice and a certain bottle of glycerine around until he left no loophole for the unlucky woman's innocence.

As obedient Britons, the jury did not hesitate in following the guidance of a Social Superior. As a man, the three plumbers, the two farmers, the milliner, the wood-turner, the grocer, the iron-monger, the house-painter and the baker brought in a verdict of guilty. Judge Stephen—with a certain rather lunatic satisfaction, perhaps?—donned the black cap and pronounced that Florence Maybrick should be hanged by the neck until she was dead.

A short time later he was himself pronounced insane.

The verdict, coming after a trial in which nothing semed to have been proved one way or the other, staggered England. It staggered the world. In a few weeks hundreds of thousands of people had signed petitions for Mrs. Maybrick's reprieve. Public opinion, in the face of what seemed like gross injustice, swung round to her side. Florence was popular at last.

For two or three weeks she lived (to use her own ill phrase) "in the shadow of the gallows." Finally, a little intimidated perhaps by the general clamor, Mr. Matthews, the Home Secretary—for there was no Supreme Court of Criminal Appeal at that time—retired the case in camera and commuted Mrs. Maybrick's sentence to one of penal servitude for life. His reasons for this clemency were that:

> "inasmuch as, although the evidence leads to the conclusion that the prisoner administered and attempted to administer arsenic to her husband with intent to murder him, yet it does not wholly exclude a reasonable doubt whether his (James Maybrick's) death was in fact caused by the administration of arsenic."

In other words, Mr. Matthews was of the opinion that Mrs. Maybrick had been guilty of attempting to kill her husband with arsenic although it wasn't certain that he had died from arsenical poisoning. This charge was something Mrs. Maybrick had not even been tried for during a court procedure at which nothing had been proved beyond the fact that James was dead—a sad eventuality which had been common knowledge before ever the slow-moving wheels of the law had got under way. If that wasn't bad luck—what is?

Whether or not Mrs. Maybrick was guilty, and how much, is no longer calculable. That she was grievously wronged is beyond doubt. The English bench has never been noted for its chivalry or its leniency toward women accused of murder, particularly where there is also a whiff of adultery. Mrs. Thompson, of the haunting love letters, and other sisters in misfortune reached the gallows as adulteresses rather than murderesses. Mrs. Rattenbury alone, that poor darling with her fatal attachment to the boy chauffeur, had a fair deal in this respect. But prudish public opinion soon snuffed her out as efficiently as the hangman's rope.

If Mrs. Maybrick learned one thing from her dismal experience, it was that virtue pays dividends when a lady happens to get mixed up in an English murder trial.

That London hotel bedroom turned out to be very expensive.

Mrs. Maybrick proceeded from one squalid penal institution to another, suffering all the hardships of an habitual and vicious criminal. But though her memory had been rinsed off the disdainful hands of British justice, she was not forgotten. Soon a tornado broke from the other side of the Atlantic. American Woman was just beginning to realize herself as a Cosmic Force in 1890. And American public opinion was beginning to mean something.

Petitions thick as fleas started to pester various, successive Home Secretaries. In England, Lord Russell himself was active on her behalf, stalwartly proclaiming her innocence. From his side, Presidents, ambassadors and their wives, notables in all walks of life signed formidable statements, one of which, penned by no less a figure than the Honorable James G. Blaine, is worthy of quotation since, with magnificent daring, it snatches the garland of "snobisme" from its traditional resting place on the coroneted British head and hurls it back like a boomerang across the Atlantic. Mrs. Maybrick, writes James G. Blaine, was guilty of no crime other than that

> "she may have been influenced by the foolish ambition of too many American girls for a foreign marriage, and have descended from her own rank to that of her husband's family, which seems to have been somewhat vulgar. . . ."

This blast at the Maybricks' social position was paralleled in the *North American Review* by the famous American newspaperwoman "Gail Hamilton" who addressed an open letter to Queen Victoria protesting Mrs. Maybrick's innocence, inveighing against her unfair treatment and begging for her release. But Gail Hamilton and the Honorable James G. Blaine received like treatment. The Queen was neither amused nor interested. Finally, however, one Home Secretary, Lord Salisbury, goaded beyond endurance by these transatlantic stabs at British justice, parried with a nettled and emphatic statement which might have been penned by the Queen herself. It read in part:

> "Taking the most lenient view... the case of this convict was that of an adulteress attempting to poison her husband under the most cruel circumstances while she was pretending to be nursing him on his sickbed. The Secretary of State regrets that he has been unable to find any grounds for recommending to the Queen any further act of clemency towards the prisoner..."

The women of America continued their losing battle with the stubborn little women who ruled England. Mrs. Maybrick's mother, the Baroness de Roques, is reputed to have spent a fortune in an attempt to have her daughter freed.

All to no purpose, however, Florence served out her sentence, penal servitude for life usually being taken to mean twenty years with three months off a year for good behavior.

She was finally released in July, 1904. On August 23, shaking the dust of England off her skirts forever, she arrived in New York.

Life held little for her. Both her children, whom she had not seen since the day of her husband's death, had died themselves. Her mother died penniless shortly afterwards. In sore need of money Florence Maybrick wrote a book, *Mrs. Maybrick's Own Story*, published by Funk and Wagnalls in 1905. In this she sang a dismal ballad of atrocities in English gaols and amassed formidable evidence of her own innocence. It is a lugubrious work, filled with lamentable clichés and poignantly trying to arouse interest in something which once had been a headache but was now only a bore. People read it for its possible sensationalism. They were no longer interested in Mrs. Maybrick's misfortunes per se. For a while she tried to lecture, largely about conditions in English prisons, but it did not go so well. After a while she began to realize (as Lizzie Borden, settled with her squirrels at "Maplecroft," had already realized for many years) that people do not take kindly to women who have faced a capital charge, even if they have been shockingly wronged.

Poor Florence. They were back not liking her again.

For several years, in Florida and Highland Park, Illinois, she stubbornly retained her married and now infamous name. But about twenty years before her death, she gave up an unequal struggle. Destroying all records of her past and reverting to her maiden name of Florence Chandler, she withdrew to a life of virtual solitude in the tiny three-room shack she had built for herself in the Berkshire foothills.

There, unknown to her neighbors, she lived on, accepted by the community and, with the years, acquiring from successive generations of South Kent boys the harmless nicknames of "Lady Florence" and "The Cat Woman."

South Kent and Gaylordsville have none but kindly memories of her. There were rumors, at times, of course, as there must be about any lonely little old lady who lives a secluded life, rumors that someone had left her a vast fortune; that a lawyer in a limousine with a liveried chauffeur appeared at regular intervals to bring her checks. But these were rumors without malice and, unhappily, without foundation in fact, for she died penniless save for an old-age pension finally wooed out of the government.

South Kent and Gaylordsville remember her as the little scurrying woman with the walnut face, the gunny sack and one loyal and indestructible brown straw hat. To them, she was eccentric, yes. It was eccentric in her that she would let no one enter her house; that, at night, there was always a single light twinkling from her window till morning—to exorcise what demons?—and that with age she had let slip in her squalid little home the niceties of hygiene. But to her neighbors, Mrs. Chandler's eccentricities bore no sinister stamp. It was cute rather than grotesque when, fighting against the loss of one of her few remaining teeth, she tied it to its nearest partner with a piece of string. She did no harm, except perhaps to leave a little too many scraps in the wrong places for the campus cats. The South Kent boys liked her.

And they knew, until the day she died, that the woman they were liking was that most magnificently unliked of women—Mrs. Florence Maybrick.

Which leads to the only really comforting feature of this long and uncomfortable life. There in the little villages of South Kent and Gaylordsville, Mrs. Florence Maybrick found good luck at last—good luck of so sensational a nature that in a way perhaps it neutralized all the tough breaks she had endured earlier.

Mrs. Maybrick was able to spend the last twenty years of her life unpersecuted. And yet, had things gone other than the way they did, this lengthy stretch of tranquility might never have been granted her.

Shortly after her arrival, a neighbor, a Mrs. Austin, was kind to Mrs. Maybrick and, to show her gratitude, Mrs. Maybrick gave her a dress which was trimmed with really good lace. It was undoubtedly the dress in the famous "wedding" photograph and to the cynical will perhaps give further proof that there is a real affinity between old lace and arsenic.

When Mrs. Austin shook the padding which stuffed the shoulders of this dress, there dropped out a cleaner's card reading: Mrs. Florence Maybrick, Highland Park, Ill. The name struck a chord in Mrs. Austin's memory. She consulted a sister who in turn consulted a female probation officer in the district. Before long these three women and the two married ladies' husbands knew all the unhappy tale of Mrs. Florence Maybrick. A family council was called; the evidence was weighed; and it was decided that she had suffered more than enough already. The Austins and their in-laws thereupon made a vow never to show by word or hint that they knew the real identity of the new arrival.

And so, from the start, "Mrs. Chandler's" future was in the hands of this small group of people. Miraculously, those people kept their vows for twenty years. Never once, at church socials, at whist drives or quilting parties or at the grocery store, did one of those three ladies succumb to the almost irresistible temptation of launching the juiciest piece of gossip in ten counties.

This was the astounding piece of good luck which came at last and enabled Mrs. Maybrick to reach the grave, unwept, perhaps, unhonored, but at least—unstoned.

On Sunday, October 25, 1941, "Mrs. Chandler" was soberly buried on the South Kent Campus. It had been her own request. Five of the students, boys of "good stock"—shades of Florence's own beginnings! —were her pallbearers. These boys, whom a local newspaper with misprinted enthusiasm termed "Socialists from the swank South Kent

School," carried her to her last resting place. And there, as if a final hand from the grave beckoned her back to respectability, her coffin lies next to that of Miss Doylan, an old friend and beloved South Kent Housemother.

R.I.P. Mrs. Florence Chandler Maybrick.

And good luck to you—wherever you are!

CRAIG RICE

For CRAIG RICE, humor and homicide always went hand in hand. The first woman to write hard-boiled crime fiction, her books read like documents from the edge where one has to "laugh, scream, or go crazy." All her novels, but especially those featuring her finest creation, John J. Malone, a cigar-chomping, hard-drinking, bet-making, womanizing attorney, are marked by wild, over-the-top improbabilities of plot and morbid slapstick humor—or as her one-time collaborator Stuart Palmer put it, "gimmicks, gadgets and slants." They were farces, and it is for this reason some critics have dismissed them as "hollow." What they've failed to realize is that mockery of the tough-guy clichés she inherited from Hammett and Co. may have been precisely her aim all along. A versatile writer (Rice worked as newspaper sob sister and radio and movie writer before turning to mystery fiction), Rice also published numerous true crime writings, the bulk of which are collected in her 1952 paperback, *45 Murders*. This story, however, a look back at Rice's days as a radio mystery writer, is about the peculiar goings-on in a gloomy old mansion, and it appeared in a collection of stories about great Chicago murders.

Murder in Chicago

"The long arm of coincidence bends a lot of elbows—"
—*John J. Malone*

It was November, 1933. I was working for a radio station, and among my many and various chores was the writing of a thrice-weekly, half-hour mystery drama. Late on Monday night, November 20th, I had been sitting at the typewriter beating my brains out for an idea. Towards morning, I came up with one—having a beautiful young woman found murdered on an operating table.

Tuesday morning I turned the script over to the stenographic department, and promptly forgot all about it.

Wednesday morning the producer called me into his office. He handed me the morning paper and said, "Are you psychic, or do little birds tell you these things?"

I looked at the paper. The body of beautiful, red-haired Rheta Wynekoop had been found on an operating table in the basement surgery of her mother-in-law's home.

The newspapers, of course, didn't put it quite so bluntly. Adjectives described the victim: "Talented young violinist"—the mother-in-law: "Dr. Alice Wynekoop, prominent Chicago physician and clubwoman"—and the house: "a gloomy old mansion on West Monroe Street..."

The story of Rheta Wynekoop's murder was a sensational one from the beginning. Elderly Dr. Alice Wynekoop was a prominent Chicago physician, clubwoman and social service worker. Rheta was a young, beautiful, red-haired and talented violinist. Her husband—Dr. Alice's son—was a handsome young Lothario who had never been able to earn enough to support his wife. Dr. Alice's daughter, Dr. Catherine Wynekoop, was a highly respected member of the staff at Cook County Hospital.

Those circumstances alone would have been enough to make the story an exciting one. But there were plenty of other details to make it dramatic from its very beginning. Rheta Wynekoop had been found face down on an operating table in Dr. Wynekoop's basement surgery, wrapped in a heavy blanket, shot through the breast. On the table, near her head, lay a revolver covered with a cloth. There were chloroform burns on Rheta's face. On the floor, at the foot of the operating table, lay Rheta's clothing.

Even before the really dramatic and fantastic details were known, it was obvious that the newspapers had hit the jackpot. Then, through the weeks that followed, while the story and speculation ran wild, little by little the history of the gloomy old mansion on Monroe Street became known. Gloomy old mansion! Let's go back, just a bit—

*　　*　　*

About noon, on a warm Chicago summer day in the year 1904, a new and happy little family arrived to take up residence at 3406 West Monroe Street, Chicago, Illinois. They were moving into a house which had just been completed, and whose construction they had watched with loving interest. Dr. and Mrs. (also Dr.) Wynekoop were bringing two baby sons into this new home.

During the first few years that followed, one of the baby sons was taken by death—but in recompense another son and a daughter were added to the household. Later on, another daughter was added, by adoption.

There must have followed days and months and years of childish prattle and laughter. Picture books. Mud pies with the usual resulting smudgy faces and hands to be washed many times a day. And playmates—yes, there must have been playmates to add to the houseful of children at 3406 West Monroe Street. Then came school days, with the young Wynekoops trudging off every morning, happily filled with tasty and nourishing breakfasts, carrying well-stocked lunch pails—and a new little one to start in the "Baby Grade" every year or so for quite a time.

Alice Wynekoop's children gave her many happy years. Walker, the eldest, became a respected businessman in a Chicago suburb; married and had two children of his own. Catherine, the youngest of Dr. Alice's own brood, studied medicine, eventually taking up surgery.

Of the adopted child, Mary Louise, who died young, we know little.

Although Earle was older in years than his sister Catherine, he seemed to be the baby of the family. Imagine him a not-too-well little boy, handsome, but just a bit on the whiney side—and demanding his own way in everything; adoring his mother, who saw to it that he was always given his way.

During the years when she was bringing up her children Dr. Alice Wynekoop was also practicing medicine, along with her husband, Dr. Frank Wynekoop. He died, however, before the job of raising all the children had been finished.

Dr. Alice carried on with her practice. She joined clubs—The Women's City Club, and others; she did charity work, most of it for children, in hospitals and clinics. She founded a sorority for the purpose of aiding women medical students in need of financial assistance. She maintained her office in her home, in a basement suite built for that purpose, accessible from West Monroe Street.

It was while Catherine was just finishing her medical training and after Walker had married and settled in Wilmette, Illinois, that Earle met

Rheta Gardner, on a visit to Indianapolis, Indiana, where she was one of the entertainers at a concert. After his return to Chicago, he started a correspondence with her.

Scarcely a year later, Earle persuaded Rheta to come to Chicago, and asked her to marry him. In spite of the fact that Rheta was eighteen years old, Dr. Alice, Earle's mother, insisted that the young couple obtain the consent of Rheta's father (Burdine H. Gardner, an Indianapolis flour and salt merchant). It was given, somewhat grudgingly, and Mr. Gardner even attended the wedding.

The marriage of the two very young people was the occasion for a family party. But Rheta refused to spend her wedding night in the old mansion on Monroe Street. After a night in a hotel the young couple left for a honeymoon.

It must be remembered that Earle was not earning his own living and certainly was unable to support a wife. The only solution was for Earle and Rheta to live with Dr. Alice in the house which she and her husband had built more than twenty-five years before. During the honeymoon therefore, Dr. Alice redecorated and refurnished a suite of rooms on the second floor to be ready for the young newlyweds.

Perhaps at this point, we'd better pause and try to picture the house at 3406 West Monroe Street. It shouldn't be too difficult to imagine it, since there are many like it still standing in Chicago, good substantial stone houses. Three stories, an English basement and a flight of stairs leading up to the first floor. Inside a lot of fine, expensive—and probably dusty—millwork, thick heavy doors and costly hardware, antiquated and inconvenient lighting fixtures which had once been the pride of the family, leaky faucets, slow drains and clawfooted bathtubs.

How about the people who lived in the house? There was, of course, Dr. Alice who was (a) a benevolent, warm-hearted and unfortunate woman, (b) an eccentric and peculiar character, or (c) a ruthless woman, who would murder her helpless daughter-in-law for a small life insurance policy—depending on which interpretation of her behavior you read. There was a daughter, Dr. Catherine Wynekoop, at that time not yet a full-fledged doctor. There was Mary Louise, the adopted daughter, a shadowy little figure—it is difficult to imagine even what she looked like. A Miss Catherine Porter—a woman of about Dr. Alice's age—was rooming there and being treated by Dr. Alice for cancer and heart disease. She shared a two-thousand-dollar bank account with her doctor and devoted friend. There was also Miss Enid Hennessey, a middle-aged school teacher and her aged father. Of Miss Hennessey, more later.

From every indication it appears that Rheta was not a happy bride. And the events following her marriage were hardly reassuring ones. Miss Porter died. Mary Louise died. Miss Hennessey's father died. Dr. Catherine left the household to become a resident physician at Cook County Hospital.

But worst of all, Earle was away from home most of the time. Later it was learned that he was interested in other women and that when, in the summer of 1933, he finally found a job at the Chicago World's Fair, his drinking and the friends he made were of great concern, also, to his unhappy young wife.

For Rheta was unhappy. What wonder—a young wife, practically deserted by her handsome husband, and left to the companionship of a devoted but aging mother-in-law and a middle-aged school teacher. Their conversations must have been highly educational, but very dull for young Rheta. She was given to introspection. Her mother had been confined in an insane asylum when Rheta was only seven years old, and had finally died there, some ten years later, of tuberculosis. It was this not very pretty picture which must have led Rheta to fear that she, too, had tuberculosis, and to instill into her mind the dread of many other diseases.

Rheta must have been afraid of a lot of things. Loss of her young husband's love. A lifetime spent in the old mansion on Monroe Street. Illness. Even insanity. But she couldn't have been afraid of murder, because according to the evidence, she was killed by someone in whom she had implicit trust.

At about ten P.M. on the evening of November 21st, Arthur R. March, a police officer in charge of Squad Car 15, received a radio call directing his car to go to 3406 West Monroe Street.

"We went directly there and were met at the front door by a lady who told us to come inside . . . The lady we met first we later found to be Miss Enid Hennessey, a school teacher and a roomer there. When we got inside we met the defendant, Dr. Wynekoop. She was seated in a chair in the library. Mr. Ahearn, an undertaker, was there. We asked the defendant what happened. She said, 'Something terrible has happened; come on downstairs and I will show you.' We went downstairs.

"When we got down, the basement was lighted and there was a light inside the operating room. Mr. Ahearn, myself, Officer Walter Kelly, Officer Wm. Tyrrell and I believe Miss Hennessey came with us. In the operating room we observed the body of the girl lying on an operating table."

The printed transcript of any evidence makes the scene of a crime seem like a rather calm and quiet place. In this one the sensitive and melancholy Rheta Wynekoop becomes, impersonally, "the body" or "the deceased." In it Dr. Alice Wynekoop, who may have been a financial conniver, a family dictator and a cold-blooded murderess—or a sick, bewildered and frightfully distressed old woman—becomes just as impersonally "the defendant."

All calm, all routine, all official. But can your imagination reconstruct the scene? Dr. Alice Wynekoop must have been terrified and possibly hysterical. The school teacher, Miss Enid Hennessey, must have been— well, at least a little nervous.

And a house where a murder has been committed tends to be full of people, most of them policemen. Sooner or later it's full of reporters.

Probably every light in the house was turned on. As for the policemen— well, let's try to estimate from Officer March's testimony:

"Officers Walter Kelly, myself and Officer Wm. Tyrrell were the first squad there. Lieutenant Peterson came in about five minutes after. A great many police officers came in. The coroner's office was there and another squad. There were maybe four or five other policemen there that night. Five or six minutes after about two squads came."

There must have been a crowd outside the house, too. That many policemen can't arrive in any neighborhood without attracting curious onlookers. There probably hadn't been that much excitement on West Monroe Street since the Chicago fire.

Later, at the trial, Dr. Catherine testified that her mother, Dr. Alice, didn't sleep a wink after the police left. To which one can only add, "And no wonder!"

No arrest was made that night, though there was the customary long period of questioning and the necessary homicide squad procedure of photographing and fingerprinting. Dr. Alice advanced the theory that a burglar was responsible for the crime. She declared that there had been thefts of drugs and money from the house. But to Captain John Stege, the manner of Rheta's slaying didn't agree with the theory. Suicide was ruled out immediately by the angle of the shot and the chloroform burns on the girl's face.

There were a lot of things Captain Stege wanted to know—and the newspapers wanted to know the same things. For instance, where was Earle Wynekoop on the night of the murder and why was he away from home?

Presumably Earle was on his way to the Grand Canyon on a color photography job, accompanied by a friend named Stanley. But there were rumors that Earle had been in Chicago not more than a day before the crime.

At this point Earle became more interesting to the newspapers than Dr. Alice. He was a tall, handsome brunet. He was taken into custody—after his arrival by train from Kansas City—along with an attractive young girl, whom he had met while employed at the World's Fair. She had known him as Michael Wynekoop and he had told her that he was unmarried. She was released, however, and vanishes forever from the story.

Earle stated that he had started west for Arizona some time before his wife's murder. He was cooperative in the matter of newspaper interviews. He gave as his opinion that Rheta had been murdered by a moron. He added other and even more interesting details regarding his married life. The marriage, said Earle, was a failure. Rheta at one time had attempted to poison the family by putting iron filings and drugs in the food. She had tuberculosis, Earle added, according to the newspaper story, and was mentally deranged.

He boasted of having fifty girl friends listed in his date book.

In the meantime, while Earle was making wild and far from helpful statements to the press, Dr. Alice Wynekoop, aged sixty-three, frail, sensitive and with a serious heart condition, was being ruthlessly questioned for an almost uninterrupted period of twenty-four hours.

During those hours, there was other material for newspaper stories. So many people crowded around the "gloomy old mansion" on West Monroe Street that the police in charge asked for another squad to come and help keep order. Burdine Gardner, Rheta's father, came from Indianapolis, and, dramatically, took his daughter's body home for burial. He had a few statements to make to the press, regarding the mansion on Monroe

Street—(it was he who first described it as "gloomy and old-fashioned");
and regarding Dr. Alice—("She struck me as a most peculiar person").

Other things helped to enliven the daily papers. A lie-detector test on
Dr. Alice: unsuccessful because of the elderly woman's blood pressure
condition. An interview by Dr. Harry Hoffman of the Behavior Clinic in
one of the city's more sensational newspapers.

But the top story was Dr. Wynekoop's confession.

Earle Wynekoop was in custody by that time. There are varying reports
of what occurred before the confession was made. According to one, Dr.
Alice met Earle in the jail and he said to her, "For God's sake, Mother, if
you did this on account of the bond of love between us, go ahead and
confess." Dr. Alice then answered—grim-faced, according to the same
report—"But Earle, I did not kill Rheta." Earle, exhausted from a night
of grilling, sobbed, "Mother, Mother—" Fortunately, the newspaper
account breaks off at this point.

Just exactly how Dr. Wynekoop's statement was obtained is difficult to
imagine from either the newspaper stories or the transcript of the trial. It
is safe to assume, I think, that, guilty or not guilty, Dr. Wynekoop was
tired and worried beyond endurance at that time when it was made. It has
been said that Dr. Alice was told that Earle had confessed to the crime.

However, here is the way Captain John Stege described, at the trial,
the scene in the police station at about 10:30 on the morning of November
24, 1933.

"She was lying on the couch in Captain Duffy's office with an overcoat
over her. I said, 'Good morning, Doctor.' She said, 'Good morning,
Captain,' and I said, 'Did you have any breakfast?' She said, 'No, I don't
want any, but I would like some coffee.' I told Officer Donoghue to go out
and get her some coffee. Dr. Hoffman was in the room. She said to me,
'Captain, what would happen if I told the story about killing Rheta?' I
said, 'Doctor, I don't want any story from you. All I want is the truth.'"

No matter how the confession was obtained, it kept the papers happy
for another few hours. As introduced at her trial it read as follows:

"Rheta was concerned about her health and frequently weighed herself,
usually stripping for the purpose. On Tuesday, November 21, after
luncheon at about one, she decided to go down to the Loop to purchase
some sheet music that she had been wanting. She was given money for
this purpose and laid it on the table, deciding to weigh herself before
dressing to go downtown. I went to the office. She was sitting on the table

practically undressed and suggested that the pain in her side was troubling her more than usual. I remarked to her since it was a convenient interval . . . for an examination, we might just as well have it over. She complained of considerable soreness, severe pain and tenderness. She thought she would endure the examination better if she might have a little anesthetic. Chloroform was conveniently at hand, and a few drops were put on a sponge. She breathed it very deeply. She took several deep inhalations. I asked her if I was hurting her and she made no answer. Inspection revealed that respiration had stopped. Artificial respiration for about twenty minutes gave no response. Stethoscopic examination revealed no heart beat. Turning the patient quickly on her side and examining posteriorly as well as anteriorly, there was no sign of life. Wondering what method would ease the situation best to all and with the suggestion offered by the presence of a loaded revolver, further injury being impossible, with great difficulty one cartridge was exploded at a distance of some half dozen inches from the patient. The scene was so overwhelming that no action was possible for a period of several hours."

If Dr. Alice's confession was the truth, that last sentence is probably at least a close contender for the world championship of understatement.

In all good mystery stories a confession ends the case. In the case of Dr. Alice Wynekoop, the confession was hardly more than a beginning. The coroner's jury reconvened and recommended that Dr. Alice be held for murder, immediately. The jury did not believe the confession was the truth. The verdict of the coroner's inquest was that Rheta had died from gunshot wounds, hemorrhage and shock. And Assistant State's Attorney Charles S. Dougherty stated that he believed most of Dr. Alice's confession was false and that Earle should be charged as an accessory.

Earle helped out at this point with the statement that "the only part of his mother's confession that was true was that Rheta used to go downstairs frequently to weigh herself. That all the rest was a pack of lies told by his mother to save him because she thought he might be in danger."

Dr. Alice then stated that if Earle loved her he should keep his mouth shut. But the damage had been done.

Assistant State's Attorney Charles S. Dougherty made the statement that he believed Dr. Alice had made up her mind to murder Rheta when she had a secret meeting with Earle the Sunday night before the murder.

No one actually knows what was said at that meeting, nor likely ever will. Yet it must have been highly important and probably highly dramatic. For, after her return home, Dr. Alice wrote Earle a frantic note.

Sunday night—
Precious—

I'm choked—you are gone—you have called me up—and after 10 minutes or so, I called and called—no answer—maybe you are sleeping— you need to be—but I want to hear your voice again tonight—I would give anything I had—to spend an hour—in real talk with you—tonight— And I cannot—Goodnight.

Dr. Alice never mailed that note. Later (according to the testimony of Police Lieutenant Samuel Peterson) she explained that she wrote it when she was hysterical, and wanted to calm down before she sent it.

State's Attorney Dougherty, who also wanted to know why Dr. Alice had waited almost five hours after Rheta's death to call the police, a doctor, or anyone, felt he had a case.

As far as motives were concerned—

First there was the "other girl." Girl? Judging from Earle's now famous date book, with fifty girls listed, and his diary, kept in code, in which he listed their qualifications, physical and otherwise, she was only one of many. But Dougherty singled out one and declared that she was the only girl Earle had ever loved. Earle had given her a diamond ring, said to be the one he had previously given to Rheta as a pledge of their engagement. For religious reasons neither his family nor hers believed in divorce.

That was one motive. Dr. Alice had wanted to insure the happiness of her adored son, by ridding him of an unwanted wife. As clinchers, however, the State's attorney added two other motives. Dr. Alive was deeply in debt, and she had taken out insurance policies on Rheta's life. Finally, said the State's attorney, Dr. Alice wanted to get rid of a person she considered unfit to live.

Earle, at this point, made five obviously false confessions, culminating in a wild story of how he had slipped into the Wynekoop home on Tuesday afternoon, lain in waiting for his wife, seized her, thrown her on the operating table, killed her and fled by plane to Kansas City. He tried to re-enact the crime, but made so many mistakes that the entire story was discounted.

Finally it turned out that Earle's alibi was correct and there was not a doubt that he had been miles away at the time of the crime.

The Wynekoop case stayed very much in the headlines. On November 28th, Dr. Alice was seriously ill, with a bronchial cough and high blood pressure. From her bed in the prison hospital she repudiated her confession and denounced the police, declaring that she had confessed only after sixty hours of questioning, during which time she had no food save for one cup of coffee. Two days later she stated she did not think she would live to stand trial, and that was why she had made the confession.

Earle promptly announced that when he got out of jail, he would take up the investigation and prove his mother's innocence.

The trial was set for January, but in the meantime the Wynekoops kept in the public eye. On December 2nd, the Wynekoop family hired a private detective to solve the mystery. Apparently nothing ever came of his investigation.

Early in December Rheta's body was exhumed in Indianapolis, and the doctors announced there was no trace of chloroform.

On December 14th, Earle ran over a nine-year-old boy with his automobile, and his sister, Dr. Catherine, was with him at the time.

Dr. Alice's brother-in-law, Dr. Gilbert Wynekoop, was adjudged insane by a jury trying him for attacking a nurse, and was sent to St. Luke's hospital for the insane.

Neither of the last two items had anything to do with the murder of red-haired Rheta, of course, but they did help keep the newspaper readers from forgetting the Wynekoops.

By the time the trial opened, Chicago was in a state of high excitement. Dr. Alice, looking exceedingly frail, was carried into the courtroom. The jury was quickly chosen—good, solid citizens: a sporting-goods sales manager, a bookkeeper, a streetcar motorman, a mechanic, a photo engraver, and so on.

The avid audience which had been waiting all these weeks for the Wynekoop trial was not disappointed. It was a highly dramatic show. Policeman March gave his testimony. During it, while the People's exhibits were being identified and arranged by the witness in the manner he first saw them on the night of Rheta's death—the operating table, pillow, blanket, thirty-two calibre, Smith & Wesson revolver, blood-stained sheets and pillow case—Dr. Alice collapsed. Then for a time the public was as interested in "Will Dr. Alice Wynekoop live?" as in "Is Dr.

Alice Wynekoop guilty?" When—according to one newspaper—she was so weak that she could not hold up her head, she protested a postponement, declaring that she wanted her name cleared before she died.

However, there was a postponement, and in the latter part of February, Officer March picked up where he had been interrupted. The rest of the People's exhibits were identified and admitted.

This first scene of the first act of a murder trial is usually fairly routine, standard stuff and Officer March's testimony does not appear to have been otherwise. But he was followed by a witness who is one of the most fascinating figures in the case, Miss Enid Hennessey. Fascinating, because in spite of the newspaper clippings and the transcript of the trial, she remains a shadowy, undefined figure, although she played one of the principal roles. It is hard even to imagine how she looked, acted, spoke and thought.

At the trial, she told, in considerable detail, her version of what happened in the Wynekoop mansion on the day of Rheta's murder.

"On November 21, 1933, I probably arose at about a quarter to seven.

"I had breakfast in the house with Dr. Wynekoop. I don't remember whether Rheta had breakfast with us or not. I don't remember whether I talked to her that morning. I left the house about eight o'clock and went to the Marshall High School. I completed my teaching duties and signed out about three-fifteen. I went to the Loop. I remained there until a little after five and went home. I got to 3406 West Monroe Street just about six o'clock or a little after. When I came into the house I saw the defendant in the kitchen.

"The defendant and I were very good friends. When I came in Dr. Wynekoop put on pork chops to fry and when they were ready we had dinner. I guess it was a little after six. Rheta was not there. She had gone downtown to get some music.

"When we sat down at the table we talked about Rheta. At the end of the meal Dr. Wynekoop went to the telephone; she was worried about Rheta. She had told me that if Rheta saw some moving picture that she liked, she would stay and see it. She said that she had left the house before Rheta did. I think she said she left the house about two-thirty or three.

"I had noticed Rheta's coat and hat on the table in the library and remarked about it. I said, 'Here is Rheta's coat and hat,' and Dr. Wynekoop answered, 'She probably wore her good coat and hat to the

Loop.' I talked with Dr. Wynekoop after dinner. She had asked me to go to the drug store to have a prescription refilled and to get her some tablets.

"The drug store is situated at Madison and Kedzic avenues. That store did not have as many tablets as she wanted so I stopped at the drug store at Homan and Madison and got a full bottle. After I completed my purchase I went back home. I arrived home about a quarter after seven, I should judge; perhaps half past. I sat down in the library with Dr. Wynekoop and we talked for about an hour.

"We discussed at least two books while sitting in the library. One was *Strange Interlude* and the other was *The Forsythe Saga*. I don't know the author of *Strange Interlude*; I am not familiar with it. I had procured a copy of it from the public library for her. I haven't ever read it.

"During the course of our conversation we discussed my hyperacidity. She said she had something in the office that she thought I could use. . . . The glass case where she kept the drugs was inside the operating room. She never got the medicine for me."

Dr. Wynekoop never got the medicine for Miss Hennessey, because the body of Rheta Wynekoop was lying face down on the operating table in the basement surgery, covered with a blanket, her clothing lying about on the floor, a blood-stained towel at her mouth and a pistol near her head.

Now here rises an interesting situation. According to Dr. Alice's confession, Rheta's murder took place sometime early in the afternoon on that tragic Tuesday in November. These are her words—remember them?—"The scene was so overwhelming that no action was possible for a period of several hours."

Yet, according to Miss Enid Hennessey's testimony, here we have Dr. Alice preparing dinner shortly after six, apparently in normal health and spirits. A good substantial dinner, of pork chops, cabbage, potatoes, a salad, peaches and cookies. A place was set at the table for Rheta. Later in the evening there was an undoubtedly leisurely discussion of *Strange Interlude* and *The Forsythe Saga*. And Dr. Alice was sufficiently self-possessed to suggest a medicine for her old friend's hyperacidity.

If both Dr. Alice's confession and Miss Hennessey's testimony were correct; if Dr. Alice cold-bloodedly murdered Rheta that afternoon and then proceeded with the normal routine of getting dinner, and chatting with her friend—well, "What a woman!" For, from what we know of Dr. Alice, she was nervous, in delicate health, even hysterical at times.

(Remember that note to Earle!) To have murdered her daughter-in-law, cold-bloodedly or any other way, and then appeared her usual self at dinner time and in the evening, must have taken a little doing. Yet, according to the case against her, that is exactly what she did—and it is interesting to reflect, at this point, that Miss Enid Hennessey appeared as a witness for the prosecution.

Dr. Alice didn't call the police, the undertaker, or the coroner's office. She didn't need to call a doctor to make certain that Rheta was dead. She called Dr. Catherine, then on duty in the Children's Department of Cook County Hospital, and said, "Something terrible has happened here . . . it is Rheta . . . she is dead. . . . She has been shot."

So, let's look at a little of Dr. Catherine's testimony at the trial (keeping in mind that Dr. Alice had previously been sufficiently calm and collected to prepare dinner and hold a conversation with her old friend Miss Hennessey about books).

"I noticed her gait was a little unsteady, her hands were trembling, her face was flushed. I helped her to a chair in the dining-room and rushed out in the kitchen for stimuli. I put a teaspoonful of aromatic spirits of ammonia in water and had her drink it.

"Mother said she just groped her way up the stairs, that on the way everything was black, she felt dizzy, that the next thing she knew she was at the telephone calling me. I went up to the room and called Miss Hennessey. She came down. After that Mother called Mr. Ahearn."

Dr. Catherine Wynekoop's testimony regarding her mother's behavior on the night of the murder came much later in the trial, she being a witness for the defense. But perhaps we should consider it now, remembering Dr. Alice's own description of her reactions to Rheta's death in her "confession" and Miss Hennessey's description of the early evening.

By all means, let us not draw any conclusions from these excerpts from testimony. But I cannot omit one comment: if both of them are true, and there is nothing to suggest that they are not, and if Dr. Alice did murder Rheta, then the stage lost one magnificent actress when a young girl named Alice Lindsay decided to study medicine!

As the trial continued, there was no doubt that Dr. Alice was far from well. She was brought in for each court session in a wheel chair, and a physician was constantly within call. This created a bit of legal argument, during which curious, non-legal minded citizens wondered if the ill and elderly Dr. Alice was being tried for murder, or for the state of her health.

This is a gruesome thing to be remembering, but it comes back to me now, how during the trial betting ran fairly high as to whether or not Dr. Alice would survive it. If you cared to bet that she would, you could get some remarkably fine odds. A bartender in East St. Louis offered thirty-to-one. And it is one of the great regrets of my life that I didn't take him up on it.

Following Miss Enid Hennessey's testimony, and some routine testimony regarding the scene of the crime, the State called the grief-stricken father, Burdine H. Gardner, to the stand.

Now there are some cynical people who have suggested that his appearance was intended, deliberately, to appeal to the sympathy of the jury, in view of the fact that his testimony contributed little that was not already known. Far be it for me to believe that "The People of the State of Illinois" would do such a thing! Had it not already been agreed that Dr. Alice's wheelchair should be kept out of sight of the jury, and that no "Physician, medical person or nurse" should be in attendance on her in their presence, in case "the incapacity of the said defendant might arouse the sympathy of the jurors?"

Burdine Gardner testified that his daughter had been in ill health, and that her mother-in-law had been worried about her. He added one highly plaintive note.

"I did not hear any more from the defendant until I learned my daughter was dead. I was first informed of her death by a reporter from the Chicago *Tribune*, who called me just before midnight on November 21, 1933."

Those Chicago reporters—they simply attend to everything!

He was followed by a witness with a lovely name—Veronica Duncan. She lived next door to the Wynekoops, and was evidently a friend of the family. She also was evidently a girl who liked fresh air and exercise, judging from a few excerpts from her testimony.

"She (Dr. Wynekoop) commented on the pleasantness of the day and asked what I was doing that afternoon. I told her I thought I might go for a walk, and suggested that Rheta go along..."

"...I...had suggested that Rheta come over to get me to go for a walk..."

"...she (Dr. Wynekoop) told Rheta she could go for a walk with me if she wanted to..."

"I talked with her (Rheta) about going for a walk..."

"I told her that I wanted to go for a walk with her . . ."

And finally, "Dr. Wynekoop suggested that I ask Rheta to go for a walk with me . . ."

The walkative Miss Duncan's testimony established little save that apparently Rheta had been not only alive but in sufficiently good spirits to be carrying a bag full of groceries at three o'clock on the day of her death, and that at seven o'clock in the evening, Dr. Wynekoop had been anxiously calling Rheta's friends to learn where she might be.

There followed the introduction of People's Exhibit 28—Dr. Wynekoop's statement to police Captain Thomas J. Duffy, made on the night of November 21st, in which she suggested that Rheta might have been the victim of a burglar. Thomas J. Ahearn, the undertaker and old friend of the Wynekoop family, testified to having been called by Dr. Wynekoop after the discovery of the body, and told of his calling the police department. Followed a parade of life insurance agents, establishing a possible motive for the crime.

More police testimony, regarding the scene of the crime. Lt. Samuel Peterson, who "took charge of the revolver," People's Exhibit 3, and turned it over to the coroner the next day at the inquest. I can find no mention of fingerprints on the revolver in the transcript of the trial; we must assume there were none clear enough for identification. And finally, Captain John Stege, who told of his examination of the Wynekoop mansion and of his questioning of Dr. Alice. This, of course, was leading up to admitting her confession as testimony, "whereupon the jury were excluded and objection made to proferred statement or confession."

After considerable argument, and a number of wildly speculative newspaper stories, the confession became People's Exhibit 32. It was followed by a cross-examination of Captain Stege, who obtained the confession. The cross-examination was, naturally, a bit on the acrimonious side, and dealt almost entirely with the manner in which it had been obtained.

Following all this fuss over People's Exhibit 32, which was Dr. Alice's confession that she had fired a shot into Rheta's body after the latter's accidental death from chloroform was false, and that Dr. Alice's financial condition was such that she would cold-bloodedly murder her daughter-in-law for her insurance.

Nothing was said, however, about Earle's "other girls" or (if that had been the motive) "other girl." In fact, Earle—who did not testify—was almost conspicuously ignored during the trial.

The State having called a number of medical experts to prove that Dr. Alice's confession could not have been the truth, the Defense opened with testimony to prove that it had been obtained by duress.

The Chicago Sunday *Examiner*, for November 26th, had carried a featured interview with Dr. Harry Hoffman, head of the Behavior Clinic of the Criminal Court of Cook County (who had testified for the State). The reporter, Austin O'Malley, had done a remarkably good job of it, and it became Defendant's Exhibit 2. It, and the testimony regarding it, indicated that Dr. Alice had been tired, ill and upset at the time the confession was made. Guilty or innocent, that information about her should not have surprised anyone.

The defense then went on along the line that Dr. Alice didn't need Rheta's insurance money, that she was too fond of Rheta to murder her for it if she had needed it and that "the general reputation of Dr. Alice Wynekoop for being a peaceful and law-abiding citizen is good."

Again and again that line appears, during a parade of character witnesses. A woman writer and lecturer. A professor of history. A social worker. A newspaper publisher. Director of a private school. The list seems endless, and always the same testimony: "The general reputation of Dr. Alice Wynekoop for being a peaceful and law-abiding citizen is good." A minister. A former Health Commissioner of the City of Chicago. A member of the school board. A prominent clubwoman. Others.

This is one of the fascinating and curious facts about murder trials. One of the most enchanting murderesses I ever personally encountered was a woman whose "general reputation, etc." was almost phenomenally good. In that case, however, the defendant was acquitted, although no one doubted that she had cold-bloodedly shot her victim while he lay sleeping. One of the jurors confided in me, some time later, "After what her lawyer told us about him, we figured the so-and-so got what was coming to him."

On the other hand, a young woman was convicted, wrongly, of murder and nearly went to jail for life, because she was proven to be "of dissolute character, one who consorted with immoral companions."

The Defense testimony does give us a new picture of Dr. Alice. Consider a few excerpts from the testimony of her younger sister. "She was born at Onargo, Illinois. . . . Our father was a farmer. . . . She attended the country school and then went to a seminary in Onargo... after she completed her course, she went to Northwestern University, to the Woman's Medical School..."

And the parade of character witnesses does show us the Dr. Alice Lindsay Wynekoop who studied the practice of medicine at a time when well-brought-up young girls were studying china painting, who did social work, taught, helped other woman medical students, was prominent in club work, all without neglecting her duties as a wife and mother.

Excerpts from the testimony of members of Dr. Alice's family give a picture of her relationship with Rheta entirely different from that indicated by the State's case. "She was very much interested in Rheta and extremely fond of her... we talked about her future some... Earle had no regular employment. My sister (Dr. Alice) supported him, and also his wife Rheta..."

From the testimony of Walker Wynekoop, Dr. Alice's son: "She was worrying about the way Earle was treating Rheta. She was worried about the crowd he started to run around with down at the World's Fair. My mother asked me to talk to him. I did talk to him about his conduct."

And Dr. Catherine: "I never heard my mother speak an unkind word to Rheta. Whenever my mother bought me a dress, she also bought one for Rheta."

At last came the moment the newspapers and their readers had been waiting for. Attorney W. W. Smith announced, "The next witness, Judge, is Dr. Alice Wynekoop."

Her story, too, describes the little farm girl who grew up to be a physician, teacher, social worker, clubwoman, and mother. It tells of the meeting of Earle and Rheta, of their correspondence and marriage, of Rheta's ill health, of Earle's restlessness, of Earle's departure for the Grand Canyon. It gives another picture of Rheta, seen through her mother-in-law's eyes. "She was fearful of tuberculosis, but there were no indications of it at all.... Rheta was always of a very quiet, retiring disposition.... I sent her to a violin teacher... she sometimes took one lesson, sometimes two, and sometimes would miss a week or two.... In the last month Rheta was rather melancholy, she was of a somewhat morbid disposition... I discussed with her about going into the open air and taking exercise. I discussed this often."

After testifying as to burglaries that had taken place in the old house on Monroe Street, Dr. Alice told her story of what had happened on

November 21, 1933. It had begun like any other day. She rose at about eight o'clock and had breakfast with Rheta. She then went to a hospital where one of her patients was to be operated on.

"I walked home, arriving at perhaps one o'clock. Rheta was waiting for me at the door. She said, 'I didn't know what time you would be home, Mother, so I waited lunch.' I suggested after luncheon that I would like her to do her shopping early. She went shopping and returned between half past two and three. I think she cleared the table and dressed. When she went shopping, I really don't remember what she wore, but, contrary to her custom, she left her wraps in the library when she returned."

So far, a rather pleasant, ordinary family day. Rheta had met Veronica Duncan on the street and been invited to go for a walk, but instead, she wanted to go downtown and purchase a certain piece of music. (There was a court recess during the telling of the story when Dr. Alice became ill, the jury was sent out of the room, Dr. Catherine administered medicine to her mother, and the jury was finally allowed to return.)

Dr. Alice left the house about three o'clock, according to her story. She walked for a bit, window-shopping. "It was an unusually beautiful day, pleasantly warm." She dropped in at a postal station and bought stamps. She paused at a hardware store. She took a street car to the hospital and examined her patient, who was sleeping. She went home, and entered by the upstairs door.

There was no Rheta. Dr. Alice took off her wraps, went into the kitchen, found groceries on the table, and began preparing dinner.

The rest of Dr. Alice's story has been told and retold by Miss Enid Hennessey, the police, and Dr. Catherine. She denied, emphatically, every detail of the "confession." She denied that she was in so serious a financial condition that Rheta's insurance would be important to her. There were other collapses during her testimony; each time the jury was excluded until she had been revived.

The trial dragged on. Cross-examination, re-examination of Dr. Alice. Other witnesses. Still no one knew exactly what had happened to pretty, melancholy Rheta Wynekoop. But at last the jury returned its verdict, on March 6, 1934. "We find the defendant, Alice L. Wynekoop, guilty of murder, in manner and form as charged in the indictment, and we fix her punishment as imprisonment in the penitentiary for the term of 25 years. We further find from the evidence that the said defendant, Alice L. Wynekoop, is now about the age of 63 years."

Everything possible was done to get the aging Dr. Alice a new trial. Nothing worked. She was sent to the Woman's Reformatory at Dwight, Illinois.

That should have ended the matter. But for naturally inquisitive minds, there are still questions. If Dr. Alice did murder red-haired Rheta, was it for rather a smallish amount of insurance money, or so that her adored son could marry again? (He never did.) Or was it for some motive that has never been told? What accounts for Dr. Alice's very calm behavior at dinner, if she knew that Rheta was lying dead, in the basement surgery? Especially when contrasted with her near collapse at the time of the discovery—if it was a discovery—of the body?

Perhaps, now that so many years have passed, one should not ask questions. Yet there are so many questions that fairly cry out for answers. First, of course, is, did the elderly Dr. Alice Wynekoop murder her lovely, melancholy young daughter-in-law? If so, just how did she commit the crime, and exactly why? Did she—being innocent—make the famous confession because she believed her adored son Earle murdered Rheta—and in that case, what led her to believe him guilty?

The alibi Earle tried to repudiate proved him unquestionably innocent. In that case, if Dr. Alice did not murder Rheta, who did?

Who did—and why? I leave it to you to do the speculating on the basis of the confused and confusing known facts in the case.

One wonders, sometimes, what happens to the people involved in stories as tragic, and as famous, as the Wynekoop Case. The real tragedy, I think, comes afterwards. In this case—

Dr. Alice is still in the Woman's Reformatory at Dwight, Illinois.

Dr. Catherine is a successful woman physician, associated with the Children's Clinic of Cook County Hospital.

Walker Wynekoop, the businessman, stayed on in business and brought up his family, despite the shadow on the family name.

The last I heard about Earle, he was working as a garage mechanic. That was several years ago.

Yet one imagines—a stranger, meeting Dr. Catherine: "Oh yes—aren't you the Dr. Catherine Wynekoop who . . . ?" Or, someone meeting one of

Walker Wynekoop's children: "Wynekoop—are you any relation to the Wynekoops of the murder trial . . . ?"

Perhaps houses suffer, too. The house at 3406 West Monroe Street, built to be a home for a young and happy family, must have suffered in the years when it was pointed out by bus drivers and pedestrians as the scene of the Rheta Wynekoop murder. Perhaps, under such circumstances, the house might even have been glad when a little item appeared on page 26 of a morning paper.

"The gloomy old mansion at 3406 West Monroe Street is being torn down now—"

JIM THOMPSON

Since his death in 1977, JIM THOMPSON has been rediscovered by a legion of readers, many of whom never read crime novels before, and by filmmakers who have seen fit to adapt five of his books to the screen: *Pop. 1280* (filmed as *Coup de Torchon*), *A Hell of a Woman* (filmed as *Serie Noire*), *The Grifters*, *After Dark My Sweet*, and *The Kill Off*, having previously adapted *The Getaway* and *The Killer Inside Me* during Thompson's lifetime. Perhaps in response to his newfound fame, some mystery critics have tried to dent his armor. They've pointed to his plot defects, and quickly dispatched, carelessly written chapters, and his use of the same themes over and over. And while some of these complaints are true, Thompson still commands our attention. Why? For starters, because nowhere else does one find this monstrous vision and laconic wit. Nor does one often come across such a sad bunch of pathetic heroes—a drawling, schizophrenic Texas sheriff, a door-to-door salesman, and a third-rate con man, to name but a few. But it is his formal experiments that truly separate him from the pulp crowd. His novel, *The Criminal*, shifts points-of-view, *Rashomon* style, and *A Hell of a Woman* uses an outlandish split narration. Robert Polito suggests in his introduction to *Fireworks: The Lost Writings of Jim Thompson*, that as-told-to stories such as the one before you now played a major role in his developing this double-voicing mechanism, for they, too, rely upon it (this particular one was told to him by Chester Stacey, Evidence Officer, La Tumara County, Texas). I agree. But in the often shadowy and contradictory life of Jim Thompson one mystery can be put to rest: he did not publish his first story in *True Detective* at the age of fourteen, as has often been written, but in 1936, when he was twenty-nine.

Case of the Catalogue Clue

At approximately 6:30 on the morning of August 6th, I was awakened from a deep sleep to find my wife shaking me by the shoulder.

"Get up, Chet. Sheriff Carter just called. He wants you to come out to the Parker-Kern Hotel right away."

When Sheriff Isaac R. Carter was in a hurry there was good reason for haste. Of the old school of frontier peace officers, he was one of those calm, drawling Westerners who find their own leisurely pace still adequate for a speeding world.

I was flinging on my clothes before the next words were out of my wife's mouth: "Mr. Trumbull has been killed!"

"What?" I paused in the act of tying a shoelace. "William Lake Trumbull?"

"That's what Sheriff Ike said."

"An accident of some kind?"

"No. Sheriff Ike said he'd been murdered."

I didn't waste time with any more questions. Jamming on my hat I raced out of the house to my car and headed for the hotel.

William Lake Trumbull was the man most responsible for changing La Tumara, the seat of the county of the same name, from a sleepy, cattle-country village into one of the busiest small cities in Texas. He had first appeared in La Tumara in the late twenties with a rickety drilling-rig and a strong conviction that there was oil in the neighborhood—and very little else. He was not a particularly likable man, but he had the rare trait of inspiring confidence. He was able to persuade several ranchers to finance the drilling of a well on a share basis. Sixty days after operations began, he struck oil.

The well was profitable but not a large producer. Hence, Trumbull was able to buy up a great deal of land in the section at a very reasonable figure. He then drilled the well a few hundred feet deeper, striking an oil sand that produced ten times the quantity of the shallower one. Naturally, his associates and the other landowners of the neighborhood felt that they had been tricked, but there was no legal measure they could take against him. Trumbull formed a stock company, drilled one well after another, and eventually built a refinery on the outskirts of the city. At the time of his death he must have counted his wealth in the millions.

The Parker-Kern Hotel is three miles northwest of the city. It was built in the wake of the oil boom and is patronized mainly by executives in the business and wealthy vacationists. As I parked my car a group of golfers came out of the lobby and headed toward the velvet-smooth links; and I heard cries of merriment coming from the swimming pool in the patio of the building. Apparently, the guests of the hotel had not been told of the murder in their midst.

The room clerk, with whom I had a speaking acquaintance, directed me to Trumbull's room on the fifth floor, and a minute or two later Sheriff Carter admitted me. He was alone in the room but in the one connecting I could hear his deputy, Joe Todd, talking to someone in a low voice.

"Well, Sheriff?" I greeted him.

He gestured soberly. "Just got here myself, Chet. Look around. There's not much I can tell you that you can't see."

I looked around as I unpacked my camera and other paraphernalia. It was a conventional hotel room of the better class. But with its furnishings all resemblance to the normal and conventional ended.

On the far side of the room William Trumbull sat slumped forward in an easy chair, his fingers almost touching the deep pile of the carpet. A pool of blood spread in front of him, over and around his feet. The top of his head was literally caved in. At his side lay a reading lamp, obviously the murder weapon. Blood and bits of hair still adhered to its heavy copper base.

Whoever killed him had also, apparently, robbed him. Business papers and clothes were scattered from one end of the room to the other. Every drawer of the bureau and dresser had been pulled open. The mattress lay halfway off the bed. The telephone stand, a few feet to the right and in front of the body, had been knocked over, and the telephone with the receiver off the hook lay on the floor. Even the carpet had been turned up in places by the murderer's search.

"This is just the way you found the room?" I asked.

Sheriff Carter nodded. "I did pull the plug on the radio, but I didn't touch the dials. It was blaring away so loud I couldn't hear myself think."

"That's all right. What about the phone?"

"That's the way I found it. I've had the operator plug out the connection on this room."

I "dusted" and examined the reading-lamp but, as I had feared it would be, the effort was wasted. There were any number of fingerprints around the bloodstained base and the shade; but the tubular gooseneck, by which it must have been swung, had been wiped clean.

While I was taking the last of the many photographs necessary in such cases, Dr. E. E. Hutchinson, the autopsy physician, arrived. He expressed a tentative opinion that Trumbull had been dead little more than an hour, and that death had been almost instantaneous. He confirmed our belief that the lamp had been the murder weapon.

Following Dr. Hutchinson's examination, Sheriff Carter and I inspected the body. Much to our surprise we discovered that the murdered man's wallet, containing $411, was intact. Moreover, his expensive watch still reposed in his vest pocket.

Carter pushed back his hat. "Doesn't look like robbery was the motive, does it, Chet?"

"Not for money, anyway," I agreed. "Who discovered the murder?"

"Mr. Durkin, a business associate of Trumbull's." Carter jerked his head toward the connecting door. "Let's go talk to him. He should be able to answer some questions by now."

Samuel E. Durkin was lying on the bed in the adjoining room. A handsome, dark-haired man of about forty-five, he was smiling rather weakly at some pleasantry Deputy Sheriff Todd had made in an effort to take his mind from the tragedy.

Upon our entry he sat up and declared he was able and anxious to help us in any way that he could.

"When did you first learn of the murder?" I began.

"At a few minutes past 6—perhaps 6:15."

"How do you place the time?"

"I was talking to New York at 6 or a little after—it would be two hours later there, of course. And I must have talked about ten minutes. Almost as soon as I hung up the hotel operator rang back and asked me if I would look in Mr. Trumbull's room. She said his telephone seemed to have been knocked over, and she was afraid he might have had an accident of some kind. I looked in, and—" He paused, gesturing toward the murder room.

"Was this connecting door unlocked between your rooms?"

"Yes." Durkin seemed suddenly uncomfortable. "As a matter of fact, Trumbull and I were talking together this morning."

"At what time?"

"Well—it was a few minutes after we got up. We both had calls for 5:30. We were catching the 6:30 plane for the East."

"How long did you talk?"

"Not very long. Two or three minutes at the most."

"Did you hear any commotion in there after you left?"

"I could hear the radio faintly, nothing else. These walls and doors are practically sound-proof, you know."

Sheriff Carter cleared his throat. "Do you know of anyone who might have murdered Trumbull?"

"No, I don't."

"Your own relations were entirely friendly with him?"

"Certainly!" Then, as the sheriff stared at him thoughtfully, Durkin dropped his eyes and a wry smile came to his lips. "All right," he admitted a little sheepishly, "we weren't friendly. He'd defrauded me out of almost every cent I had. I tried to get him to square up this morning, and when he refused I called my attorney in New York."

"Suppose you tell us the whole story," Sheriff Carter suggested.

Durkin nodded soberly. "I retired from the retail drug business about three years ago because of ill health, but I wasn't satisfied to sit around the rest of my life with no financial interests. A friend introduced me to Trumbull, and the next thing I knew I'd invested just about all my capital with him. It amounted to $85,000, to be exact. Well, I never received the return that I should, and these last few months I got nothing at all. I had what is known as a divided interest in the Trumbull properties. It was in certain specific wells, not the entire property. Trumbull tried to tell me the wells I was interested in had to be shut down indefinitely. Said they'd been overproduced and unless they got a rest they'd be ruined. That sounded pretty fishy to me, and I insisted on coming down here and looking around.

"I got an entirely new light on Trumbull from the people around here. I found that he'd pulled these shakedowns before, and I told him he wasn't going to get away with it with me—"

Sheriff Carter held up his hand. "Just what was it he was trying to get away with?"

"Why, he was going to make my investment so unprofitable that I'd be glad to sell at any price!" Durkin's voice rose indignantly. "He actually had the nerve to offer me $10,000 for it! And he had my hands tied. He'd kept controlling interest in those wells, and had the say-so about their operation."

Carter shook his head sympathetically, and glanced at me. I arose and picked up the telephone. Without lifting the receiver, I walked as far as the cord would allow me toward the other room. At the connecting door I was brought to a halt. I could stand on the threshold of the other room but could not enter it without releasing the telephone.

Durkin was watching me anxiously.

"It looks like you're in the clear, Mr. Durkin," I said. "Providing, of course..."

"You can check my story with the telephone operator," he offered.

"We'll do that, of course," I nodded. "One thing more. Was the hall door of Trumbull's room unlocked?"

Durkin hesitated. "Well—I don't know whether it was or not. It easily could have been, though. We were both expecting the bellboy to come up after our baggage."

"It was unlocked when I got here, Chet," the sheriff added.

Durkin readily agreed to fingerprinting, although, to tell the truth, I could see little point in it. Obviously, he and Trumbull had been in and out of each other's rooms throughout the week they had been stopping at the hotel. Moreover, no matter how angry he might have become with Trumbull, he couldn't have killed him while he was talking over the telephone.

Leaving him with the admonition to remain in town until the affair was cleared up, Sheriff Carter, Todd, and I went back into the other room. There, I saw something that had evaded me on my first inspection.

The reading lamp with which the murder had been committed did not belong on the writing desk or radio as I had first supposed. There was no outlet for it on that side of the room, the side on which Trumbull had been murdered. The only outlet for it was on the reading-stand near the connecting door.

Todd and Carter were quick to seize on this fact.

"Whoever did it," Todd pointed out, "had to pick the lamp up over here, walk across the room, get behind Trumbull, and then hit him over the head."

"And Trumbull was too smart a man to sit there and wait for it to happen," mused Carter. "He'd have put up a fight or hollered or tried to get away. Probably all three."

"Maybe he was asleep."

"He'd just got up; barely finished dressing. And he was listening to the radio." The sheriff shook his head. "No. Trumbull must have seen what was happening, but for some reason he wasn't alarmed by it."

"Which poses quite a problem," I said. "If it was someone he knew—Durkin or practically any of his former associates—he would have been alarmed. On the other hand, if it wasn't anyone he knew—well, he'd certainly never let a stranger pull anything like that."

Carter slapped his thigh suddenly. "One of the hotel employees! One of them could have found an excuse to move the lamp, and Trumbull wouldn't have thought anything of it!"

"Let's go!" I said.

Todd was left to guard the room and supervise the removal of the body. Carter and I caught the elevator for the basement.

I should say here that the management of the hotel in general and Mr. J. E. Parker, resident manager, in particular, gave us the utmost cooperation throughout our work on the case. At the sheriff's request, Mr. Parker had detained the night employees of the Parker-Kern until they could be questioned, and they were now waiting for us in one of the locker rooms.

Miss Nina Fair, of 3457 Burk Street, was the night operator. She confirmed Durkin's statement that both he and Trumbull had had 5:30 calls.

"The keys are right together on the board, and I rang them both at the same time," she declared. "Mr. Durkin answered first, then Mr. Trumbull."

"You're positive it was Mr. Trumbull?"

"Why—who else could it have been?"

Sheriff Carter hesitated. "Well," he drawled, at last, "it could have been Durkin. Their rooms connect. I'm not saying that it was him, and all this is in strict confidence. But—"

"I know Mr. Trumbull's voice." The girl was positive. "Anyway, Mr. Trumbull and Mr. Durkin were both on the wire at the same time."

"But you said Mr. Durkin answered his phone first."

"I don't mean when I first called them," said Miss Fair. "It was a couple of minutes afterward. Right after Mr. Trumbull hung up some lady called him from outside. I connected her right away, but she hung up as soon as he answered, and Mr. Trumbull accused me of cutting them off. While I was trying to explain, Mr. Durkin picked up his receiver and put in a call to New York."

There could be no doubting that kind of testimony.

"Do you know who the lady was who called Mr. Trumbull?"

"No, I don't."

"What time was it when Durkin started talking to New York?"

"It was 6:02 when I finally got his party for him. He talked until 6:10."

"Do you know what the conversation was about?"

"I know he was talking to his lawyer, and it was about suing Mr. Trumbull." The girl colored slightly. "I don't listen in on calls, of course; I just cut in a few times to see if he was still talking. You see, the signal lights don't always work as they should on these long-distance calls, and I was worried about Mr. Trumbull's phone being knocked over. So—"

"So you wanted to tell Mr. Durkin about it as soon as he was through," Carter concluded, soothingly.

"Yes, sir."

"One more question," I said. "After Trumbull's phone was knocked over, did you hear any sounds of scuffling or anything of that kind in his room?"

Miss Fair shook her head. "No—just the radio and—" Her voice trailed off thoughtfully.

"And what?"

"I heard the door open and close. The hall door."

Sheriff Carter pounced on this. "How do you know it was the hall door? Why couldn't it have been the connecting door?"

"Because on cutting into Mr. Durkin's wire I would have heard the radio going in Mr. Trumbull's room if the connecting door had been open. I had the cords up on both rooms and I switched from one to the other in just a fraction of a second. I couldn't listen in on both rooms at the same time but it was so quick that it might just as well have been."

The room clerk, Frank E. Corbert, who lived at the hotel, was not able to add greatly to our store of information. He had remained behind the desk all night and knew nothing of the crime until Durkin called him. According to Corbert, there had been a number of people going to and fro through the lobby during the last hour of his shift, from 5:30 to 6:30. Many of the guests of the Parker-Kern liked to get in a round of golf, some swimming or horseback riding before the day became too warm. Corbert would not pretend to remember who they were. He did declare that no one had checked out of the hotel.

Harry Knox, of the Cuyamaca Rooms, 119 East 4th Street, was the night elevator operator. A smiling middle-aged man, he had been crippled since birth and could not walk without assistance. He had left his car only once during his shift—for his relief. He "supposed" that he had taken several people to and from Trumbull's floor between 5:30 and 6:30. He named two of them, but subsequent investigation proved them entirely blameless in the affair.

The remaining night employees, with the exception of those who worked in the coffee-shop and whose duties confined them there, were the lobby porter and the two bellboys. The porter, as practically every other employee could testify, had been occupied in the lobby all night, and had been too busy to be interested in the pleasure-hunting guests.

The attitude of the two bellboys was somewhat puzzling. I will not say that they were secretive or uncooperative, but certainly they were relieved when their interviews were over. They had a record of the guests they had waited on between 5:30 and 6:30, but that, of course, was only a partial list of those who had been up and around; and it was incredible that a murderer would have sought the services of anyone who might later have an opportunity to identify him.

Neither boy had visited Trumbull's or Durkin's room during the shift. Instructions had been left from the previous watch for one of them to pick up the baggage from those rooms at 6:20. But by that time the murder had been announced, and the pick-up had never been made.

Leaving my car behind for Deputy Todd's use, I rode back into town with Sheriff Carter.

"Well, Chet, it doesn't look like we've made much headway."

"Not unless those pictures show something," I admitted. "Frankly, I don't know what it would be, though."

"Neither do I. There might be something in the call Trumbull had from that woman this morning. From what the operator told us, it sounded like she just wanted to make sure Trumbull was in his room."

"And when she found out that he was she came up and murdered him? That could be. But we can't trace the call."

"She might not know that. I suggest we drop a story in the paper to the effect that we know who she is and that she'll save a lot of trouble for herself by coming in voluntarily."

"It's worth a try," I told him.

Stopping at the plant of the La Tumara *Tribune*, we found the editor-publisher, J. Lee Rowan, busily engaged in getting out an extra on Trumbull's murder. Naturally he had little information beyond the bare fact that the millionaire oil-man had been killed, and he welcomed the chance to run the story about the mysterious phone call. While he was talking with Carter, I went back to the photographic laboratory at the rear of the shop.

As a daily newspaper and the owner of the largest job-printing plant in the country, the *Tribune* could afford a much greater investment in photographic equipment than the sheriff's department. I had an improvised darkroom and other essentials in my home; but Mr. Rowan had placed their facilities at my disposal and frequently I used them. In return for this courtesy, we made available to them such of our pictures as were news.

L. A. "Red" Craig, the photographer, promised to develop the films and send them over to the sheriff's office at once.

"Now, I really am in a hurry today, Red," I told him. "Don't waste time in pulling any tricks on me."

"Certainly not, Chet," he said solemnly. But there was a twinkle in his eye.

Red and I had practically grown up together in La Tumara, and he seldom lost an opportunity to play a practical joke on me. On one occasion, which I remember particularly well, he superimposed the portrait of a bathing beauty upon a picture I had taken of a wrecked car. He did not change the negative, of course, and the only harm done was the temporary shock to my nervous system.

Since it was now mid-morning and neither Sheriff Carter nor I had eaten, I ran into a restaurant on the way back to the courthouse and got a carton of coffee and a few sandwiches. We were just sitting down to eat in the sheriff's office when the phone rang.

He picked up the receiver, talked for a moment, then motioned for me to take the extension phone.

J. E. Parker, the manager of the Parker-Kern Hotel, was on the wire. "I've just been talking to those two bellboys you interviewed this morning. I find they concealed something they should have told you."

"Yes?" There was a snap to Sheriff Carter's voice.

"One of our day bellboys had arranged with them to come on shift early so that he could carry down Mr. Trumbull's baggage. It seems that he waited on Mr. Trumbull regularly, and he could get a much bigger tip than they could. Of course, the hotel doesn't approve of mixing shifts for such reasons, and the boys were afraid they might be fired. But when they got to thinking it over—"

"Where is this other boy?" Carter interrupted. "Is he on duty now?"

"Well, he should be. According to the time-clock, he punched in at 5:50 this morning. And his street clothes are still in his locker. But no one has seen him—or remembers seeing him. Apparently he dressed in, and got out of, the locker room before any of the other boys got down."

"Don't you have a man on duty at your service entrance?"

"We do. But he's principally concerned in seeing that everyone who comes in punches the clock. After they're once in and in uniform he just watches to see that no hotel property is carried out. Our employees have to use the rear entrance all day in the course of their work."

Sheriff Carter groaned audibly. "What about the night elevator operator, Harry Knox? If this boy had gone to Trumbull's floor wouldn't Knox have seen him?"

"Not necessarily. The boy could have used the stairs. More than likely, however, he would have borrowed the service elevator. The operator doesn't come down to work until 6:30; employees use the front car at night."

Mr. Parker gave the boy's name as Jack Sibbons and his residence as 453 South Main Street.

Leaving our food almost untouched, Carter and I sped the few blocks across town to the address. It was in one of the dingier sections of the city, bordering on the business district. Once the home of a pioneer rancher, it had, in recent years, been converted into a rooming house. The proprietor was Mrs. Olaf Walling, the wife of a refinery company employee.

"Jack left for work at 5:40 this morning," she stated. "I looked at the clock when I heard him go out because he and Olaf usually left about the same time and I thought, perhaps, Olaf was late. About 6:15 he came back in his uniform; said he'd forgotten to send his washing to the laundry. He ran upstairs, and came down a minute or two later with a suitcase. He put it in his car and drove off, and that's the last I saw of him."

"Do you know what laundry he patronizes?" I asked.

"Yes. But I'm pretty sure he didn't go there. I looked in his room a while ago, and everything's gone that was worth taking. Fortunately, I'd collected my rent in advance."

A brief inspection of Sibbons's room revealed that he undoubtedly did not intend to return. Nothing had been left behind but a pair of worn-out socks and a few magazines.

Using Mrs. Walling's telephone, Sheriff Carter dispatched a pick-up request to the State Highway Patrol. Largely due to Mrs. Walling, he was able to give a minute description of the suspect and his car, and it seemed certain that it would be only a matter of time until he was picked up.

The "extra" issue of the *Tribune* was already on the streets as we drove him back to the office. And as we walked down the corridor of the courthouse, County Attorney Max Radford called to us from his quarters. We entered and he led us back to an inner room.

"This is Mrs. Brock, boys," said Max, nodding toward a smartly dressed woman of about thirty. "She's the lady who called Mr. Trumbull this morning."

The woman patted her blonde hair uneasily. "All I did was call him. I never went near the hotel."

"Suppose you tell us the whole story," suggested Carter.

The woman gave her name as Jane Brock, and stated that she lived at the Empire Hotel at Main and Elm streets. She was a waitress in the Ramble Inn.

"Mr. Trumbull used to drop in at the Inn quite frequently when he was in town," she began. "He was kind of flirty, like some men get at his age, and he was always kidding me about taking me back to New York with him. Well, yesterday he came in and, as I'd been having a little trouble on the job, I asked him if he really meant it about going to New York. He said he did, and I told him I'd think it over and let him know the first thing this morning." She broke off, blushing. "It wasn't like it sounds. I just thought I might be able to get a better job in New York."

"So you called him this morning?" I prompted, after a moment's pause.

"Yes. I was going to tell him I didn't think I'd better go. When he answered the phone, though, he sounded so angry I got scared and hung up."

Drawing us to one side, County Attorney Radford revealed that he had checked Mrs. Brock's story with the night clerk at the Empire Hotel. He declared that she had called the Parker-Kern from her room at about 5:30, and that she had not left her room at the time he went off duty at 7 o'clock.

There was no reason for detaining her, and she was excused with our thanks.

Not more than an hour later, the highway patrol notified us that they were bringing in Jack Sibbons. He had been picked up less than forty miles away from the city while trying to repair a tire on his jalopy. He had only twenty dollars in money on him, and no valuable papers of any kind. He professed to be in ignorance of the fact that Trumbull had been murdered.

Around noon, the arresting officers, Mike Kindle and J. P. Rhodes, arrived in La Tumara with their prisoner. A rather slender youth of about twenty-two, he was still dressed in his bellboy uniform. He was so badly frightened that he was almost in hysterics.

Before he was well inside the office he was shouting accusations that he was being framed.

Carter sat looking at him silently, and Sibbons suddenly grew quiet. Sheriff Ike had that effect on people.

"That's better," he drawled, approvingly. "No one's going to frame you, Sibbons. We are going to ask you some questions. The answers to those questions will decide what's going to happen to you. It's up to you, not us. Understand?"

Sibbons gulped. "Yes, sir."

"Good. Now, you went to Mr. Trumbull's room this morning, didn't you?"

"Yes, sir."

"What time did you go up there?"

"I don't know exactly. It was around 6 o'clock—earlier than I was supposed to have been there. I thought I'd help Mr. Trumbull do his packing and stall around a little and by that time it'd be all right for me to be seen in the lobby."

"How did you get up there?"

"I walked. His room's just on the fifth floor, you know."

Carter nodded. "All right. What happened after you got there?"

"Nothing." The youth's glance wavered. "I decided maybe it would be better not to go in after all."

The sheriff shook his head soberly.

"That's foolish, Sibbons. It's not helping your case to pretend you didn't know about the murder. You must have known. If you didn't, why did you try to leave town?"

"Well, I didn't kill him, anyway."

"We're waiting to hear your story," observed Carter.

"I—I just rapped on the door and walked in. That's the way we usually do when it's a man's room. We don't wait for them to answer the door.

"As soon as I looked in I knew something was wrong. The room was all torn up like someone had been searching it. Then, I saw Mr. Trumbull and I knew he was dead. I figured I'd better get out of there fast."

"Why didn't you report the crime?"

"I was afraid to. I didn't have any business being there."

"You've been in trouble with the law before, haven't you?"

"No, I haven't!" Sibbons protested.

Carter ignored the answer. "What was the other trouble about? Murder?"

"No! It was for—they said I stole a watch from a man at a place I was working at. But that's a long time ago! I was only seventeen when that happened!"

"Why did you run away this morning? Can't you see you made things worse for yourself?"

Sibbons started to speak; then, he bit his lip sullenly and remained silent.

"Have any reason to kill Trumbull?" Carter persisted.

The bellboy shook his head nervously. "No. Why should I?"

County Attorney Radford, who had been listening in on the interview, spoke up.

"You've got a bad case against you, Sibbons," he said. "Let's see how it stacks up. Point number one, you sneaked into the hotel and up to Trumbull's room. Second, you were in there between the time he was killed and the time the body was found."

"Point three, no one but an employee, such as yourself, could have taken that lamp and got behind Trumbull without putting him on guard. Four, you pulled a sneak on us. And finally, you have a record. Now, if you've got anything to say for yourself you'd better say it—and fast!"

The youth licked his lips nervously but said nothing.

Radford leaned above him and demanded, "Did you kill Trumbull?"

Sibbons shook his head in a frantic, scared way. His voice trembled. "No. No! I had no reason to kill him. Honest to God! Look, gents, gimme a break. Honest, I didn't touch him. I got a record but I'm not a murderer. I—I want a lawyer!"

He stopped talking and no amount of questioning or prompting could get him to say more.

Carter and I saw him lodged in the county jail on a charge of suspicion of murder. We then had our long delayed breakfast and returned to the office.

While the sheriff thoughtfully rolled a brown-paper cigarette, I opened the package of photographs which had arrived from the *Tribune* and began to go through them. I came to the third one and the hair stood up on the back of my neck. Then, feeling foolish, I threw down the print and reached for the telephone.

The sheriff looked at me inquiringly. "What's up, Chet?"

"Just look at that! Red Craig's been monkeying with our pictures again. I'm going to call him and pin his ears back."

Carter inspected the print closely. "Red got that sense of humor from his father. The old man got shot in the leg for it, too, when he was about Red's age—" His voice stopped and he pulled open a drawer and took out the magnifying glass we used in comparing fingerprints. After studying the photo for several seconds he laid it on the desk before me. "That picture hasn't been doctored, Chet. It's a picture of Trumbull's room before the murder—either his room or one just like it. Red might have had an artist paint out the body with an air-brush but he couldn't have put the room in order and show the bed made up."

He was right. By this time I had cooled down enough to look closely. It was simply a picture of a room in the Parker-Kern Hotel, identical to the one occupied by the mining magnate. But how had it got in with the pictures I took of the crime scene?

I got Red Craig on the wire.

"Hi, Chet," he said cheerfully. "How'd you like the body-snatching stunt?"

I started to tell him just what I thought of it when he stopped me.

"Wait a minute, Chet. Don't get on the prod yet. Let me tell you about it. We're getting out a new advertising folder for the Parker-Kern—we do all their job printing for them.

"Well, a few weeks ago I was up there shooting stuff for it, indoors, outdoors, view from the roof terrace, everything. This new piece is more like a college catalogue than a resort folder. No—let me finish telling you. One of the shots was of a deluxe bedroom, same as Trumbull's. The management tries to make them look like guest rooms in a wealthy home but they're all as much alike as peas in the pod. Every ash tray, every flower vase—they're all alike. Lamps, bureau scarfs, do-dads, everything. Well, I just couldn't resist giving you a 'before and after' view of your murder room. No hard feelings, I hope."

"I wasn't listening to Craig after this. Sheriff Carter had made a sudden pounce on another picture in the group and was comparing them with the lens, the smoke from his cigarette curling up one side of his face unheeded.

"Okay, Red," I told him, "you owe me a dinner for that one. I've got to get busy." I rang off.

The sheriff straightened up, took the corn-shuck butt from his mouth and dropped it deliberately in the cuspidor. He laid the magnifying glass away in the drawer and gathered up the pictures carefully into their envelope. His face was grim but the lines of uncertainty between his eyes had smoothed out. "I've got him, Chet."

"You know who did it?"

"Yep. He's a pretty fancy dodger and we've made a couple of bum casts and nearly got our rope on the wrong critter. But I've got him hog-tied and ready for the iron quicker than you can say 'scat.'"

"You want me to bring Sibbons back for another talk?"

"Sibbons? Hell's fire, son, he's one of the mavericks that come near leading us clean off the trail. No. We'll want to hang onto him as a witness but he's not the killer."

I still couldn't realize what new element had entered the case to make the sheriff so positive. "You don't mean that woman who got bashful at the last minute?"

Carter pulled his hat down a little further over his eyes. Then he reached back and flipped his short-barreled .45 from its leather pocket holster on his hip. He swung out the cylinder, checking the load, and returned it. "No. She was never in it at all."

I followed him out of the office, knowing the old man had his own way of breaking a case, and was content to let him handle it in spite of my curiosity. When we got in the car all he said was, "Back to the Parker-Kern. And this is definitely the last time."

Arriving at the hotel Carter and I made our way through the gala dinner-dance through to the manager's office. He was in his usual evening conference with the house staff but on seeing us enter the anteroom he excused himself and came out at once.

"I'd like to talk to your housekeeper," the sheriff announced quietly.

"She'll be in her room at this hour, but I can have her down in a few minutes."

"Don't bother. I think I can find out what I need over the house phone."

The old man wedged himself into one of the booths and spoke for perhaps two minutes. When he came out he nodded to me and we caught an elevator.

At the door of the murder room Carter knocked; it was opened by Deputy Joe Todd. Behind him I saw a straight chair tilted against the wall, looking strangely out of place in the lush setting. Beside it on the floor was a tray containing the dishes from Todd's dinner and a large pot of coffee. "Nobody's tried to get in, Sheriff," Todd whispered. "Nothing's been touched, either."

"Fine, Joe. Let's get your chair and the tray out in the hall. I want the room just the way it was. Durkin in his room there?"

"Unless he went out quietly. You want him?"

"Yes—to tell us about one thing in the arrangement of the room."

Durkin seemed to have recovered entirely from the shock of sudden death striking so close to him. He was freshly shaved and wearing a dinner jacket. "I understand you've caught the murderer, Sheriff, and that congratulations are in order. I was sorry to hear that it was young Sibbons—he seemed like a decent kid. What on earth could have been his motive in bludgeoning the old man?"

"The motive for the killing is clear enough to me," Carter said, drawing out the envelope of photographs. "What I'm interested in right now is neither why or how Trumbull was killed. I want to know where he was killed."

Durkin frowned and looked at me but I simply shrugged and waited for Sheriff Ike to tell us more.

"You mean he was killed somewhere else and brought back here into the bedroom?" Joe Todd exploded.

"I didn't say that. But this is a good-sized room. Tell me this, Mr. Durkin; that armchair where Trumbull was sitting when you found him—was that always in the same location? Ever since Trumbull moved into the room?"

Durkin frowned. "Now that you mention it, Sheriff, I seem to recall that it was somewhere else, but Trumbull wasn't the kind of man to let anything stand in the way of his comfort. He'd have moved the bed into the middle of the floor if it suited him better that way."

"I see. How long would you say the armchair has been over there?"

"Several days at least."

The old peace officer nodded as if satisfied.

I found my own attention fastening on the armchair with its sinister dark splotches. Where the dead man's body had rested was marked with a chalk outline on the upholstery, and two chalk ovals on the fleur-de-lis pattern of the rug showed where his feet had touched the floor.

"The thing that bothered me from the beginning," Ike Carter mused, as if thinking out loud, "was why in thunder a man like Trumbull didn't get the wind up when he saw the killer heading for him with a loose lamp. Any other sort of bludgeon might not be suspicious but the killer had to pick up that lamp, jerk out the plug, rip off the shade, up-end it and swing it at Trumbull's head. Bellhops don't come into a room at 6 in the morning and start monkeying with the lamps. Here, Joe—you go in and unlock the connecting door between this room and Mr. Durkin's. I want to get another angle of view on this room."

Joe went out the corridor door and reentered through the connecting door, the sheriff meanwhile having slipped off the catch from our side. Through the open door I could see the neighboring room, exactly like the one in which we stood.

"Now, then," the sheriff continued, "let's try to reconstruct this business. If I were to stand here, in this doorway, and Trumbull was sitting with his back to me—if that armchair was just reversed—I could hit him with a lamp or anything else. If I could get the lamp."

Joe Todd was looking more and more bewildered. Durkin was blank and I must confess that I was still in the dark.

"However crazy that may sound I think it's just the way the thing was done. I think Trumbull was sitting over here—"

"But the bloodstains!" I interrupted. "Look at that pool of blood. There's not a drop over there where you're standing!"

"That's right, Chet. But look at these photographs." He handed them to me. "Red Craig's 'before and after' joke turned out to be the truth. These rooms are furnished alike and to specification. The housekeeper told me that just now. Look at the rug patterns in those two photos. All the flowers in one rug—the undisturbed room—point toward the windows. But the ones in here point back toward the door. Trumbull was moved after he died. But the killer moved the whole works—rug, chair, and body. He couldn't quite get away with it because the legs of the bed are in the way and he didn't have time. So he left the rug scrounged up that way and upset everything else in the room to keep it company. Whoever killed Trumbull stood in this doorway, where I'm standing now."

Durkin snorted. "Obviously you are implying, Sheriff, that while I was talking on long distance, I calmly allowed someone to pass through my room and murder the man next door!"

Ike Carter leaned back against the door jamb. "You might. And then again you might be in it even deeper. You know what I think happened? I think Trumbull's telephone was upset after he was killed. I think the killer took that long bureau scarf there and took a hitch around the base of the telephone with it—the end of it is creased like it had been tied around something. That way the killer could stand in your room, pick up your phone and start talking and, by giving the scarf a yank, upset the telephone in here."

Durkin's face had turned an ashy gray. "It's insane! It's the most idiotic thing I ever heard of! You said yourself that the—the person who did it would have to pick up the lamp first and Trumbull would have seen him and tried to defend himself. If you think I did it, what about the lamp?"

"I'm coming to that," Carter went on, his voice a low, even drone. "Nobody touched Trumbull's lamp until after he was dead." The old man left his post by the connecting door and knelt beside the murder weapon, picking up the plug. "This lamp never came out of that base outlet over there. The metal of the plug prongs is soft. They're scratched by the contacts in the base outlet. If we photograph these scratches and enlarge them, every base outlet in the hotel will be found to leave a different pattern on the prongs of a plug. Now, are you going to make us go to all that trouble of collecting the evidence or are you going to admit that you took your own lamp, from your own room, and beat Trumbull to death with it?"

Joe and I had been so absorbed with Ike's analysis of the intricate modus operandi that Durkin managed to dash past both of us. In a split second he had vanished into his own room, slammed the door and bolted it.

Sheriff Ike crossed the room with a single bound. His .45 appeared in his gnarled right hand and the air of the bedroom jarred with the concussion as he fired a slug into the lock. His shoulder against the door sent it crashing in and we heard a sharp crack and a howl of pain.

When we got in Durkin was holding his right wrist. A little .25 Colt automatic lay on the floor. Sheriff Carter stood by easily, his right wrist braced against his hip, the muzzle of his revolver covering the cowering man.

"Get that little popgun, Joe, and then put the cuffs on him. Then you might tell the hotel doc to hurry up here. This fellow looks like he's going to faint."

Durkin did, indeed, seem on the point of collapse. When he had been handcuffed the sheriff pushed him back onto the bed and spread a blanket over him. "You ought to be glad this is 1939 and not 1879," he told the trembling prisoner. "In the old days when two fellows had a falling out and settled it with artillery the one that came out alive was pretty sure of getting a square deal. But what our folks never did like was the kind of killer that would snake around and try to pin it on an innocent man. You'll have your chance in court but I'm telling you that in the old days you'd have worn a rawhide necktie quicker than I can tell you about it."

Durkin stopped trembling and suddenly sat up, his eyes gleaming. "He deserved killing! He beat me out of every cent I had. And he had millions!"

"Take it easy, son. You don't, by law, have to say a word from here until they strap you into a chair."

"I want to talk. I've got to. I'm guilty. I killed him. But it wasn't planned beforehand. If I'd planned to kill him, I'd have used my own gun, wouldn't I? Well, I didn't. I went into his room this morning and tried to persuade him to do the right thing by me. I warned him that I was calling my attorneys and was going to start suit. He laughed at me. He admitted he'd swindled me but he'd kept within the law. I tried to plead with him but he turned the radio up and drowned me out. I ran back in here. Then I opened the door to try arguing with him and he was sitting there laughing at the ceiling in triumph. I snatched up my lamp and hit him!" The man's breath was coming back and a little color returned to his lips.

"Everything else happened just the way you guessed it. I switched the lamps afterward. I tried to switch the rug and the old man with it. I couldn't quite make it so I tore up the rest of the room and I rigged the telephone with the bureau scarf. The radio was still blasting away and I closed the door and left one corner of the scarf under it. I lay down on the floor while I was talking to New York and could just reach that corner under the door and I pulled it and upset the phone. I—I had to think fast. I didn't figure anybody would be charged with it; I thought that it would be unsolved. All I wanted was time to get away."

Taken before County Attorney Radford, Durkin unprotestingly signed a formal confession to the crime. He was lodged in the cell only recently vacated by the bellboy, Jack Sibbons.

On October 18th, 1939, in the District Court of Judge Robert Lee Arrowman, Samuel Durkin was allowed to enter a plea of guilty to a charge of manslaughter in the first degree. After the brief technicality of a trial, he was sentenced to twenty-five years' imprisonment in the state penitentiary where he still remains.

Six months ago an ingenious jail-break plot was uncovered in the penitentiary. The details have never been made public but the warden has intimated that the brain of Samuel Durkin was behind it.

LAWRENCE TREAT

Few writers can claim to have sired a genre. LAWRENCE TREAT is among the exceptional few. Before Ed McBain, J. J. Marric, and Dell Shannon, Treat was dazzling readers with his police procedural novels—and he's continued to do so for nearly forty years. Always taut, always engrossing, he's focused upon the detailed investigation of a crime told from the standpoint of the police. Whether concentrating on forensics, the mind-set of various detectives, or the painstaking checking and following of leads, Treat's books have always been starkly realistic in detail. The story you are about to read is also a police procedural, a real one. Not content to present a drab account of a policeman's heroics, Treat brings us the story of a New York City cop's first big murder investigation—his sense of doubt, purpose, insecurity. And, sure, the noble cop ultimately triumphs against evil (it wouldn't have appeared in *Master Detective* if he didn't), but it is a harder-fought battle than most, and it is we, the readers, who reap the spoils of his victory.

The Body in Sector R

At 8:07 A.M. on September 10th, 1942, a police car drew up in front of the big apartment house at 252 West 87th Street and parked alongside a pair of radio cars. Detectives Clarence F. Cassidy and Walter Nitkin, of the New York police, got out, followed by two patrolmen.

Cassidy was a veteran officer, twenty-two years on the force and fourteen of them with the rank of detective. Homicides had rarely come his way. He'd worked on several of them in a subordinate capacity, but only once before had he had a real murder case all to himself, and that had been a routine stabbing, with the identity of the criminal as obvious as a red hat.

Cassidy had just passed his forty-seventh birthday, but he looked older. His hair was completely gray; his face was lined and patterned like a piece of ancient leather. His eyes blue-gray and keen, seemed the only vital part of him. You'd have taken him for a sea captain, just off a long, tired stretch on the convoy routes.

He was the first to enter the building. At the foot of the steel fire steps he spotted the insignia of the Air Warden Service tacked over a sign reading "Headquarters, Sector R." An arrow pointed upwards and Cassidy climbed up the stairs.

A uniformed patrolman from one of the radio cars was guarding the door to a rear apartment. There, too, Cassidy noticed the air wardens' insignia.

"Where's the body?" asked Cassidy.

The patrolman motioned inside. "In the back room. This guy found it."

"It's Clyde Warner, one of our wardens," piped up a small, dapper man.

Cassidy studied him. He had good, even features and a neat little black mustache. His face was tanned, as if from a sun lamp or a vacation. Cassidy noted the fact with the same precise observation that took in the room. A plank table with some stationery and a large, black ledger on it. Three charts tacked on the bare walls. A few bridge chairs, a broken down couch. Buckets, stirrup pumps, a shovel. Blackout curtains.

He crossed the room, went through a second room that was bare of all decorations and contained a long bench, a dozen chairs and another makeshift table of boards on which stood a half empty whiskey bottle and glass. Cassidy scowled at it and went on into a smaller room at the back. There he stopped.

Here, too, there was the same barrenness of discarded and insufficient furniture. But on the floor next to a canvas cot lay the body of a man.

He was about thirty-five and powerfully built. He had dark, straight hair and thick, flat lips. The body lay on its face, one arm outstretched. There was blood beneath it, apparently from a chest wound, and the blue eyes stared sightlessly.

For form's sake, Cassidy bent down and felt for the pulse. There was no beat to it and the wrist felt cool. When he released his hold, the arm dropped with a thud. Rigor mortis hadn't started yet.

Cassidy touched nothing. The experts would be here soon and he'd have to wait till they did their stuff. His job was to get spot impressions and to start things rolling. He'd do the leg work and then later on he'd have all the headaches. Right now, there was the sunburnt man in the front room. Cassidy turned his back on the corpse and retraced his steps.

He asked his questions in a dry, patient voice that seemed interested in eliciting facts and nothing else. He kept jotting down the endless information in a small notebook with a torn cover.

The dapper man said that he was an air-raid warden, that his name was Arthur Kraus and that he was married and lived at 298 West 86th Street.

"Know Clyde Warner's address?" asked Cassidy.

"No, but you can look it up. In the file box." Kraus approached the table and halted suddenly. "That's funny," he said.

"What?"

"The file box. The cards with the names and addresses of all the wardens. It's always there, on the table."

"Maybe it's in the next room. What did it look like?"

"A cardboard box, mottled like marble. It was about sixteen inches long and five inches wide. We used four-by-five filing cards. The box has to be there."

Cassidy turned to one of the precinct patrolmen. "See if you can find it, Jim." He stared thoughtfully at Kraus. "All right—go ahead."

The warden explained that sector headquarters, under the reorganization which had taken place a few months previously, had to be manned twenty-four hours a day. The men divided up the night work. Some of them took two four-hour shifts a week; others, like Warner, preferred to put in a single eight-hour stretch and get it over with. At 8 A.M. they went off duty, in time to freshen up and reach their offices on schedule. Since the women who manned headquarters during the day didn't report until nine, there was a gap of one hour. Kraus, being his own boss, filled in three times a week. If he was late getting to his office, it didn't matter.

Cassidy frowned. Kraus was full of meaningless details, but the detective didn't stop him. There might be something of importance, something unusual. Like the missing file box.

The patrolman returned and reported that he couldn't find it. There were no places in the sparsely furnished apartment where a file box could get lost or be hidden. Why wasn't it there? Who'd want to take a thing like that? What for?

Kraus kept talking. He liked to report a few minutes ahead of time. It meant nothing to him, but the men who were on duty all night were tired and—

Cassidy interrupted. "Men?"

"Yes. There are always two, except when I'm here from eight to nine."

"Who was on with Warner?"

Kraus picked up the big black book. There were blanks for names and hours of duty. He pointed to the last item.

"Clyde Warner, David Schirmer. 12:01 A.M. till—" No further entry had been made.

Here was something at last. Two men had signed in at midnight. In the morning only one of them was there, and he was dead.

"Where does Schirmer live?" asked Cassidy.

Kraus shrugged. "His address is in that file box," he said. "Listen—it must be here."

Cassidy walked over to one of the charts. On it, he read, "Sector Commander, Herbert Streit, 267 West 87th Street. Trafalgar 7-0800." The Sector Commander—he might know.

He instructed a patrolman to call Streit from outside. Nobody must touch the phone here. There might be fingerprints.

The next hour or so must have been a nightmare for Cassidy. The Headquarters staff arrived, the Medical Examiner arrived, the inspector of the division, the acting captains of the district and of the detective division arrived. The experts snapped pictures, dusted for fingerprints, examined the corpse. And meantime the Sector Commander and the Zone Commander of the Air Raid Service showed David Schirmer, the missing warden, lived in a furnished room at 323 West 88th Street.

Cassidy transferred himself to the meeting room with the long wooden bench. He asked his questions methodically. The brass hats interrupted and he had to bring all of them up to date, but he kept doggedly to his line of inquiry.

Herbert Streit, the Sector Commander, was a tall, serious man with thin shoulders and a tired face.

"I'm Streit," he drawled. "Of Streit and Galbraith, Advertising."

"So? What do you know about these two men? David Schirmer, Clyde Warner."

Streit sat down. He was too tall to be comfortable in the folding chair and he kept wrestling with it, twisting his long legs around it and sliding gradually toward the edge.

Schirmer, he stated, was waiting for his induction notice and had volunteered to take charge of headquarters whenever necessary. He was on twice a week. Streit hadn't met him until a few months before, when the air-raid service had started to function, but he had found him exceptionally likable.

Streit shifted to Clyde Warner. The latter was without question the most disliked man in the organization. He was bossy and aggressive and had threatened to resign unless he was made a squad leader. As a jewelry salesman, he was accustomed to carrying valuable merchandise. For that reason he had a pistol permit. When he reported for duty, he always placed his gun ostentatiously on the table, as if he were the real stuff and everyone else an amateur. His manner had made him many enemies. Streit was one of them.

He hesitated, as if he were not sure whether it was wise to proceed. Then, after a short pause, he hooked his leg through the chair rung and went on with his story.

Headquarters had been furnished almost entirely by the wardens and their families, he explained, and it was they who had contributed money for office supplies, phone service and other basic essentials. Despite a specific order to the effect that the Air Warden Service had no right to collect funds, Streit had written to a few residents in the sector suggesting that donations would not be amiss. Warner had heard of this and reported it to the Mayor, who had demanded Streit's resignation. He had tendered it yesterday. The incident had caused considerable ill-feeling.

"You mean you had an argument with Warner?"

Streit smiled for the first time. "I was more inclined to thank him. The headaches I've had over this, the responsibility and the demands on my time and purse—they're over at last. Do you know that I haven't had a free evening since the war started?"

It sounded plausible and Cassidy made no comment. He picked up the log book and read off the names of the two men who had been on the eight-to-twelve shift.

"They'd know who came on at midnight," he said. "See if you can locate them and get them here, without telling them why."

Streit nodded and, with an expression of relief, got up and went toward the phone. Cassidy headed for the back of the room to examine the small pile of objects taken from the dead man's pockets.

Besides the pistol permit, there was only one thing of interest—a printed form, reading, "In case of accident, please notify—" The blank had been filled in with the name of Mrs. Clyde Warner, 50 West 79th Street, and then crossed out and the name of Harold Warner, 286 West 89th Street, substituted for it. The 89th Street house was Clyde's address, too. Cassidy ordered Detective Francis Hanrahan to go there and hold Warner until questioned. Then he addressed the Medical Examiner.

"When was he killed?" he asked.

The Medical Examiner shrugged. "You guys always expect magic. I'd say around two or three in the morning. That's a guess. I'll check on it later and let you know."

Cassidy swung around. "What about prints?"

A discouraged little man who was working with fingerprint powder and a brush looked up. "Either we don't find any at all or we find too many," he said glumly. "This time it's too many. There've been a lot of people in and out of this place."

"What about that whiskey bottle and glass?"

"Half dozen nice clear prints. But they all match up with the guy who was shot."

The detective stood there gloomily until a patrolman called from the doorway.

"Hey, Cassidy—Schirmer's here."

Davis Schirmer was a well-built man in his twenties and he answered questions in a slow, earnest manner.

"Let's have it," Cassidy said. "Everything you did between eight last night and now."

Schirmer's account was brief. He said that he'd gone to bed at eight o'clock the previous evening, since he had expected to be up most of the night. He woke at eleven and started to dress. Then he heard the bell on his floor ring three times, which meant a phone call for him down in the basement.

It was Clyde Warner, declared Schirmer. Clyde told him there'd been a change in schedule and that Schirmer didn't have to report. Schirmer had gone upstairs without speaking to anyone. He had read for a while and then gone to bed. He'd got up shortly before a policeman had knocked on his door and told him what happened.

Cassidy showed him the log book. "How about this?"

Schirmer studied the entry—"David Schirmer, 12:01 A.M. till—"

"That's not my handwriting."

"Let's see your air-raid warden's card."

Schirmer took it from his wallet and Cassidy compared the signatures. There was no doubt that someone else had written Schirmer's name in the log book.

"You say you spoke to no one after getting that phone call?" asked the detective.

"No. No one. I live alone."

"You sure it was Clyde Warner you spoke to?"

"You couldn't fool me on that voice. It's always harsh and abrupt, as if he were giving orders."

Cassidy frowned. "Your only alibi is a phone call that you say came from Warner, and the only proof it was Warner is your own statement."

"I guess that's right. But it's the truth—I swear it! Look—why would I shoot Warner?"

"I don't know," said Cassidy, "but if you did, I'll find out." He turned and went out and down the stairs.

He walked the two blocks to Warner's address. There, in an apartment on the tenth floor, he found Harold Warner glowering at the detective he had sent on ahead. The two brothers resembled each other. Like Clyde, Harold had dark, straight hair and thick lips.

At sight of Cassidy, he snapped angrily, "Why am I being kept here? You have no right to hold me—what are you trying to get away with?"

"I just want to ask you a few questions."

"Sure. Go ahead. I don't have to answer."

"Where were you last night, from eleven o'clock on?"

Warner frowned and his chin stuck out obstinately. "That's my business."

"You can get in an awful lot of trouble," said Cassidy quietly. "Either you talk, or you go right down to Headquarters in a patrol wagon. Better make up your mind quick."

Warner's small, brown eyes darted at Cassidy. "I was in Brooklyn."

"What time did you get back?"

"Pretty late."

"What time?"

"I just told you. Late." His voice dropped and he added grudgingly, "Around four."

"Whom were you with?"

"A friend," Warner said. "Look, I got a right to know what this is all about, don't I?"

"Sure." Cassidy hesitated and then let him have it. "Murder."

Warner scowled, started to speak and stopped. Finally he repeated, "Murder? Who?"

"Your brother."

"Clyde? He got killed?" Harold gave the detective a calculating look. He took a gold cigarette case from his pocket, opened it, selected a cigarette, tapped it on the back of his hand, and then seemed to forget all about it. Suddenly his closed-mouthed attitude vanished and he began to talk—so rapidly that Cassidy's pencil had trouble keeping up.

"I haven't seen Clyde since eleven o'clock last night," he said. "We both went out together. He said he was going on duty at air-raid headquarters. I took a cab to Brooklyn—388 Farragut Avenue. I spent the evening with a friend of mine, Joseph Poletti. I got back here around quarter after four and went to bed. The elevator man can tell you that."

"Any idea who might have wanted to kill your brother?"

Harold shook his head. "Well—no. But he was married and he'd had trouble with his wife. They were separated and Clyde came here to live with me. He wanted to go back to her, but she wouldn't have him. She was hell-bent on a divorce. That might have something to do with it."

Cassidy's pencil noted the name. "Where does she live?"

"At the Barbizon-Plaza, but she'll be at work now. She's with the Municipal Life Insurance Company."

"Thanks," said Cassidy. He motioned to the other detective. "Come on—let's go."

But downstairs he halted. "I'm going to send someone over to trail Warner. You stick here so you can point him out. Then go to the Farragut Avenue address, find Poletti, and check the rest of that story. I'm going to locate this wife of Clyde's." He rubbed his chin. "I wish I knew why somebody went off with that file box."

A phone call was all Cassidy needed to learn that Bertha Warner was not at her office, and fifteen minutes later he was knocking at a door in the Barbizon-Plaza. The woman who answered was dressed for the street. She was smart and attractive, with frank, clear eyes.

Cassidy introduced himself and stated his business. She gasped and turned away from him.

"Clyde—murdered?" she exclaimed. "That's horrible! How did it happen?"

"That's what I hope you can tell me. Where were you last night?"

"Me? I had dinner with my parents. But you—you can't suspect me!"

"What time did you leave?"

She sat down heavily. "Please—you don't really think I could have killed him, do you? We were separated, but we were friends. There was no bitterness. We still liked each other. We hadn't even decided definitely on a divorce. We were going to wait and find out. You can see I couldn't have had anything to do with it, can't you? All I want to do is help."

"Then just answer my questions. Everything you did last night."

"Yes, of course. I'm sorry." She took a miniature handkerchief from a small, initialed pocketbook and dabbed at her eyes. "I had dinner with my parents. They live on 90th Street, off Broadway. I stayed there until about ten. We played three-handed bridge. Then I took the subway to Fifty-ninth and walked across to the hotel. I read a little, took a bath and went to bed around midnight."

"Why didn't you go to work today?"

"I had the morning off. I'd worked late last Friday and I had time coming to me. I was going to shop and do some odds and ends. I have an appointment with the hairdresser downstairs. I made it a couple of days ago."

"When was the last time you saw your husband?"

"I don't know exactly. One evening last week. He had some papers for me to sign. The car was in my name and he was selling it. I had to sign the license or something. We had a friendly drink and then he left."

"He wanted to live with you again, didn't he? What did you have against him?"

"I? Nothing. It was just our marriage that didn't work out. He wouldn't let me live my own life, and I insisted."

"What do you know about his brother?"

"Harold?"

Cassidy thought he detected a note of reticence in her voice. "I haven't seen him since quite a while before Clyde and I separated. We used to see a lot of him, but—" Her voice trailed off and she shrugged.

"But what?" the detective insisted.

"I didn't like him. I didn't like him or some of his friends he used to bring up to our apartment. That's all."

Cassidy wasn't sure that was all, but he didn't press the point at the moment. "He and Clyde get along all right?" he asked.

"Do you mean did he have the motive for killing Clyde?"

"You can put it that way if you want to."

Bertha Warner looked down at the floor and frowned. "I don't know," she said slowly, "but it wouldn't surprise me. Harold has a vicious temper and if he and Clyde had a fight, it might very well end in—in murder."

Cassidy spent ten minutes trying to pin down these rather vague accusations and get something concrete. But about all he actually got was Mrs. Warner's statement that she believed Harold capable of murder. She either didn't have or wasn't giving out any fact that could be counted as evidence.

The detective spent another half-hour in the hotel trying to find out what time Bertha Warner had come home. Nobody remembered her. The doorman said he'd been trying to get a couple of taxis around ten-thirty, which was when she claimed she'd returned. The desk clerk didn't recall seeing her, but she carried her own key. The elevator man didn't even know who Bertha Warner was. There were so many people.

Cassidy located the night clerk and the night elevator man. Some time after two—had they seen Mrs. Warner? The detective described her. The clerk admitted he'd dozed off a few times. The elevator operator, however, was definite. An attractive dame at two in the morning? Sure he'd have remembered her, but he hadn't taken her up. Could she have walked up? He laughed. Climb nine flights of stairs when there was a car running? What for?

Cassidy bore down. He didn't want to know what the operator thought a dame would do. He wanted to know whether or not she could have done it. The elevator man shrugged. He didn't spend his time watching the stairs. If she wanted to walk up, she had a pair of legs. While he was on one of the upper floors, he wouldn't have seen her.

Cassidy returned to Sector R headquarters. His brain must have been spinning by then. Three red hot suspects—Schirmer, Harold, Bertha. And Harold and Bertha Warner were practically accusing each other.

Why?

And yet, Schirmer loomed as the Number One possibility, except that no motive had been unearthed. But Cassidy didn't care what the motive was. He wanted to know who had shot Clyde Warner, and how.

Schirmer might have done it. But the two wardens on the eight-to-twelve shift had been located and stated that Warner had arrived alone, saying Schirmer would be along any minute and that they should go. When they had pointed out that headquarters was supposed to be manned by at least two men he'd gotten angry. They'd obeyed him to avoid a fuss.

Harold Warner was a guy who didn't seem to like cops for some reason and he'd claimed to have an alibi which might or might not be okay. Mrs. Warner didn't look like the kind of woman who would shoot a man, but she didn't have anything that could be called an alibi, either.

Cassidy collected reports. The fingerprintmen had developed innumerable prints, mostly blurred, but they had no hope that any of them would be of much use. At least fifty wardens had been in and out of the apartment during the last twenty-four hours. They had rubbed their hands on chairs and tables and walls. A dozen different persons had used the phone and there wasn't a decent print on it. Just smudges.

The Medical Examiner had phoned in that Warner had been drinking and that death had taken place between two and three in the morning. He had been shot in the heart and killed outright.

Ballistics had the slug. It came from a .45 which was the caliber of the gun for which Clyde Warner had a permit. But you can't tell from which gun a bullet has come unless you have the gun, and the murder weapon had disappeared.

It was Streit, the Sector Commander, who had the only item of real interest to report. He came in suddenly from the hall and announced excitedly, "The cards from the file box. I've found them!"

"Where?"

"In the trash basket out in the hall." Streit's narrow shoulders straightened up. "What do you think of that?"

"I think," said Cassidy, "that I'd like a duplicate of that file box. Come on out and help me get one."

Cassidy returned to the precinct house with a duplicate file box under his arm. He had a glimmering of an idea, but he was far from sure.

Inspector Kennedy, in charge of the division, and Captain Lauterback, of the precinct detective division, were waiting for him. They had the facts now on Harold Warner's alibi and it apparently left Cassidy with only two suspects. When questioned by Detective Hanrahan, Poletti had corroborated in every detail Warner's statement that they were together all evening.

"Hanrahan's doing a check on Poletti now," Lauterback finished. "And we're keeping a tail on him, too, just in case."

Cassidy made his report, describing his conversations with Harold and Bertha Warner. Then he leaned back and listened as his superior officers discussed the case. But he said little himself. He wanted more facts. For one thing, he wanted to know why someone had dumped those records in the trash basket and walked off with the file box.

The day wore on. Every patrolman in the precinct who wasn't needed elsewhere had been put on the case. Cassidy did paper work and stared at a box. The Captain was handling things and giving the orders.

Around four o'clock, Patrolman Keenan knocked on the door. He had been canvassing the neighborhood under instructions to find out all he could about wardens, and he'd struck pay dirt.

"You know that lunch counter around the corner from Number 202?" he said. "The Greek who runs it said Schirmer was in there for a cup of coffee around 4 A.M. He knows Schirmer and identified him from the photo."

The Captain smiled grimly. "Bring Schirmer in."

Schirmer, when he arrived, didn't try to deny the fact. Instead, he changed his story. He still insisted that Clyde Warner had called him and that he had never been to sector headquarters. But now he stated that he had wakened around three in the morning and couldn't get back to sleep. He had gone to bed at eight, he kept repeating, he'd had enough sleep. He'd gone out for a cup of coffee. That was all. Why hadn't he mentioned it? He answered that he hadn't thought it important enough.

In the middle of the questioning Cassidy was called out. Hanrahan, whom he had sent to check on Poletti, was on the phone.

"I think I've got something," he reported. "I start checking on this Poletti and I run into an OPA investigator who's doing the same thing. It seems they got a hunch that he might be tied in with the mob that's been dishing out those phony gas coupons that hit the East Coast a few weeks back. If they've got a case and if Warner spent the evening with Poletti—well, it has possibilities."

Cassidy agreed. "I see what you mean. I'll contact OPA and find out just what they've got. See what else you can dig up."

He returned to Captain Lauterback's office. The Captain hadn't been able to break Schirmer down, but there was too much against him to turn him loose. He was being held as a material witness. They wanted a confession before making any formal charge.

"I got the laboratory reports, too," said Lauterback. "They looked over his clothes for bloodstains. There weren't any."

"There was no struggle," said Cassidy. "Warner was shot down in cold blood. You can't expect stains."

"I didn't expect them. I was just hoping."

There was another knock on the door and Detective Redfern called in excitedly, "Captain—we've got the gun!" He shoved in a short squat man in the drab uniform of a street cleaner.

Cassidy's face lit up. The street cleaner was carrying a cardboard file box under one arm.

In broken English he told how he had been on a Department of Sanitation truck that was picking up refuse from the rubbish bins along Broadway. He always put his hand in first and felt around. He'd heard of somebody who once had found a gold watch that way and he'd always thought it might happen to him, too. So when he'd seen the file box he had picked it out and opened it, and here it was.

Cassidy lifted off the cover. There was a gun inside. A .45 Colt revolver. He exchanged a look with Lauterback and then he noticed a few tiny slivers of glass.

"What else was in there?" asked Cassidy.

"A drinking glass, but it was no good. Broken. I throw away."

"Well," Cassidy said philosophically, "we're not exactly getting the breaks this trip. Unless the fingerprints that were probably on that glass are also on this."

He took a pencil from his pocket, pushed it through the trigger guard of the gun and lifted it from the box. Captain Lauterback went upstairs with him and watched as he dusted it with fingerprint powder. It was a discouraging process. Not a sign of a print showed.

"Wiped clean," the Captain said disgustedly. He reached for the revolver and examined the chambers of the cylinder. One cartridge was missing. Then, squinting and holding the gun at an angle, he read off the numbers. It was the weapon for which Clyde Warner's permit had been issued.

Lauterback wrote out a tag for identification and tied it through the trigger guard.

"I'll send it downtown to Ballistics," he said. "There's not much doubt that this is the murder gun, but they'll confirm it. I think, too, that I'll have another session with Schirmer.

"We know now pretty much how it happened. Warner got there first. Maybe he really called Schirmer so that the latter wouldn't come, or maybe not. That's something we don't know—yet. Anyhow, this is the way it was.

"Clyde Warner takes out his gun, like always. Then this other person comes. They have a couple of drinks and then they get into an argument. The gun is there, staring them both in the face. Maybe this other person grabs it and that's why Clyde runs all the way to the back room before he gets shot.

"The murderer is pretty cool. He's lucky so far because nobody noticed the shot. Maybe a truck went by, maybe people thought it was a backfire. That's happened plenty of times. So the murderer picks up the glass and the gun and looks around for something to put 'em in. That file box is just the thing. He empties it. Then he sneaks downstairs without being seen, drops the box in the nearest rubbish basket and goes home."

Cassidy nodded. "Sure," he said. "But I wouldn't use a file box. Would you?"

Lauterback stared at him, and Cassidy went on.

The following morning a brain trust gathered in the detectives' room at the precinct station. Present were Captain Lauterback, Inspector Kennedy, in charge of the division, Assistant District Attorney Charles H. Burns, Cassidy and two other detectives.

Cassidy arrived late and had to be told the latest developments. Schirmer hadn't broken yet. He had been questioned most of the night and had stuck obstinately to his story of the phone call. His landlady, Mrs. Ruth Kaminov, had corroborated the fact of the phone call and said it was a man's voice, but more than that she couldn't say.

Some of Clyde's actions on the night of the murder had been painstakingly traced. He had left his house shortly after eleven and stopped at a bar just off Broadway. The bartender remembered him and said he'd had a Scotch and water. The bartender was vague as to the time he'd left, but was fairly certain he had not made a phone call. It was obviously possible that he had phoned elsewhere, although none of the shopkeepers remembered him.

Both Bertha and Harold Warner were brought in and questioned again. Each stuck to his original story and hinted again that the other might be responsible. Clyde Warner's papers shed no additional light on the case, nor could any of his acquaintances add anything relevant. The case, therefore, had to rest on the evidence already at hand.

Cassidy coughed nervously. "I think I can swing it," he said. "I've got an idea, and if it works we may get a confession. I need somebody to fake an identification. Redfern can do that. All he has to do is pretend he isn't a cop and pick up the cue from me. And I need this." He reached for the murder gun, pressed his finger on the trigger guard and dusted it with powder so that even an amateur could see the clearness of the print. "That's why I had Ballistics return the gun," he added.

"This is kind of screwy," said Burns, from the District Attorney's office, "but I might go along if you tell what's behind this idea of yours."

Cassidy looked miserable. "I'm not sure," he said. "But we're up against a stone wall and we've got nothing to lose. I just want to question Schirmer and Harold and Bertha Warner together, and show them the print on the gun."

Lauterback looked at the faces gathered around the table. "All right," he said. "Go ahead." He raised his voice and called out, "Bring 'em in!"

Harold and Bertha Warner entered, followed by Schirmer. They all looked tired, but defiant. Cassidy knew that what he planned wasn't going to be easy. He pointed to the empty chair at the large table.

"Sit there, Mr. Warner. We've turned up a lot more evidence since the last time anybody talked to you. For one thing, we have the gun."

Harold Warner sat down, scowling. "I wasn't anywhere near that air-raid headquarters last night and you know it. I was in Brooklyn. You talked to Poletti. He told you that, didn't he?"

Cassidy nodded. "Yes, I saw him. He corroborated your alibi. He said you were together until about three-thirty in the morning. But there's one little difficulty. Poletti may not be on hand to tell that story for you in court."

Warner jumped to his feet. "What? Why not?"

"He's not at home this morning. He packed up last night and took it on the lam. He skipped."

"But—but you've got his statement."

Cassidy nodded. "Yeah. But the OPA is after him on a gas coupon counterfeiting charge. When that comes out, the jury may not want to pay much attention to his statement."

Warner looked at Cassidy and said nothing.

"And," the detective continued, "when the OPA agents went through Poletti's rooms they found evidence that gives them a charge against you, too." Then Cassidy added ominously, "But you may not have to worry about that after I get through with you." He shoved the file box forward and opened it so that Warner and the others could see the gun that lay inside. "This is the murder weapon," he added, lifting the revolver out and turning it so that Warner could see the smudge of fingerprint powder on the trigger guard.

"The killer tried not to leave any prints. But a gun isn't too easy to wipe clean. He missed this. It's not a complete print, but it'll be enough to send him to the chair."

Warner's jaw tightened. "It's not my print," he insisted.

"We'll see about that," Cassidy said. He turned to one of the detectives and ordered, "Take him out and get his prints."

Warner got slowly to his feet, an obstinate look on his face. "You can't—" he began.

But Cassidy paid no attention. He looked at Schirmer. "I think I'll have yours, too. Any objections?"

Schirmer seemed anything but pleased at the prospect, but he didn't argue about it. There was a brief hesitation before he answered, then he said, "No," and stood up.

The detective jerked his thumb toward the door and the two men left with him.

Cassidy watched them go, then sat silently looking at the gun on the desk, frowning a bit. He leaned forward, picked the gun up and studied the fingerprint in a satisfied manner.

Then, suddenly, Mrs. Warner stood up and the noise her chair made as it scraped along the floor when she pushed it back was loud in the stillness. "You don't need Harold's prints," she said in a tight, tense voice. "Someone else might have touched that gun. The fingerprint is probably his, but even if it isn't—Harold killed Clyde. I know he did. And I know why!"

Cassidy said, "Yes?"

"Clyde threatened to tell the police about Harold's black-market racket. He thought Harold had something to do with our separation. He thought Harold and I—" Her voice stopped and she looked at the floor.

"Did you?" Cassidy asked.

"No. But Clyde thought so. And—"

"And," the detective broke in, "when you and Clyde separated, he moved in to live with the man he suspected of having come between him and his wife. That sounds a little bit odd, doesn't it, Mrs. Warner? You aren't a very good liar.

"And trying to pin it on Harold is another mistake. I wondered if you might try that when you thought his alibi wouldn't hold up. You see, there's really nothing much wrong with Harold's alibi. I just tried to make it sound that way. When I said Poletti had taken it on the lam, I neglected to mention one little thing. Poletti skipped, all right, but he didn't get far. My men and the OPA agents were on his tail. They picked him up when he tried to shove off by plane from LaGuardia Field. He'll be in court, all right."

Bertha Warner sat down again. She stared at Cassidy and her hands gripped her chair until her knuckles were white.

Cassidy didn't give her any time to think. "Never try to pin a murder on a man who couldn't have done it," he went on. "Besides, even if he didn't have an alibi, I wouldn't suspect him too much. The real clue to the murderer is not that fingerprint on the gun, at all. You're wearing the same clothes you wore last night as I asked you to, aren't you?"

She nodded wordlessly.

"And that's the same purse you carried?" He pointed to the small cotton bag.

She looked at it in bewilderment, but she nodded.

"That," Cassidy said, "is the clue. That and this file box. If Harold Warner had killed his brother and had wanted to remove the gun from the scene, he wouldn't have needed to conceal it in that file box. He'd have simply stuck it in his pocket. But you haven't any pockets big enough to hold a .45 and your purse is much too small. That's why you used the file box."

Some of Bertha Warner's fear dropped away. She almost smiled. "That's pretty thin," she said. "That might apply to any woman. You can't prove that I—"

Cassidy raised his voice. "Let's have Redfern," he called.

The door opened and a uniformed patrolman came in with Redfern. Cassidy asked, "Is that the woman you saw come out of 252 yesterday morning, some time after two o'clock?"

Redfern studied her. "Yes," he said.

"Was she carrying a file box like that one?"

"Yes."

Mrs. Warner shrank away from Redfern, shaking her head. "No!" she exclaimed half hysterically. "No, no!"

Cassidy merely said, "I'll have your prints now, Mrs. Warner."

The calm, completely confident way he said it apparently told Bertha Warner that she was licked. She broke. Hysterically, disconnectedly, prodded by Cassidy's swift, unrelenting questions, she told her story.

She left her mother's around ten. Passing a movie, she had an impulse to go in. She left the theater around eleven-thirty and was on her way to the subway when she met Clyde.

He told her he had to speak to her. He said it was important, something about Harold, and that he was on his way to Sector R headquarters and that she should come with him. He said they'd be alone, that all he had to do was phone Schirmer and tell him not to report.

Bertha Warner, believing that Clyde had some family problem concerning Harold, consented. Clyde went upstairs first and told her to follow in about five minutes and not let the elevator boy see her. Only wardens, he said, were supposed to be in the apartment.

She obeyed his instructions and he was alone when she arrived. He had a flask of liquor with him and he set two glasses on the table. They had a couple of drinks and he kept postponing the matter she'd come to discuss. Presently he began to plead with her to come back, and tried to make love. She said all she wanted from him was a divorce. He refused to let her leave the apartment. She ran to the back room, intending to lock herself in. Then she saw his gun, partly concealed under the pillow of the cot.

He followed her and she raised the gun. Suddenly it occurred to her that if he were dead, she wouldn't have to worry about the divorce. He shouted at her, and in a blind fury she fired.

She knew at once that she'd killed him. She thought of putting the gun in his hand to make it look like suicide, but she was afraid of a slip-up. She decided to remove all traces of her presence. She hadn't been seen coming in, and it was a simple matter to wait until the elevator had gone upstairs and then to run out.

She threw the file box containing the gun and glass into the nearest rubbish basket. Then she went back to her hotel, sneaking in and walking all the way up.

In December, 1942, Bertha Warner was tried in Special Sessions for the murder of Clyde Warner, her husband. She admitted she had shot him but she pleaded self-defense. The prosecution pointed out that there was absolutely no evidence of a struggle and that the position of the body indicated Clyde had been shot suddenly without warning.

After six hours, the jury brought in a verdict of guilty of murder in the second degree. Several of the jurymen intimated later that the cold-blooded way in which she had sought to make Harold Warner pay for her crime weighed heavily against her.

She was sentenced to a term of from twenty years to life.

S. S. VAN DINE

Today's reader, more accustomed to flawed heroes (or antiheroes) might find S. S. VAN DINE's Philo Vance insufferable. Indeed, even during Vance's heyday, some, including Dashiell Hammett, loathed him: "There is a theory that any one who talks enough on any subject must, if only by chance, finally say something not altogether incorrect. Vance disproves this theory; he manages always, and usually, ridiculously, to be wrong. . . . His conversational manner is that of a high school girl who has been studying the foreign words and phrases in the back of her dictionary." But Vance's aristocratic, rugged good looks, sophistication, and encyclopedic knowledge of the arts, painting, religion, and music won him great favor with readers. And in 1926, while Hammett, Caroll John Daly, and Erle Stanley Gardner were breaking new ground in the pages of *Black Mask*, Van Dine was, according to Howard Haycraft, "breaking all modern publishing records for detective fiction" with the publication of *The Canary Murder Case*. Vance was so fashionable that literally dozens of movies were adapted from books in which he appeared, and eight different leading men played the role of Vance on the screen. And as you are about to find out, true crime editors, too, seeking to capitalize on this fictional hero, thought up strange new ways of incorporating him into seemingly unrelated yarns.

Germany's Mistress of Crime

"I see that Madeleine Smith, the tarnished heroine of the famous old Glasgow poison drama, died yesterday in New York."

John F. X. Markham, New York's district attorney, was enjoying his post-prandial cigar in the lounge room of the Stuyvesant Club. With him were Philo Vance and I. It had long been our custom to forgather at the club for dinner and chat on Sunday nights; and it was here that Vance had related to us many of the more famous criminal cases of Europe, with which he had familiarized himself during his criminological studies.

"I could never quite understand," Markham asked, "why the jury permitted Madeleine to escape with a verdict of 'not proven.' Perhaps it was because they could find no sympathy for the victim."

"Don't be so legalistic, Markham old dear," Vance drawled. "What can one expect when a defendant is young and attractive? Even Scotchmen are of the *genus masclinum*. . . . Still," he went on, "a fascinatin' culprit of the unfair sex sometimes gets her just desserts. For instance, there was Grete Beier—the last woman to be executed publicly in Germany. I've always considered the blond and toothsome Grete the most accomplished woman criminal of modern times."

And then Vance told us the astonishing story.

Grete Beier (he began, settling himself comfortably) was a genius in both the broadest and narrowest definition of that term; for there can be criminal genius as well as aesthetic genius. Was she sane? Well, Nordau tells us that all genius is insane. But Grete was legally sane beyond any doubt. In the deeper sense, however, her sanity can well be questioned.

The fact is, Markham, that a few more, or a few less, or a few different glandular secretions might have made her a great writer, or a great musician, or even a great painter. Her talents and her imagination were misdirected.

In the field of forgery alone she was most remarkable. She could look at any person's handwriting for a few moments, and then, through some instinctive process of memory, record the calligraphy so accurately that not even an expert could detect the imitation.

In the course of her criminal career she forged the handwriting of no less than eight different people, not once but many times; and in each instance she completely deceived the nearest relatives of her victims. These voluminous forgeries are still preserved in the German police archives, a constant source of study and amazement for the experts.

But forgery was only one of her accomplishments. After she had been arrested and accused of murder, she told a series of stories each of which was so plausible and logical, so carefully worked out to the most minute detail, that it was obvious she could have become a great writer, if she had directed only a part of her genius to literature.

Moreover, she bolstered up these stories with the most elaborate and convincing evidence, which she herself concocted. Her instinctive histrionic gifts were amazin'—she might even have been one of the world's greatest actresses. And her power for plotting was positively Machiavellian—the execution of her criminal acts was almost perfect.

For sheer talent and unscrupulousness, for ingenuity and boldness, for cold, calculating deviltry, for unadulterated wickedness, for subtle and farsighted chicanery, Grete was perhaps the most astounding figure of criminal history. And, as I say, she might have been a great creative artist and left us an enviable heritage of beauty, if her endocrines had been different. A staggerin' number of books and pamphlets have been written about her by psychologists and criminologists in Europe.

(Vance lay back in his chair and blew a spiral of smoke upward.)

Marie Margarete Beier—to give this resourceful gel her full name—was born on September 15, 1885. She was the daughter of the mayor of Brand, a small town in Saxony. The upholders of the theory of heredity have long pointed to her as a triumphant vindication of their doctrines, for not only was her father a grafter and a criminal, who at the time of his death was under arrest for the embezzlement of the city funds, but her mother had been sentenced to several years in jail for abortion and perjury.

Grete's youth appears to have been the somewhat uneventful existence of the daughter of an influential citizen in a small town. In passing, it may be mentioned that she had an extraordinary musical talent. She was an accomplished pianist and did a considerable amount of composing even as a child.

Here we have the genius motif. Perhaps if her creative will had continued to function along the lines of the tonal art ... but something went awry with her internal secretions.

When Grete was sixteen, she attended a dance and met there a young man who became her beau. For several years her parents permitted their—I speak technically, of course—innocent association. Finally, though, her mother objected to the youthful swain on financial grounds.

This maternal interference quite naturally resulted in the usual clandestine meetings of the lovers; and within a few weeks Grete became the lad's petite amie. But aside from the fact that it vexed her mother, whom she had always disliked, her *Fruhlingserwachen* was a dismal failure; and young Fritz—or whatever his name was—received his walking papers.

In February of 1905, when Grete was barely twenty, she met at a masquerade ball a young salesman, Hans Merker, who was destined to play an important and contemptible role in the coming tragedy of Grete's perverted genius. And here enters Grete's dominant sex instinct—an instinct which, Freud and Stekel tell us, is at the bottom of all creative genius. Grete and Hans were immediately attracted to each other, and a month later became secretly engaged.

In July, Merker was caught in a series of embezzlements from his employer, and Grete was able to persuade her father—who undoubtedly had some sympathy for this sort of pastime—to advance half of the stolen sum in order to save Merker from criminal prosecution. Papa Beier even went so far as to find a good position for him at the Saxonia Mines in Brand, after having extracted from him a solemn promise not to see or communicate with Grete.

Did he keep his promise? Alack for human frailty! I regret to say that Merker promptly became Grete's lover; and that Grete rented a *pied-à-terre* where she could meet her adored Hans in comparative security.

This river of bliss, however, did not run a halcyon course for long. Merker, alas, was a polygamous soul, and Grete herself felt that a change of amorous association would do her no harm.

Early in 1906, just a year after her meeting with Merker, she went to another ball—this time in Chemnitz—where she met Chief Engineer Kurt Pressler. At the end of a short courtship, conducted strictly along what we euphemistically call "honorable lines," Pressler was able to announce their engagement, the date of the nuptials being set for October, 1907.

Grete's parents were enthusiastically in favor of Pressler, who was a quiet, studious, hard-working bourgeois Johnny in good standing. A perfect son-in-law.

But Grete, with the proverbial perversity of woman, now began to turn her eyes longingly back to Merker, who was reported to be pining away for his lost love. And in an incredibly short time her emotions for Pressler passed from tolerant affection to aversion.

Grete made various efforts to break off the engagement, but Pressler refused to be dislodged. Even when Grete prompted Merker to write to Pressler and tell him of their former relations, he clung stubbornly to his determination to marry the unwilling lady of his choice. Frau Beier assured him that her little Innocenza did not know the meaning of such things as Merker had caddishly revealed, and Pressler—staunch, trusting soul—believed her.

In the summer of 1906, Grete, having renewed her amour with Merker, became pregnant. She was elated, for she felt that now Pressler would agree to break off the engagement. She confided her condition to her mother, and was straightway advised to become Pressler's mistress so that the joyous event could be credited—or is it debited?—to him.

Grete, who evidently was somewhat under her mother's domination despite her antagonism for the older woman, reluctantly fell in with this plan and began seeing her loving Kurt regularly. But to her chagrin he nobly rebuffed her advances and remained to the end the chaste Teuton.

Incidentally, Grete's child never arrived in this vale of tears; it would be indelicate to inquire into its fate, but I might mention that a certain midwife in the neighborhood was sent to jail.

Merker was furious. I can't say, y'know, whether he felt that he had been cheated out of his paternal office, but it's certain he had counted on Grete's condition to foster his own matrimonial ambitions. He wrote an indignant letter to Papa Beier, threatening to inform the authorities; and he was placated only after the ingenious Grete had unfolded to him a most amazin' fairy tale.

It was at this point that the diabolical creative genius of the gel was set in operation. She told him of secret potions that Pressler and her mother had administered in her food, and even produced a letter ostensibly from Pressler, giving instructions to Frau Beier about the dosage necessary to forestall the childbirth.

This letter was her first forgery, and it constitutes one of the most astonishin' documents in the modern records of criminology. Grete naturally had seen Pressler's handwriting, but when she wrote the letter she had no original before her. And yet this letter—now in the German archives—is considered one of the most perfect imitations of another's penmanship in existence.

In the meanwhile, Grete's engagement to Pressler was left dangling—an unsatisfact'ry state of affairs which irked the ardent Merker. He objected violently and Grete began to evolve a scheme wherewith to pacify him.

Anon she hit upon a plan, which, fantastic as it appears, was successful for a long time and almost permitted her to reach her goal.

She invented a purely fictitious wife of Pressler, and named her "Leonore Ferroni." Then she began writing a series of letters to herself, in which the forsaken "Leonore" warned her weepingly against the wiles of the unspeakable Pressler, whom she vividly described as a sort of Minotaur who fed on young, innocent maidens.

I might remark that here, too, the girl's creative genius was apparent; for while these letters from the nonexistent Leonore were not precisely forgeries, they were written in a consistent imitation of a feminine hand entirely unlike Grete's own handwriting or that of any of her actual victims. Indeed, they were purely creative efforts, conceived and executed in the most masterly fashion.

Merker read these communications with gloating satisfaction. Let his rival Kurt press his suit now, if he dared! But the exaltation was short-lived. Before long he began to doubt the authenticity of these lurid epistles—not, however, from any intrinsic evidence—and taxed Grete with wanting to get rid of him in order to marry Pressler. Grete indignantly denied the charge, and instantly evolved another scheme more bizarre than the first to convince Merker of her innocence.

She proposed to go to the hymeneal altar with Pressler, and have the deserted "Leonore" appear and dramatically denounce the bridegroom for his perfidy, accuse him of attempted bigamy, and thus turn the ceremony into chaos. Grete could then, she assured Merker, abstract heavy damages from Pressler; and she and the skeptical Hans could live happily forever afterwards on the proceeds thus acquired.

("But how was she to produce her fictitious Leonore?" asked Markham.)

The whole scheme (Vance answered) was a kind of psychological hallucination; and it's a question in my mind whether Grete did not actually believe her own fantasies. Certainly the term "lying" seems hopelessly inadequate for her astonishin' inventiveness. Having fabricated an imagin'ry wife for Pressler, she eventually thought her real. If she had been confronted with the actual necessity of going through with her outlined melodrama at the altar, she no doubt would have concocted still another tale to account for "Leonore's" failure to appear.

But events soon shaped themselves so that there was no necessity, or even opportunity, for her to meet the conditions of her proposed extravaganza.

In April of 1907 an uncle of Grete's mother, named Kastner, died in

Freiberg. Among his belongings was a steel box containing seven savings-bank books, 500 marks in cash, and two wills. In one of the wills Kastner's sister, a Mrs. Schlegel, was named the sole beneficiary; in the other the sum of 3,600 marks was left to his grandniece, Grete.

A few days later Grete's mother took possession of the box and Mrs. Schlegel retained the key—a kind of check on each other's honesty. I imagine—until the estate was legally settled, which, according to German civil procedure, would require about a month.

Grete at this time was behaving herself according to her kaleidoscopic lights. Her affair with Merker was going merrily on, and Pressler apparently had taken a distinctly second'ry position in her scheme of things, although she saw him occasionally.

And then on the fourteenth of May—three weeks after Uncle Kastner had been gathered to his fathers—Kurt Pressler's dead body was found by his landlady, who immediately notified the police.

The dead man was reclining on a couch, a napkin wound about his eyes, and a revolver, with one chamber discharged, lying beside his right hand. The bullet had passed through his mouth and embedded itself in the back of the brain. On a table by the couch were two liqueur glasses and a bottle of egg cognac.

The post mortem was performed by the police surgeon in Chemnitz, who turned in a report of suicide—a verdict with which the assisting physician fully concurred. Thereupon, in accord with the known wishes of the departed, the body was cremated.

Now, on the table near Pressler's body resting against the bottle of egg cognac had been found an envelope addressed to Fraulein Grete Beier. The contents consisted of a will, dated five days before, in which Pressler left all his belongings to his beloved fiancée. The letter begged her to forgive him for his deed; stated that neither his wife nor any member of his family had any claim whatever on his estate; and divorce him so to choose this road to forgetfulness.

Among his effects was found another letter purporting to come from Leonore Ferroni, wherein this mythical lady indicated her intention of resuming her marital life with Pressler, and bitterly reproached him for his villainous deception toward the innocent Grete. Since the authorities knew little of the dead man's past, this letter was not questioned.

On the day of Pressler's death, Grete and Pressler's brother Otto deposited the will with the civil court. Otto, as well as Pressler's mother and one of his sisters, swore that the will was genuine and in Kurt's handwriting. Whereupon Grete at once took possession of everything she could find in Pressler's apartment, including the couch on which he had died!... Need I mention that the will and the letter from the stubborn Leonore were both elaborate and perfect forgeries on the part of our skillful heroine?

Ten days later Uncle Kastner's steel box was officially opened, and it was discovered that one of the savings-bank books and more than 300 marks were missing. Moreover, the box now contained a third will—ostensibly written by the departed Mrs. Kastner and dated "1905"—leaving her entire fortune to her husband on condition that at his death all the money should go to Grete.

A bit of investigation was instituted, and before long it was ascertained that the missing bank book had been collected by an entrancin' young lady signing the name of "Erna Voigt, née Kastner," who had explained that the book had been given to her by her uncle shortly before his death.

"Erna," of course, was none other than the wily Grete; and the bank teller positively identified her. Grete thereupon nonchalantly admitted that she had surreptitiously made a wax impression of the key and obtained a duplicate, and that early in May she had opened the box in the very room where her father lay ill in bed and had abstracted the bank book and the 300 marks! That act in itself eloquently reveals Grete's cool-blooded resourcefulness.

In extenuation she explained that Mrs. Schlegel, who was very poor, had persuaded her to steal the money, which amounted to 4,500 marks, and give it to her—an act of benevolence which she magnanimously performed. And she stated further that she had asked Pressler to convey the money to Mrs. Schlegel.

Grete, who never did things by halves, wrote several letters to Mrs. Schlegel and deposited them in the woman's desk, where they were discovered when Grete requested that a search be made of the Schlegel apartment. In these letters she discussed the entire transaction, and thanked Mrs. Schlegel for the receipt.

So perfect was the handwriting of Mrs. Schlegel on the receipt that the lady herself was half convinced that she had written it. And Grete had seen only one letter of Mrs. Schlegel's, yet had recreated the handwriting so well that experts could not say definitely that Mrs. Schlegel had not written the receipt.

(Vance smiled musingly and lighted a *Regie*.)

It's very distressin', Markham, but the hard-hearted German *Polizei* looked upon this entrancin' romance as related by Grete with deep suspicion; and on June 27th they decided that it was the part of wisdom to lodge her in jail for safe-keeping.

But Grete was nowise disheartened. She immediately began a regular correspondence with Merker, smuggling her letters to him in the laundry and clothing that she gave her mother. But all her epistolary attempts to prove her innocence and good faith in the looting of her steel box were in vain. Mrs. Schlegel tenaciously held to the statement that she knew nothing of the whole matter.

Grete then wrote to Merker requesting him, with matter-of-fact calmness, to kill Mrs. Schlegel in such a way as to make it appear like suicide, and enclosed a note to be left beside the body. This note—another startlin' imitation of Mrs. Schlegel's handwriting—stated that Mrs. Schlegel had induced her poor innocent niece to commit the theft, and preferred death to the disgrace of a public confession! Grete gave Merker meticulous and expert advice about how to disguise himself and how to commit the murder, and threatened to take her own life if he failed to carry out her wishes.

Merker, however, had no intention of risking his precious hide, and refused to do anything. When his reply to Grete was intercepted by the police he promptly confessed the whole plot, and was straightway arrested as an accomplice to the theft, for he admitted having accepted from Grete a large part of the purloined money.

Hearing of her lover's predicament, Grete herself indulged in a bit of confession. She alone had stolen the money, she said, and forged all the letters and the receipt, as well as Mrs. Kastner's will.

This confession was Grete's first tactical blunder, but then it was undoubtedly the result of her ardent affection for the pusillanimous Merker. It was *ex animo*, not *ex capite*.

The effect of her confession at once raised the question in the examining magistrate's mind whether Pressler's will and farewell letter and the letter from his wife were genuine. Merker was put on the tapis, and he—a true gallant—was only too willing to assist the police in the hope of escaping from his own precarious position. He turned over to them a number of Grete's letters, whose contents practically amounted to a confession of Pressler's murder.

Grete, even now, with the tentacles of the law closing tightly about her, was undismayed. A stout lass! She began to unroll a new series of fairy tales, in which the hypothetical Leonore Ferroni figured conspicuously.

She even produced a long letter from this mysterious lady confessing the murder of her faithless husband—and this letter contained a perfect counterpart of the handwriting that Grete had formerly used in letters supposed to have been written by the fictive Leonore. And she wrote the letter in jail, without any of the former letters to guide her! I tell you, Markham, that if such genius had ever been directed into the field of the graphic arts—but this is not an aesthetic discussion.

Not content with this new version of the crime, Grete acknowledged soon afterwards that Leonore was but a product of her imagination, and asserted that Pressler had committed suicide in her presence upon her definite refusal to marry him. She also admitted the forgery of the will and the Ferroni letter, explaining that she saw no reason why she should not derive benefit from the self-inflicted death of a man whom she cordially disliked.

(Vance smoked awhile, then continued.)

It's quite clear, y'know, that all these rococo tales that Grete concocted were in the nature of a compulsive neurosis—but isn't all artistic creation the result of a compulsive neurosis?

Once Grete had started on her fictions she was unable to stop. Even when her stories could be neither contradicted nor disapproved she felt the irresistible urge to elaborate and alter them. It was, therefore, inevitable that sooner or later she should confess to the murder of Pressler.

The examining magistrate, a shrewd gentleman with a deep understanding of psychology, allowed Grete to talk to her heart's content. He neither interrupted her nor expressed doubts as to her veracity.

His patience and perspicacity were rewarded early in October when the young lady, of her own accord, admitted the shooting of Pressler. The reason she gave for her act was that she was unable to repulse his amorous advances. No doubt she still harbored a deep resentment for that stodgy Teuton's chastity when she had attempted to seduce him at her mother's behest.

Grete's details regarding the method of killing varied considerably, as was natural. Truth, in the moral sense, was not in her. At first she said that she had administered morphine to Pressler and had shot him while he slept. Then she stated that she had given him potassium cyanide with his egg brandy, and that, when he had collapsed five minutes later, she had shot him in the mouth. The creative *litterateur* was revising and copy-reading her novel!

In January of 1908 Grete was sent to the Asylum of Waldheim for examination. Here, needless to say, her extravagant tales continued without abatement. Despite all her imaginative efforts she was declared sane but of very low moral repressions—a typical "expert" opinion since it was meaningless and left the real problem of Grete's creative but twisted mentality unsolved.

An interesting side light on the girl is that during this period she wrote many really beautiful letters of tender love and devotion to her unspeakable Hans. Whether they were true expressions of her feelings or merely the outpouring of a romantic imagination, is another question.

Also at this time she wrote several poems which would not have disgraced the pen of a Heine. Once more we see the basic talent of the girl coming to the fore. Perhaps for a brief period her glandular secretions were functioning normally.

In the asylum she appeared perfectly happy, unrepentant and even proud. The attention paid to her and to her tales flattered her vanity; she genuinely enjoyed being an "interesting case."

Grete's trial—or trials, for there were two of them—took place in Freiberg in June. She was first convicted of theft, forgery and incitement to crime in connection with Uncle Kastner's steel box, and sentenced to five years. Three weeks later she was tried for the murder of Pressler and the forgery of his will.

The result was one of the most thoroughgoing pieces of legalistic absurdity on record. She was found guilty on both counts, and was sentenced in the following ludicrous manner: first, death by beheadal for removing Pressler from this earth; secondly, eight years in jail for forging the will; and thirdly, the perpetual loss of her civil rights!

The fact that Grete with her severed head in a basket, could not conveniently serve the eight years, made not the slightest impression on the judge. And lest she might somehow manage the miracle and later go free in her decapitated condition, he concluded, by some weird and unearthly process of logic peculiar to lawyers, that she should have no civil rights!

The only loophole overlooked by this modern Rhadamanthus was when he omitted to order her to report annually to an officer of the court. Maybe he would have done so had he been acquainted with Ichabod Crane.

The proceedings against Merker were dropped for lack of evidence, and when he stepped out of jail he disappeared completely from the pages of history—*Gott sci Dank!*

Grete's last days were passed quietly. She showed neither fear nor compunction. Indeed, she was haughty and cheerful; and her courage held up even under the final ghastly preparations for her death.

On the twenty-third of July, 1908, her scheming blond head fell under the executioner's knife. (The executioner it seems was partial to blondes.)

A strange and baffling case, Markham. In studying its numerous documents, one is forced to doubt practically everything that concerns Grete herself—except, perhaps, the fact that she murdered Pressler—and even here the motive is obscure. Her impulses, her mentality, her feelings for her parents, for Pressler, for Merker—nothing is wholly certain, for she lied to herself as consistently and vividly as she lied to the world.

In fact, it is problematical whether Grete could ever have been convicted without her own voluntary confession. Nobody could have disproved her first versions of Pressler's death; and her forgery of Pressler's will was so cleverly done that his own family acknowledged it to be genuine.

Grete was caught and punished only because of that supreme optimism which characterizes all true egoists. She was unable to keep her triumphs to herself. Her "urge to tell" was irresistible. And this "urge to tell" is the basic impulse of all creative art.

LIONEL WHITE

LIONEL WHITE didn't just dabble in true crime; he spent the better part of his writing career in pulp purgatory. During the 1940s, he published *Underworld Detective, Detective World,* and *Homicide Detective,* magazines whose tawdry, hyperstylized layouts and unusually violent stories make for astonishing reading even today. In the early 1950s, White turned to fiction. He wrote several straight crime novels, the boldest of which, *To Find a Killer,* is a book of such brutal rage that it would make Mickey Spillane blush. ("My beautiful wife turned to me in her sleep and softly murmured, 'Harry—Oh Harry.' It was right then, in that very second, that I made my decision. Me, Marty Ferris. I decided to kill my wife.") In the mid-1950s, White began writing caper novels which dealt with the meticulous planning and execution of heists—and in the years that followed, this subgenre would become his own private turf. His best books, *Death Takes the Bus, Clean Slate* (filmed by Stanley Kubrick as *The Killing*), and *The Big Caper,* endure not just because of the ingenuity of the knockovers but because of his ability to bring out his characters' fears, desires, and fatal flaws. Though his fiction was revered by readers and critics, he never left the world of true crime behind. And he would still crank out an occasional yarn when the mood struck or his creditors knocked. This one, however, appeared back in 1942. It is quintessential White—from the first dark, brooding sentence to the last.

Clue of the Poison Pen

This time he had made the move alone. He couldn't help but think of this one fact above all the others as he sat there in the small, conventionally furnished apartment at 536 Boulevard in Atlanta, Georgia.

Tall, broad of shoulder and stocky, brown hair already receding and shot with a few gray strands, he was only 26, but already, within these last weeks, Perry M. Williams had aged rapidly. He was a harassed, lonely man—a man who spent his days and nights in a maelstrom of fear and worry.

Across the room from where he sat slumped in a deep upholstered chair, was the dressing table at which Mildred Seymour Williams, his 22-year-old wife, had sat so many mornings during those five years of their marriage. On it were the fragile bottles of perfume, jars of makeup material; the dainty, oddly disjointed French doll which she had loved. And in the polished mirror, where his own image made a shallow reflection in the dim light of the room, he saw nothing but her lovely face as he had seen it so many times in the past. Hers was a slender, oval face with soft brown eyes beneath a curtain of fine auburn hair.

He tried not to think of Mildred. Tried not to think of the past at all. But little things kept coming back like so many shadowed ghosts to haunt him until his tortured mind was a mad kaleidoscopic pattern of the years of their life together.

He had thought this latest move might help, but it really hadn't at all. And yet he knew he couldn't have stayed on at the old address where they had last lived together. The house at 640 Mayland Avenue, S.W., from which she had disappeared back on November 21, 1941. Everything in that place had constantly reminded him of her and so he had moved. He hadn't intended taking her belongings with him at all, but then at the last minute had told the truckman to bring them along. He wanted to see her things, even though he knew to do so was an exquisite torture.

He remembered now how happy they had been when they made the move from the furnished rooms at 1117 Stewart Avenue to the Mayland Avenue apartment. She had loved having her own furniture, their own apartment, their privacy. And now she was gone and he had nothing. Nothing but his memory of her and that was worse than nothing because it was something to remind him constantly of his loss; something to twist and embitter and ravage him.

He was a strong man but was unable to cope with the ruthless disaster which had overtaken him. His friends could give him no help; not even the police could do anything about it.

Worst of all, of course, was the uncertainty, the terror of not knowing where she might be: the agony of mind and heart brought about by the wild and uncontrollable imaginings of a heartsick soul—this was what was wrecking him. She was gone and now he didn't know where to turn.

Instinctively his eyes went to the telephone and for a passing second it occurred to him to call the police once more. He started to get up but then a second later slumped back helplessly. He knew what the answer would be. It would be what it had been each time he had called these last few weeks. They would know nothing. They could do nothing.

And then, as his eyes slowly closed and his heavy face seemed to relax into a mask of utter futility, the sharp, imperative jangle of the telephone disturbed the dead air of the room. Within brief minutes Perry Williams was to find the answer to his enigma. He was to find the peace of knowledge. But it was to be a peace distilled of tragedy and blood and violence.

High winds and sheets of rain beat with an unrelenting violence across the breadth of the city. Great sign boards keeled beneath the wild fury of the storm, wires were down and the facilities of Atlanta's sewage system were incapable of coping with the tons of water which flooded the gutters until the streets ran in mad torrents.

It was the middle of March and the entire South was being lashed with the pre-spring gales. Hardest hit was Georgia. Down Atlanta's Stewart Avenue flowed a veritable river of mud, water and debris. And into the cement basement of the old-fashioned frame dwelling at number 1117, water seeped in a turgid, never-ending flow until it reached a height of more than six feet.

Odds and ends of old, discarded furniture floated in silent, drunken fashion. Mud and silt and the accumulation of years intermingled to give off a dead, musty odor.

And then on March 18th the winds suddenly died and the heavens cleared beneath the crashing orange of a rediscovered sun. The storm was ended and once again the city settled down to clear away the aftermath of the rains and fury of the weather.

In the house at 1117 Stewart Avenue, Tom Griffin, 26, and for these last six years unselfishly carrying the burdens of the eldest son, turned to his widowed mother and smiled down at her frail figure as she sat rocking gently back and forth in the kitchen chair.

"Ma," he said, "it's a mess downstairs. If we weren't so busy, me and the kid would get down there and clean up. But I guess we better hire a couple of men to do it."

Minnie Lee Griffin looked up at her son and shook her head. A slight figure, tired and with slender, drooping shoulders, her face was thin and weary with the years of struggle. The almost black eyes made deep shadows in her face and there was an odd, downward twist to her small, worried mouth.

"Don't worry about it, lad," she said. "You boys just keep on working and let me take care of the house. This is my job and I can still manage it all right."

Tom nodded and smiled back at her. But, he decided that he would still make the arrangements. His mother, only 46, had of late shown signs of premature age. Always frail, she had worked hard for her children since her husband's death. She had kept house and cooked for them and had even taken in boarders. She had worked too hard and worried too much. Her withered hands, gray hair and the lines around her eyes were visual proof of it. He knew that she would likely enough forget all about the cellar.

Later that afternoon he hired two Negroes to come in the following day and drain out the basement and clean it up.

Minnie Griffin left early the next morning to go downtown and get in some shopping. She and a neighbor decided to go together and make a day of it. Tom and his younger brother, J. W. Griffin, 16, left the house a few minutes afterward for work. Meantime, the hired men had arrived and Tom had sent them into the basement to start cleaning it out.

The big fellow, his shoulder muscles bulging beneath the thin cotton fabric of his shirt, stood at the top of the wooden steps and shook his head. He turned to the little man at his side.

"Boy," he said, "is that some dam' mess. Look like this here basement been the meeting place of a hurricane. She's going take some back labor to straighten out."

His eyes made out the outlines of the broken debris, the mud and silted floor and the stained cement sides of the cellar. Already the water itself had receded until there were but isolated puddles in a desert of filth and muck and trash.

"She's dirty, all right," his companion said. "Goin' be plenty of work here," he added as he started down the stairs.

*   *   *

First they righted the overturned work bench and then stacked broken furniture in one corner. Everything was mud-encrusted and they made little effort in the beginning to do more than move things to one side so that they might be able to clean out the silt in tin buckets. They worked hard and it was long past noon before they made much headway.

"The junk that folks can hang onto," the little man said. "Now why do you suppose they want that ol' sewing machine?"

"Why they want anything down here is more'n I know."

They worked on and by mid-afternoon their labor had reduced the shambles to some degree of ordered arrangement.

"Take this here trunk," the little man began, pointing at an ancient metal automobile luggage carrier which looked as though it had been removed from some sedan of the early 1920s. "Now what you suppose they keeping this for?"

"Probably filled with somethin' or other," his big companion said. "Let's put it in the corner."

They leaned down and started to lift it. The little man grunted and then dropped his end.

"Dam'," he growled. "If this ain't the heaviest dam'..."

"She sure is. Now what you s'pose is in this thing to make it weigh like this?"

The small man wiped the perspiration from his brow. He sat down on the trunk for a minute and then looked up.

"One way to find out," he said. "Han' me that bar an' I'll pry her open."

Less than one minute later they burst through the cellar door at the top of the stairway and went running across the kitchen. When they reached the open air both began screaming.

It didn't take long. It seemed as though there were hundreds of people there in less than five minutes. Somewhere, in a house down the street, a woman, seeing the rush of people and having heard those awful yells, had the sense to call the police. She thought it might be some sort of riot.

The men were hardly coherent, but the first ones to arrive realized through the terrified shrieks that down there in the basement they had come across a dead body. Oddly enough, no one went into the house— they just stood and waited for the law to arrive.

The first cop on the scene went downstairs and came back in a hurry.

He closed the door behind him and then sent a brother officer to the telephone. Within minutes, Detective Superintendent J. A. McKibben, accompanied by Homicide Detectives D. L. Taylor and J. M. Austin, were pushing their way into the house and down the rickety basement steps.

The dim light of the naked electric bulb hanging from a slender cord in the center of the basement was supplemented by the powerful police flashlights as they bent over the trunk. The little Negro had thrown the lid back and had pulled the gray worsted woman's coat from the ghastly burden which had made the trunk so heavy. Brown hair matted and stained a mottled red covered her disintegrated face. A frayed rope had been tied about it to pull the slender body into a gruesome huddle as it lay there in the trunk. The nauseating odor which rose from the decayed corpse sent the officers reeling back.

As hundreds converged outside the house of death, and reinforced police fought to keep back the ever-increasing crowd, a trackless trolley car slowly made its way down Stewart Street and passed the house. The windows on the left side were crowded with the morbidly curious, attracted by the mob and the sight of a dozen squad cars and an ambulance. A heavy, package-burdened female turned to the slender, elderly woman at her side.

"Why, Mrs. Griffin," she exclaimed, "it looks like they're in front of your place. Yes, I'm sure it's your home where something's happened."

Mrs. Griffin looked out the window. She nodded as she started for the exit door.

Morgue attendants were carrying their gruesome parcel across the cement sidewalk in a canvas stretcher as Mrs. Griffin approached. Stopped by a burly officer, she told him in a low voice that it was her home. She asked what had happened. The policeman looked down at her and felt a surge of pity. He took her arm and then forced his way through the crowd.

Flanked by detectives, Perry Williams followed Coroner's Physician J. C. Blalock into the morgue. His right arm was couched in a white sling which went over his shoulder. His cheek was scratched and the red marks made livid rivers in the dead white of his haggard face. Bloodshot eyes automatically sought out the marble slab and the pathetic outlines of the figure beneath the starched sheet.

His steps faltered and the detective half supported the heavy man as he slowly went on. A sigh escaped his bloodless lips. Fingernails cut deep furrows in the palms of his clenched hand.

They pulled the sheet back, and the sigh crescendoed into a high wailing sob which was suddenly choked as Perry Williams rocked back on his heels. The officers saved him from falling.

Later, in the outer room, he muttered a few broken words to the detectives.

"It's Mildred, all right," he said. "Mildred—oh, my God..."

They had taken the rope from her once lovely throat. They had unwound the coils from beneath her knees and straightened her body. With alcohol-soaked gauze they had cleansed the ugly wounds on her face and breast. There was nothing they could do about the deep indentations of the skull. The black vacant hollows where her front teeth had been battered back into her throat were charitably concealed by her bruised and torn lips. Little was left of the face, but even as it lay in a pathetic heap on the morgue table, the girl's body still looked from a distance slender and young and oddly alive in death.

That night Perry Williams once again repeated all he had gone over so often before. He told it in a broken, harsh voice. A voice which seemed to cry out for vengeance.

"That day, November 21, Mildred went to work as usual in the Whitehall Street shoe store where she was a clerk. She left before noon, and that is the last I ever saw of her until tonight. I can't understand it—how she happened to be in that trunk in the Griffin house. We used to live there a few months back, you know. And police had searched that house looking for her after those mysterious telephone calls."

Officers nodded gravely. Later, they questioned Williams about his injured arm and the scratches on his face. He explained that he had fallen and hurt himself.

Williams was permitted to go home and detectives were at once assigned to check his story about falling, as well as to establish his whereabouts on the day his wife disappeared.

Meantime, officers were holding three men and a woman for questioning. Within the last few hours they had interviewed more than a dozen persons, and they had turned up a mass of amazing evidence. The difficulty was, unfortunately, that it might be of inestimable value once they had found the killer—but it failed to point to the killer himself.

Detective Superintendent McKibben called a conference in his private office with detectives and plainclothesmen who had worked on the case, before interviewing the people he was holding.

"Here's what we know," he began, "at this point. These are the facts we have without dispute. To begin with, Mrs. Williams disappeared on November 21st. She started for work and that was the last seen of her, until the day her body turned up in the Griffin basement. The only clues we have are negative, with the exception of one. The positive clue is the fact that rope has been found in the Griffin house similar to the rope which bound the corpse.

"The negative clues are the facts that the girl's expensive wedding and engagement rings, as well as a valuable breastpin, were still on the corpse when she was discovered. That and the medical examiner's report that she had not been criminally attacked.

"This would tend to eliminate either a robbery or a sex motive for the crime. There is no insurance angle; she left virtually no estate. She was not murdered for money.

"The wounds would indicate that she was killed on or near the spot where the body was concealed. Now a strange angle enters the case at this point. You all remember that at the time of her disappearance, that is, a few days later, her relatives began receiving telephone calls saying that she was being held captive in the Griffin house."

He stopped for a minute and eyed the detectives listening to him.

"I'm not blaming anyone," he went on. "But two of you men searched the place at that time. Unfortunately you were looking for a live woman— not a dead one. Now I want to know one thing—does anyone remember seeing the trunk in the cellar at that time?"

A tall, thin detective stepped forward.

"Yes," he said. "I helped search the house and I saw the trunk. I didn't investigate it. The fact that she might have been murdered never even occurred to me. I wasn't looking for the hiding place of a dead body. But the trunk was there then."

"Which," McKibben said, "adds another unusual angle. The killer must have made the phone calls. And it is a strange thing for a murderer to first conceal a victim and then attempt to tip off the place of concealment."

He stopped to light a cigar and the officers could feel a tightening in the room's atmosphere while they waited for him to go on.

"So far," he continued, "we have no known motive for the crime. But somewhere there must be a motive. Murders don't just happen. From this point on, I will review exactly what we know of the victim herself, of her husband and of the people who were connected with them in one way of another.

"Detective Taylor has interviewed the girl's mother, Mrs. J. J. Allen; her grandmother, Mrs. W. W. Smith; and her aunt, Mrs. J. T. Neal. Each of these three relatives were very close to the Williamses. All three agree on two definite points.

"The first point: Perry and Mildred Williams were a happily married couple. They were never known to fight, there was no jealousy of any kind between them. They were very much in love with each other. The second point: Neither Perry Williams nor his wife had any relations with any other person. Mildred was a perfect wife and neither before nor after marriage had gone with any man other than her husband. They were a model couple.

"On the other hand, Mrs. Smith, the grandmother, has one unusual piece of information to contribute. For a period of three to four months before the girl's murder, she had received a series of poison pen letters. Frequently the letters were accompanied by clippings from Dorothy Dix's newspaper column. The clippings were all along one line—advice for women to stay away from other women's husbands. The letters were vicious indictments against Mildred herself—warnings that she must stay away from another woman's husband.

"Now, from what we know of the victim, it is a complete mystery why she should have been sent the letters. We are certain that she never did go near another woman's husband. Thus, we can draw but one conclusion at this point. Whoever sent the letters must have been a psychopathic case who imagined that Mildred Williams was a bad woman."

Again the chief of detectives stopped for a minute. His assistants by this time realized the technique he was following. Unable to draw any leads from the clues he had at hand, he was, by a series of psychological deductions based on definite facts, attempting to discover the criminal by the process of elimination.

"There is just one more thing," he went on. "I refer now to the telephone calls which were made to relatives of the dead girl soon after she disappeared. The calls were all along the same line. The phone would ring and then whoever was making the calls would either hang up, or else would wait a minute or so and offer the information that Mildred Williams could be found at an address which later was to prove mythical. The only time the correct address was given was the time the Griffin house was mentioned.

"There is but one of two deductions here. First: The calls were made to mentally torture the husband and relatives of the girl. Second, the more logical, the person making the calls, probably the killer, was having a battle with his conscience and intended to confess or at least see that the body was found and put the family free of anxiety. And then, at the last moment he lost courage.

"Inasmuch as the phone messages likely came from the person who had, previous to the murder, written the poison pen letters, we can safely assume that our killer not only suffered from a persecution complex but very likely suffered from a bad conscience as well.

"There is just one more pertinent fact. Analysis of the handwriting of the letters indicates a woman. A man's technique in a like case would have been more direct action. And, as far as the victims of the phone calls are concerned, the voice, although highly muffled, sounded to be that of a child or a woman!"

As he stopped talking, Detective Taylor, who had accompanied Williams home, entered the room with Motorcycle Policeman G. Herbert Williams, the young husband's brother.

"I can add one possibly salient factor," Taylor said. McKibben nodded for him to go ahead.

"Williams told me a few minutes ago," he began, "that once Mildred received a poison pen letter accusing her of having relations with Ken Hubert. Hubert is married to Mrs. Griffin's daughter, Ruth. Williams, knowing how upset his wife was, at once took her to see the Huberts. They talked the letter over. The two young couples had always been very friendly, and after discussing the matter, all agreed that the charges were ridiculous and completely without foundation."

"Ken Hubert and Ruth have been married for about a year. Their marriage, from all I have been able to find out, is as ideal as was that of the Williamses. It doesn't seem possible that whoever wrote the letter could have been right. But whoever did must have had the idea he or she was protecting Ruth and Ken's marriage."

As Taylor stopped talking, McKibben again took the floor.

"Inside," he said, "we are holding four persons. Virtually everyone else who might be involved has been eliminated. But the four we are holding—three young men and a woman—either lived in or had access to the Griffin home. All knew the victim and her husband. Any one of them might have had the opportunity to commit the crime. Any one of them might have been the voice on the telephone; any one might have written the letters."

"Those four are Mrs. Griffin; her 26-year-old son, Tom; her 16-year-old son; and Hubert, her 22-year-old son-in-law. I want them brought into this room!"

Mrs. Griffin, her head held high, entered first. She was followed by the boys, defiant and at the same time bewildered. Once seated, they looked toward the chief of detectives.

McKibben waited a minute and then started talking. He looked directly at Ken Hubert.

"Hubert," he rasped, "someone wrote Mildred Williams warning her to stay away from you. You were living at the house the same time the Williamses had rooms there. Now I want you to explain..."

He didn't have a chance to finish. Mrs. Griffin had leaped to her feet.

"He didn't," she screamed. "He didn't have a thing to do with it. You leave Hubert alone."

Quickly she was calmed and McKibben waited a minute until the woman had relaxed. He turned to the youngest Griffin boy.

"Son," he said, "you have a high-pitched voice. I want to listen to you make a phone..."

Once more the place was in an uproar. Once more Mrs. Griffin had leaped to her feet. Once more she was defending "one of her boys."

But this time, McKibben changed his tactics. He had the three young men sent from the room. He and two detectives were alone with the woman. Speaking with a deep kindliness, he turned to her.

"Mrs. Griffin," he began, "don't you see, they were the only ones who could possibly have done it, could possibly have concealed the body..."

But this time the interruption was completely without hysterics. Mrs. Griffin didn't get to her feet, didn't scream. She merely stopped him in a dead, calm tone that from the very first syllable demanded attention.

"No," she said. "Not one of them. What was done was done to protect my family, and they shall be protected still. Not one of them could have done it. They were all working. But I was at home that day!"

With the exception of the thin, high voice, endlessly going on in the weird monotone, there was the hushed silence of a tomb in the room. At one side, before a battered table, a police stenographer sat, taking down quick notes on a long sheet of legal foolscap. A dozen high police officials and detectives, representatives from the district attorney's office, a man from the coroner's department, all stood breathlessly and listened.

The voice continued from deep in the chair.

". . . and it was just after noon when she came in answer to my phone call. I hated her, but this time I was glad to see her. I wanted to tell her some things—a lot of things. I had talked it over with God and now I was going to talk it over with her.

"She hadn't taken my warnings. Yes, it was I who had sent her those clippings and those letters. I had tried to threaten her and I thought it would be enough. But it wasn't—she kept right on. So then I decided to see her and have a talk with her.

"When she arrived, I asked her in and then took her to my bedroom. We sat down and I told her just what I thought of her. I suppose she did look surprised. Yes, she denied everything. But doesn't any criminal deny a charge?

"She wouldn't let me finish. She jumped to her feet and she started for the door. But I stopped her. I stood right in front of her and defied her. I can't remember now for sure which of us first reached for the broom. But I think she did and I took it away from her. Tore it out of her hands.

"I know I struck her across the face with it. I remember thinking it strange the way the blood suddenly welled up in her mouth and then ran over her chin. Yes, I suppose that was when her teeth were knocked out. I was surprised, otherwise I would have been on guard. But she got past me and ran out of the bedroom and through the kitchen.

"I caught her there and I struck her again—this time on the back of the head. I hit her two or three times. She ran down the cellar steps then. The last thing she yelled was for me not to follow her. But I did. I dropped the broom and I went down after her.

"She was on her knees, as though she were praying, only I knew that it wasn't prayer. She was frightened and weak, that's all. So I picked up a club, or at least it looked like a club. I drew it back and it crashed into the top of her skull. It twisted her head around, but because of all her hair, it didn't knock her out. Then I struck her in the face.

"After that I kept on hitting her until she crumbled. She kept whimpering, but I didn't feel anything. Just hate.

"I sat over on the bottom step for a while and then I went to the work bench and got a length of rope. I tied it around her throat, then I doubled up her knees and pulled them up with the rope. After that, while I was planning what to do, I remembered the old auto trunk. I pulled it out from the corner and got the lid open. I hauled it across the floor and pushed her down in it. Then I went upstairs where she'd left her coat in the bedroom. I took it down and piled it on top of her.

"I shut the lid and locked it. I hauled the trunk back to the corner. By this time I was tired so I sat there and rested for a while. Then I once more went upstairs. It was late in the day now and I had a lot to do. But I was tired and so I went in and fell asleep for an hour."

The voice came to a sudden stop. And the frail, gray-haired woman opened her eyes and looked around her. Then she spoke again.

"My oldest boy, Tom, likes his dinner on time, and so I slept only an hour and then got up and started cooking supper for him."

Officials were stupefied as the confession came to its grimly ironic end. It was unbelievable to them that this slender, hard-working widow, a good mother and an honest, God-fearing churchwoman, could have made this confession.

Later Mrs. Griffin was to elaborate.

She had had, she maintained, biblical admonitions that Mildred Williams was trying to lure her son-in-law away from his wife. That was why, she said, she had asked the couple to move from her home. They had moved to an address less than 60 yards from the cellar where the girl's murder had taken place.

She had tried to warn the girl with letters; later she had talked it over with Ruth, her daughter, and her son-in-law. But no one had paid any attention to her. And so, finally, she had taken matters into her own hands.

Mrs. Griffin's sons and Hubert were at once released. Following several hours of sleep, the aging widow summoned officials and went on to explain how, following the crime, she had had no regrets and no remorse.

She said that each afternoon, as soon as her housework had been completed, she made a habit of going down to the basement and sitting for several hours while she knitted on a quilt she was making for her daughter. She liked to keep an eye on the trunk.

Officers, at first perplexed that the body had lain in the cellar so long without giving off telltale odors, explained it when they realized the trunk had been of such construction that, when closed, it was virtually hermetically sealed.

On the morning of March 21, 1942, Mrs. Minnie Lee Griffin, head high and eyes defiant, stood erect and unflinching as she was indicted on charges of first degree murder and held without bail for the grand jury.

HARRY WHITTINGTON

HARRY WHITTINGTON is remembered as the "King of the Paperback Original," and not without reason. From 1950 to about 1970, he published more than 150 novels in categories as diverse as detective fiction, horror, science fiction, westerns, backwoods romance, hospital confessions. More remarkable than his sheer output is the fact that each of them (or at least, each of the more than 50 I've been able to hunt down) were written with grace uncharacteristic of the genre. Fast-paced, well-plotted, unimaginably sparse, bleak, and always suspenseful. Whittington's heroes were always disillusioned, tragic men, tarnished angels in the heat of personal battle. (See *Forgive Me, Killer; Ticket to Hell, A Moment to Prey, Murder Is My Mistress*). Maybe that is what attracted him to this true case about two high-flying pilots, desperate men who make one last desperate gamble. If "Invaders from the Sky" appears familiar, that's because he later "structured the true events" of this "botched, bourbon and laced crime" into the 1960 novel, *The Devil Wears Wings*.

Invaders from the Sky

The small, silver Cessna cabin plane cleared the Tampa airfield at 5:45 A.M., and cut radio contact with the operations tower. Daybreak, October 24, 1957, was crisp, and in the Florida flatlands, sudden and complete.

The man at the controls glanced earthward with a faint grin. Thirty, he was stocky, handsome. His companion in the Cessna two-seater was four years younger, fair-haired, lean, long-legged. One thing they shared: a look of unbearable tensions, anxiety, inner pressures.

By nature both were gamblers, but had never hit the jackpot which they considered their right; now they were determined to play for high stakes. Their plan was new, even fantastic, full of risk, and this showed in their faces. They were risking everything in one wild gamble—they would no longer be denied: they were desperate men!

The taller, younger chap pulled a whiskey bottle from his jacket.

"Don't start that!" the pilot shouted.

The other laughed, removed the cap, drank deeply. "You run the plane. I'll do my part."

"Just be sure you can."

They followed the black lane of the city's Campbell Causeway west across upper Tampa Bay, where they would execute the next play in their carefully plotted Operation Invasion.

At the Clearwater airfield, the pilot set the silver Cessna down on the strip occupied by other private planes. His scheme included the stealing of another airplane; two were needed for this maneuver.

The fair-haired younger man took one more drink, as if sucking courage through the mouth of the bottle.

He sauntered around the Cessna, checking it. From a distance it might appear that the silver and yellow-trimmed ship had developed some minor defect and that its owner was concerned about its condition.

The stocky pilot took a brief gander at the deserted field. It was so early in the day that the attendants hadn't come out when the plane had landed. He strode to a larger, more horse-powered airplane which was parked nearest the Cessna. He swung into the cockpit quickly, moving with the assurance of a man who lives planes from jennies to jets. He set the controls, pressed the starter.

His companion's head jerked around at the balky engine whine, face stark. Twice the motor almost caught, then died noisily.

Suddenly the fair-haired man ran around the Cessna, voice tense. "Come on!" he yelled. "Forget that plane. Let's get out of here. One of those grease monkeys has spotted you—"

Faintly angered because he'd been frustrated in his theft by any plane motor, the stocky man unwillingly swung out, and in a moment the Cessna was airborne again, moving inland south by west. It was not yet 6 A.M. . . .

By 9:30 A.M. they raised Winter Haven's Gilbert Field, about 70 air miles inland from Florida's Clearwater. The pilot had now been drinking, too.

His voice betrayed the anger still rankling at their first failure to steal a

second plane. "We've got to do better than that. I hope the rest of this
plan goes better. Couple more slips like that—"

"Forget it." The fair-haired man laughed. "We've been over it. Every
step. Plenty. It's not about to go wrong."

"Just the same, I don't like this plane being spotted down here. We've
got to get another one that can't be traced to us. My boss thinks I
borrowed it for a business trip. I've got to get it back safely."

"So what? Who'll be out this time of day? We've got a right to fly where
we want."

The pilot muttered something, pinpointed the silver Cessna to a spot
beside a bright yellow Aeronca parked on Gilbert Field. He left the
Cessna's engine purring, swung out, raced across the runway. The
fair-haired man changed seats and took over the controls of the Cessna.

This time the plane theft was accomplished quickly. The Aeronca
sputtered to life, the pilot waved his arm in a motion that said more
clearly than words: "This time we got a break, let's get the hell out of
here."

Both planes took off without mishap. Flying the Cessna, the younger
man kept his companion's stolen yellow Aeronca in sight as the two fliers
returned westward. Excitement was building in the fair-haired youth now.
Another detail was complete, they were moving nearer to that jackpot
which they both needed so urgently. His pulse raced. A vein throbbed in
his temple. He could not control sudden bursts of laughter.

He watched the Cessna settle to the broken runway of an abandoned
airstrip that they'd cased days ago outside Plant City, Florida. They'd
returned to within 30 miles of Tampa now, but it was all planned—it was
going to work.

He knew his partner was still cobbed about that plane's not starting in
Clearwater. Sure, it would have been smarter to abandon a stolen plane in
Winter Haven in exchange for the Aeronca; it would have covered their
trail a lot better, but that was a minor matter, no longer important.

He put the Cessna down on the strip, realizing that he didn't fly as
expertly as the older man. This fact didn't upset him either—few men
could fly that well.

There was little concealment on this abandoned airstrip, but he taxied
the Cessna near the hedgeline, killed the engine. He swung out and ran
across to the Aeronca, carrying his bottle. He was laughing as he
clambered in.

"You happy now?" he said. "Let's go."

"We've got plenty of time. Let me have a drink."

The two thieves had cleared Gilbert Field at about 9:45 A.M. It was now almost 11. The pilot checked the radio, but so far as he could learn, the loss of the Aeronca had not been reported.

"Slick!" the tall man said, laughing. "Not a hitch. They might not miss this plane all day. Come on, fellow, let me see you laugh. What's the matter, you hate bein' rich?"

The noon sun glinted on steel towers and high-tension wires strung across the stubbled field on the outskirts of Fort Meade, Florida. The two men cruised the Aeronca low over the area, circling the high-piled gray sand hills of the fertilizer company beyond a wooded area.

It was about 12:10 P.M. when the pilot set the plane down in the field, sailing in beside the high-tension power wires, bouncing across the stubbled, rutted earth. The tall man tossed an empty bottle into the weeds.

At 711 West Broadway in Fort Meade, Ex-Chief of Police, L. M. Roberts, who had retired in 1953 after 14 years of law service to run a filling station/beer tavern, noticed two strangers in coveralls strolling in from the Sand Mountain Road, headed downtown.

Fort Meade, a placid, sun-blasted town well inside the Florida cattle country, has less than 4,000 town residents; strangers attract attention. Ex-Chief Roberts had that faint sense of something being wrong, an intuition developed in years of law work; but it was nothing he could pin down. Two strangers walking into this isolated town was odd. He thought perhaps they'd had car trouble on the Sand Mountain Road, which had been the route to Wachula before the new highway was built. He expected that the newcomers would ask aid, but they strode past, sweating in the noon heat.

They crossed the railroad tracks, strode east on Broadway. Mrs. Maxine Johnson and Mrs. Neil Heath, in the drugstore, noticed them when they bought dark glasses, because aside from being strangers, both appeared to be drunk. The taller was especially taut and nervous, almost as if he were hopped up.

Across the street the Fox Theater advertised its Saturday feature, "For Whom the Bell Tolls," but neither man glanced toward its marquee. The girl behind the soda fountain warned the smaller man he'd better watch his friend or both would be arrested for being intoxicated.

"Tough town, huh?" the tall man said sarcastically. He marched to the pay phone at the front of the store, and, though he could see the police headquarters building across the street, he dialed its number.

The girl watched open-mouthed as he asked for the police chief. Told that Glenn Baggett was home at lunch, he asked, voice slurred, who was speaking? "This is Constable Harry Godwin," came the reply.

"Well, Constable Harry Godwin, you better get down here on East Broadway. Couple men acting drunk and mighty disorderly."

Laughing, the two men walked out to the street as Harry Godwin pulled his patrol car up alongside the curb and got out.

The constable was a stout, well-built officer. He beckoned to the two strangers, who were staggering, and said with good humor, "All right, fellows, get in my car and we won't have any trouble."

Meekly the two coveralled men obeyed. Godwin got behind the wheel, pulled away from the curb.

Suddenly his passengers sobered. "Drive outside town," the taller one ordered.

Constable Godwin frowned at the sight of automatics which the men carried. They forced him to surrender his own pistol, stop the squad car in a wooded area off Highway 17. The tall man gouged his gun into Godwin's side. "You don't think we mean business, do you?"

He jerked his gun upward, fired it within inches of the lawman's face. "Now do you think I mean business?"

Godwin said, "I think you do."

The tall bandit announced, "We're going back into town at two minutes of 1:00. You're going to drive us."

Godwin drove slowly. As he turned his car into Highway 17 his heart lifted. Coming toward him in his official car was County Patrolman Herbert Goodson. Godwin swerved his car into the patrolman's lane, but Goodson, riding with another man, laughed and made way for him, waving as he passed.

At the intersection of Highway 17 and East Broadway, Constable Godwin pulled into the path of another oncoming car. Courteously, the driver gave way for him.

"You want to get hurt, bad," the tall man threatened, "pull a trick like that one more time!"

It was now 12:58 by the constable's watch. The tall man could no longer sit still. He and his stocky companion pulled women's stockings over their faces and ordered Godwin to pull his car into the side street beside the First State Bank of Fort Meade. The building has a drive-in teller window in its west wall.

Just beyond the glass doors of the First State Bank entrance, the building wall was being torn down as part of a remodeling job. Thinking Halloween had come early, J. T. Smith, Winter Haven contractor in charge of the project, stared at the masked men herding the constable ahead of them.

Smith no longer thought it a prank, however, when one of the men jabbed a gun in his ribs and ordered him into the bank, along with Grover Altman, a Fort Meade garageman, who happened to be passing.

Twenty-four-year-old Morris Lunn, assistant cashier, saw the group enter the front door. The taller man held Constable Godwin by the belt, kept his pistol at the back of the lawman's head.

Four women tellers, Mrs. Cleo Brown, Mrs. Lila Crews, Mrs. Leona Cloid and Mrs. Patricia Futral, were speechless at the sight of Constable Godwin held helpless and in danger of being slain by the grotesquely masked men.

The smaller man tossed several cloth bags at the tellers. The other gunman shoved Godwin forward so that he stumbled. "You dames start shoveling money into those bags or I'll blow his brains out!"

Morris Lunn stared at the tall gunman. This was no fear of robbery he felt, but realization that the nervous bandit was a potential killer at the moment. The tall hold-up man began cursing at Lunn. From the moment he entered the bank, the desperado talked continuously, cursing and pistol whipping the constable to demonstrate how serious he was in his threat to kill the officer if his commands weren't obeyed. He threw a sack at Cashier Lunn, ordered, "Fill it up!"

Worried for the lives of the women and the people in the bank, Lunn told the tellers to comply.

"Don't put in anything less than tens," the tall gunman pressed.

Lunn turned around. "You've got all the big currency," he said.

The cashier's words seemed to infuriate the bandit. He struck Lunn across the back of his head with the gun. The cashier slumped to the floor, his head almost at the doorway.

Head clearing, Lunn saw a man standing outside the bank door. He muttered, "We—we're being robbed!"

The onlooker simply stared, uncomprehendingly. Lunn cried out, "Get the police!" but when the man didn't move, he murmured, "Get on away from here!"

Rolling out of the doorway, Lunn stared at the robbers. The smaller crook had collected the money-ladened bags, was pleading with his companion to leave. "Let's scram before our luck runs out."

The tall desperado stood in the center of the room as if receiving a charge from this moment of evil triumph that might never come again. They'd been inside the bank no longer than seven minutes. Their loot consisted of more than $26,000.

"Come on." The stocky man moved toward the door. "Do you have to put on a show for 'em?"

The tall gunman backed toward the door. He glanced at Cashier Lunn, jerked his gun up, fired a shot to cow the witnesses. The bullet lodged in a window sash.

Before the sound of the shot had died, before the hold-up victims had recovered from the paralyzing effects of the raid, the two bandits leaped into Constable Godwin's car and sped west on Broadway.

Alton Bourne, employee of the hardware store beside the bank, had been alerted about the robbery by bank Vice-President J. H. White. He in turn had called police headquarters, where the alarm had been radioed to Chief Glenn Baggett.

The police chief arrived at the bank as the two bandits piled into Constable Godwin's car and sped away. Baggett gave chase.

Drawn outside his filling station by the sound of the speeding getaway car, Ex-Chief of Police L. M. Roberts saw the man at the wheel, still wearing his stocking mask. The bandit was driving too fast to make the turn into Sand Mountain Road, and he skidded into the mud beyond it.

Gears grinding, the desperado thrust the car into reverse. When the car didn't budge, the two thugs leaped out and fled on foot.

At this point, Perry Johnson, a Fort Meade wholesale dealer, pulled into the service lane of Roberts' filling station. And at just this moment Chief Baggett braked his car behind Constable Godwin's abandoned sedan.

Johnson rushed to assist Baggett, who was already crouched in the thick growth of a hedgerow, firing at the criminals running across the fields with the bags of money.

Chief Baggett tossed Johnson a gun while he continued to blaze away with his police automatic. The bandits, streaking across the field, returned his fire. By now the thugs had reached their plane.

The pilot clambered into the Aeronca. The tall man threw the money bags in ahead of him, stumbled as he turned to shoot at Chief Baggett and Perry Johnson. The pilot caught his companion by the shirt collar, dragged him into the plane.

As Johnson and Baggett ran forward, the plane was being revved, jerked about. The tall man fired once again to force them back.

The lawman and his courageous associate were stunned by the short run which the plane made before it was airborne—almost as if it were lifted bodily by that pilot's know-how and frantic skill. . . .

Within minutes, word of the daring daylight bank robbery and unique getaway was radioed throughout that section of the state. All law-enforcement agencies, including the FBI were converging on Fort Meade.

Meanwhile, in the yellow Aeronca, the tall bandit stuffed the loot into two suitcases he had brought along as part of the operation.

And, while this was taking place, the standard-band radio was broadcasting the following through Station WGTO, Haines City: "At noon today, John Parker of Lake Alfred reported the loss of his yellow Aeronca, pocketed at Gilbert Field, Winter Haven. Aw, come on, fellows, bring back John's plane!"

The tall bandit could not stop laughing at the announcer's witticism. Of course, the radioman had no idea of the use to which the plane had been put.

The bandit-pilot was not so happy. His radio was reporting that planes from Bartow Air Base, two Florida Forest Service aircraft and a Coast Guard helicopter from the St. Petersburg base were in the air search. Forest Service fire towers from Fort Myers to Gainesville were alerted to watch for the Aeronca.

Avon Park and Sebring announced that a plane answering the description of the Aeronca had been spotted. State and local police checked these reports, but the Bartow Air Base stated that one of the search planes had spotted the Aeronca on an abandoned airstrip near Plant City.

Hillsborough County police raced to the airstrip, found the Aeronca pitted with bullet holes. The robbers had vanished, leaving behind as clues nothing but shoe prints leading away from the Aeronca. Deputy Leon Thornton brought bloodhound trainer Carl Andrews and some of his best tracking dogs to the airstrip. Lieutenant J. J. Mitchell, fingerprint expert of the Hillsborough County sheriff's office, searched the plane for fingerprints, while other law officers made plaster casts of the shoe tracks.

Sheriff Ed Blackburn of Hillsborough County was in his office in conference with Pinellas County Sheriff Sid Saunders when a break in the case came. Witnesses reported that they had seen the two fugitives abandoning the Aeronca and continuing their flight in the small, silver Cessna. A description of the two-seater plane was furnished.

A check of the aeronautic records revealed that only two planes were registered in the State of Florida in that particular silver with yellow-trim color combination. One of these was quickly checked out. The other was supposed to be in its Tampa hangar.

Sheriff Blackburn's telephone rang. A man named Eiler said he'd heard that the police were seeking his Cessna; he'd called as soon as possible. He had lent the plane to an employee of his named Don Thompson, who had told him that he had some urgent business across the bay in Venice.

Thompson was no stranger to the Hillsborough County authorities. He'd come to Tampa as an Air Force pilot at McDill Air Field, was esteemed as an excellent flier in both speed and acrobatic planes.

Thompson's wife and seven-year-old daughter were not home. Lawmen doubted that the war hero was connected with the crime, but radioed descriptions of him and the silver Cessna throughout Florida.

Shortly before 5 P.M., Tampa police were called to the intersection at Cypress Street and Howard Avenue. Two cars had collided. A man named Irvin U. Suits was arrested for drunken driving.

Suits, youthful, handsome, 26-year-old son of a respected Hillsborough County family, was routinely questioned by the city police. Because he was known to be a friend of Don Thompson, was a plane broker, had more than $300 in fresh bills in his pockets and resembled the man described as the taller of the two Fort Meade air bandits, he was turned over to Sheriff Blackburn and the FBI.

At 5:06 P.M. Don Thompson landed at Tampa International. An airport attendant called Sheriff Blackburn, told him that "Bugs" Thompson—as he was familiarly known on the airstrips where he was a flying instructor—had just flown in with a silver Cessna.

"Keep talking to him," Blackburn directed. "Hold him until I can get somebody out there."

Thompson was arrested by sheriff's deputies. While he admitted that he had been drinking, he maintained that he had been giving Irvin Suits flying lessons all afternoon and knew nothing of the Fort Meade robbery. There were no guns on him or in the plane, no trace of the $26,000. Nevertheless, Thompson was detained.

Brought from Fort Meade, Constable Harry Godwin picked Irvin U. Suits from a line-up, definitely identified him as the man who had cursed and pistol whipped him in the Fort Meade bank. Godwin, however, failed to identify the stocky Dan Thompson in another police line-up.

Confronted with the fact that Godwin, as well as other Fort Meade witnesses, had definitely named him as one of the hold-up men, Irvin Suits confessed to the crime, implicating Donald J. "Bugs" Thompson as his accomplice.

He said that he and Thompson had cased a number of banks in central Florida, and had chosen the one at Fort Meade because they figured they could fly in and out of a small city with little difficulty and with no chance of pursuit.

Suits stated that after the running gunfight with Police Chief Baggett and Perry Johnson, he and Thompson flew back to Plant City. At the deserted airstrip, they'd switched planes and flown to Boca Grande Island near Sarasota. Thompson had brought the Cessna down on the fairway of an abandoned golf course. He'd taxied the small plane into a patch of tall grass and weeds where the two suitcases—one containing most of the stolen back money, the other the coveralls they'd worn, plus a quantity of ammunition—were dropped.

"I was so drunk at the time," Suits claimed, "that I really am a little hazy about the entire matter. I don't know whether or not I can take you to where those suitcases are."

After hiding the loot, they'd then flown back to the Peter O. Knight Airport on Davis Islands in Tampa, where Thompson had let Suits out.

Suits had next stolen a car, and was to pick up Thompson at Tampa International when the flier returned his employer's Cessna. But coincidence—and heavy drinking—intervened; Suits crashed into another car at the corner of Cypress and Howard, and suddenly all the luck of the daring duo ran out.

Don Thompson maintained his innocence in the face of all this evidence. However, his shoe exactly matched the cast made from the tracks left on the Plant City airstrip.

Suits accompanied the lawmen when they went to Boca Grande Island.

It was a matter of five hours' search, however, before the two suitcases were located.

Thompson and Suits were returned to Bartow in Polk County, where the robbery had occurred. Here Sheriff Hagan Parris charged them with armed robbery and assault. They would also face charges of bank robbery, a Federal offense; plane theft; and car theft.

Two days after the daring bank robbery, Don Thompson admitted his part in the crime.

"We'd been casing airports looking for planes to cover our trail," Thompson began. "There was one we saw in Clearwater. We were going to steal it, then change to the Aeronca. If we'd done that you'd never have caught us.

"But the plane in Clearwater—it just wouldn't start. So we had to fly the Cessna into Gilbert Field at Winter Haven and leave it there when we took the Aeronca. We flew that job to Plant City and went on with the bank robbery.

"I understand that somebody saw us when we came back to Plant City for the Cessna, and reported us. That's where we made our first mistake."

Thompson shook his head sadly. "The second tough break," he muttered, "was the weather." There was supposed to be a cold front moving in, with rough winds and a lot of rain. We figured that there would be no other light craft flying that day. But the rain didn't come."

The two accused men were returned to Fort Meade, where they directed the lawmen to the weeds along the road they'd taken after their gun battle with Police Chief Baggett and Perry Johnson. It wasn't long before the revolver which Thompson and Suits had taken from Constable Godwin was found. The bandits had tossed it away before climbing aboard the Aeronca.

Thus the career of the two Jesse Jameses of the air came to an end. Thompson's great war record will likely stand him in little stead when he comes to trial with Suits, first in Polk County, then in Hillsborough County, and finally before the Federal Court.

It must be remembered, however, that Donald Thompson and Irvin Suits are entitled to fair trials, at which time it will be determined whether they are innocent or guilty of the charges against them.

PERMISSIONS